HANDBOOK OF HISTORY

BY THE SAME AUTHOR

Agriculture, 1730-1872 (1971)
Trade Tokens: a social and economic history (1971)
Commemorative Medals: a medallic history of Britain (1972)*
Coming of the Railways, 1808-1892 (1972)
Gloucester Besieged, 1640-1660 (1974)
Prison Reform in Gloucestershire, 1776-1820 (1975)
A House of Correction (1978)

*This book won the Royal Numismatic Society's Lhotka Memorial Prize.

A HANDFUL OF HISTORY

J.R.S. Whiting

ALAN SUTTON 1978

Alan Sutton, Dursley, Gloucestershire

First published 1978

© J.R.S. Whiting 1978

All rights reserved. No part of this publication may be reproduced, stored in a retrieval system, or transmitted, in any form or by any means, electronic, mechanical photocopying, recording or otherwise, without the prior permission of the Publisher.

ISBN 0 904387 21 6

Printed in Great Britain by
Redwood Burn Limited
Trowbridge & Esher

Bound by Cedric Chivers Limited
Bath

Contents

	Illustrations	v
	Preface	vii
	Introduction	1
ONE	The Spanish Armada, 1588	7
TWO	The Knavery of the Rump, 1647-1653	19
THREE	All the Popish Plots, 1588-1688	36
FOUR	The Horrid Popish Plot, 1678	50
FIVE	The Meal Tub Plot, 1679-1680	64
SIX	The Rye House Plot, 1683	79
SEVEN	The Monmouth Rebellion, 1685	89
EIGHT	The Reign of James II, 1685-1688	105
NINE	The Reign of James II, the Revolution	116
TEN	The Reign of Queen Anne, 1702-1704	125
ELEVEN	Marlborough's Victories, 1702-1707	138
TWELVE	Dr. Sacheverell, 1709-1711	150
THIRTEEN	The South Sea Bubble, 1720	164
FOURTEEN	All the Bubbles, the Bubble Companies, 1720	174
	Bibliography	189
	Card Collections	191
	Index	193

Illustrations

The cards were photographed from *Playing Cards of Various Ages and Countries* by C. Schreiber and A.W. Franks by kind permission of the Bodleian Library, with the exception of the Rye House pack which was photographed by kind permission of the Trustees of the British Museum and the South Sea Bubble and Meal Tub packs which were photographed from the Phillips Collection in the Guildhall Library with the kind permission of the Worshipful Company of Makers of Playing Cards. The cover was photographed by Jack Farley.

All the cards have been reduced in size for the purposes of this book.

Spanish Armada	Plate 1	page 9
	Plate 2	12
	Plate 3	14
	Plate 4	17
The Rump	Plate 1	21
	Plate 2	24
	Plate 3	28
	Plate 4	31
All the Popish Plots	Plate 1	39
	Plate 2	42
	Plate 3	45
	Plate 4	47
Popish Plot	Plate 1	52
	Plate 2	55
	Plate 3	58
	Plate 4	61
Meal Tub Plot	Plate 1	65
	Plate 2	69
	Plate 3	72
	Plate 4	76

Rye House Plot	Plate 1	80
	Plate 2	82
	Plate 3	84
	Plate 4	87
Monmouth's Rebellion	Plate 1	90
	Plate 2	92
	Plate 3	96
	Plate 4	99
	Plate 5	101
Reign of James II, 1685-88	Plate 1	106
	Plate 2	109
	Plate 3	111
	Plate 4	114
Reign of James II, Revolution	Plate 1	117
	Plate 2	119
	Plate 3	121
	Plate 4	123
Reign of Queen Anne	Plate 1	126
	Plate 2	129
	Plate 3	131
	Plate 4	135
Marlborough's Victories	Plate 1	139
	Plate 3	141
	Plate 3	145
	Plate 4	147
Dr. Sacheverell	Plate 1	152
	Plate 2	155
	Plate 3	158
	Plate 4	161
South Sea Bubble	Plate 1	165
	Plate 2	167
	Plate 3	169
	Plate 4	171
All the Bubbles	Plate 1	176
	Plate 2	179
	Plate 3	181
	Plate 4	184
	Plate 5	186

Preface

It is the historian's duty to leave no stone unturned in his search for truth. Historical evidence can be found in many 'off beat' places, such as trade tokens, commemorative medals, — and playing cards. Of course such evidence must be handled carefully and only valued for what it is worth, but that still means that the evaluation should take place and not be brushed aside without further thought.

In this book I have taken fourteen packs of cards which depict events in history and put them to the test, not only to see if they tell the truth, but also to find out if they reflect the feelings and rumours of their period and of their subject. The result proved more exciting and fascinating than I had dared to hope. All sorts of curious points emerged as I researched into the pictures on these cards. Careful detective work proved essential.

Plots, rumours, propaganda, victories, disasters, inventions, all came alive in a new way. In the classroom I have found their use a stimulus to learning and understanding the subjects they deal with. Classes have constructed their own historical sets to mirror subjects not covered by these packs.

I am indebted to the late Oliver Warner, David Chandler, Miss M. Packman, the staff of the British Museum and the Guildhall Museum, and the young ladies of the reference section of the Gloucester Library for all the assistance they have given me. I also own a debt of gratitude to my pupils at King's School, Gloucester, for the enthusiasm and interest which they have shown.

Introduction

This book is not intended to be a history of playing cards, but a study of history from certain packs of playing cards. Nevertheless, a brief history of playing cards and the games they were used in as far as England is concerned would not be out of place.

Playing cards originated in the East and were probably adapted from chess in India or China about 450 A.D. Originally the court cards were the king, the horseman, the camel and the footman. No queen was included. As their use spread westwards and reached Europe in the fourteenth century, so the king became the queen of the west, the horseman the knight, and the camel the bishop. The Italians chose to have king, queen, knight and valet in their 56 card packs. The Germans took to using animals or flowers for suit signs and had kings, queens and upper and lower knaves as court cards.

The earliest mention of cards in England occurred in 1463, in the reign of Edward IV, when an act of parliament prohibited the import of cards as English manufacturers needed protection. This implies that they had existed in England for some time.

Both Henry VII and Henry VIII forbad their use in order to encourage long bow practise in spare time. In the accounts of Henry VII are found such references as, 'To King to pley at cardes, £5', and, 'To King which he lost at cardes, £4'. These were large sums in those days. In 1495 Henry VII allowed servants and apprentices to play cards during their Christmas holidays. Incidently, the court costumes on English cards are those of the reign of Henry VII.

Not only did Elizabeth I play cards, but she enjoyed watching card tricks. On 12 May, 1602, we read, 'There is an Italian at Court that doth wonderful strange tricks with Cards, as telling of any card that is thought, or changing one card from another though it be held by any man never so hard under his hand. The Queen gave him 200 crowns for showing his tricks, and divers gentlemen make meetings for him where he getteth sometimes 20, sometimes 40 crowns, and yet they say he spends it so strangely as he cannot keep a penny in his purse'.

In December, 1591, Robert Greene's *Books on Conny-Catching* were on sale. For the Art of Conny-Catching, or 'coseining at card play', three rogues are needed, he tells us. The 'setter' to 'draw in' the conny (the person who is to be cheated) by chatting him into playing with him; the 'verser' to join them and offer to play too; the 'barnacle', who pretends to be a stranger, and is willing to complete the foursome. 'The barnacle and the verser begin to cut the cards, and the verser, asking the conny secretly by signs if he will help him to cheat the barnacle, begins his game, and at the first winneth the stakes until the conny is also drawn in and venturing a high stake, by some sleight the cut falls against him and he is cheated of all'.

During a debate on a monopolies' bill on 20 November, 1601, Dr. Bennet said card monopolies among others were hurtful 'at which Sir Walter Raleigh blushed'. On November 28 a proclamation was issued which included the statement that anyone who is grieved by card monopolies may take the matter to the courts.

In Samuel Rowlands' *The Four Knaves,* 1611, the knaves plead for a change of fashion for their clothing, which was already out of date! By 1628 there were so many card-makers in London alone that they formed a company called the Worshipful Company of Makers of Playing Cards of the City of London.

Puritans referred to cards as the 'Devils's Picture Book'. But in 1665 a set of 52 fortune-telling cards was on sale, with two cards giving explanations for use. On this set the court cards were called Cupid, Wat Tyler, Mahomet, Hewson (see Chapter Two, nine of hearts). Earlier, in 1656, F. Jackson, M.A., had published *Scholer's Practicall Cards,* a little book teaching one to spell, write, cipher and cast accounts by means of cards.

English geographical cards first appeared in 1675, the cards having county maps on them. The thirteen northern counties were clubs, the western counties spades, the eastern counties hearts and the southern counties diamonds. Each card gave the chief towns, compass bearings and a scale, together with details on length, breadth and circumference of each county, latitude of the county town and its distance from London (a) as generally accepted, and (b) as measured by 'Esquire Ogilby'. A number of geographical sets followed this one. In 1665 H. Winstanley produced a set describing far off lands and their inhabitants. Pictures included Jamestown and Boston. In 1684 appeared a pack entitled, *The Arms of the English Peers,* and several similar sets appeared about this time.

It was at this period that the fourteen packs which form the subject of this book began to appear. Samuel Pepys had the Popish

Plot and the 1688 Revolution packs and mounted them as momentoes in his scrapbook (*London and Westminster* Vol II, 2973). He also had a copy of *The Compleat Gamester,* which first appeared in 1674. This pocket-size volume also included detailed instructions on training horses and cock-fighting as well as the rules of contemporary games. In the section entitled 'The Character of a Gamester' we read:

'Some say he was born with Cards in his hands, others that he will die so; but certainly it is all his life, and whether he sleeps or wakes he thinks of nothing else. He speaks the language of the Game he plays at, better than the language of his Country; and can less indure a solecism in that than this .... He loves Winter more than Summer, because it affords more Gamesters, and Christmas more than any other time, because there is more gaming then'.

The cards games it deals with include Picket, Gleek, Cribbidge, and 'Ruff and Honours (alias Slamm) and Whist, are Games so commonly known in England in all parts thereof, that every Child almost of Eight years old hath a competent knowledge'.

The six of hearts became known as 'Grace's Card' when Richard Grace, Governor of Athlone, wrote on one 'Tell your master I despise his offer' in reply to William III's request that he desert James II. In 1692 the nine of diamonds became known as the 'Curse of Scotland' as it was on such a card that the Duke of Cumberland, during a drinking bout, wrote the order to wipe out the Macdonald clan for failing to swear allegiance to William III by 1 January, 1692. J. Dalrymple, later Earl of Stair, got the order, and his coat of arms has nine lozenges or diamonds on it to mark the subsequent massacre of Glencoe.

Card playing was very popular in Queen Anne's reign. Sir Roger de Coverley gave a pack of cards to every poor family in his parish as a Christmas present. Dr. Johnson regretted he had never learnt to play, saying, 'that it is very useful in life; it generates kindness, and consolidates society'.

In 1731 the *Gentleman's Magazine* contained a 'List of Officers established in the most notorious Gaming-houses'. It included, for example, '*An Operator,* who deals the Cards at a cheating Game called *Faro*'; 'Two *Puffs,* who have Money given 'em to decoy others to play'; 'A *Squib,* is a Puff of a lower Rank, who serves at half salary, while he is Learning to deal'.

In 1728 a set of cards was printed for Carrington Bowles with the lyrics and music of the *Beggar's Opera* on them. In 1759 *Aesop's Fables* appeared on a set marketed by I. Kirk. Astronomical cards and 'London Cries' were produced in 1795.

Duties were imposed on playing cards for two reasons, namely, to prevent the importation of foreign cards, and to raise revenue. On 20 July, 1615, a duty of 5/- (25p) on every gross of imported cards was imposed and the office of 'Inspector of all Playing Cards imported' established. The first inspector was Sir Richard Coningsby. When the Worshipful Company of Makers of Playing Cards was established in 1628, they were given power to seize foreign cards and 'cards defectively made or unsealed', on condition that they paid 2/- (10p) on every gross of packs they made and 1/- (5p) to the officer who collected the duty. But in 1631 the Commons complained that the duty was 'arbitrary and illegal' as it was levied without their consent. Orders against foreign cards were issued in 1638, 1643 and 1684.

On 11 June, 1711, it was announced that for the next thirty-two years 'all playing cards made in or imported into Great Britain' should pay a duty of 6d (2½p) per pack as a means of financing Marlborough's campaigns. To break this law was a serious offence, and if one forged a pack's seal one was liable to be executed. One engraver, Harding, was executed for this offence.

The reaction came in the form of petitions such as this one:

'Reasons Humbly offer'd by the Card-makers against the Tax upon Playing-Cards.

The Card-makers in and about the City of London are about One Hundred Master Workmen. For some time past (Paper having been double the Price as formerly) the trade is much Decayed.

The most they sell their Cards for to the Retailers (one sort with another) is Three Half-pence the Pack, and their Profit not above an Half-penny. So that the Tax intended will be double the value of the Cards and six times their gain.

The generality of the Card-makers are Poor men and out of the Small Gains above can hardly maintain their families: And therefore to impose a Tax to be immediately paid upon making by the Cardmakers (whose Stocks and Abilities are so very mean, that they now make hard shift to forbear the Retailers the Ordinary time of Credit) will be a direct way to Ruine these Poor Men.

Besides there is at present a Stock of Cards in the retailers hands sufficient for the consumption of Four or Five year; and they will assuredly sell all the old stock off before they take any at the New advanced rate: The consequence whereof will be:

First That the Cardmakers till that stock be sold off can make no new ones

Secondly That during that time they and their families must needs starve

Lastly That until the card-makers can make new ones no money can arise by such Tax'.

The result was an announcement that cards made before 12 June, 1711, were to be sealed for 1s 2d (6p) per pack, but from 12 August,

1712, no cards were to be sold unless the wrapper was 'sealed and stamped or marked', and one of the cards 'stamped or marked on the spotted or printed side'.

In 1719 a £10 penalty was put on anyone reissuing or using old stamps or seals. Then in 1756 an act (29 Geo II c 13) was passed imposing the charge of 'the sum of 6d (2½p) over and above the duty of sixpence payable for the same'. From 5 July, 1765, the ace of spades became the card to be marked for duty purposes. An extra 6d (2½p) duty was put on periodically in the eighteenth and nineteenth centuries. A man who forged ace of spades was hung for doing so in 1805. Then in 1828 a new duty of 1s (5p) was imposed and the ace of spades was specified as the card to be marked. On 1 September, 1862, the duty was reduced to 3d (1p), and this was only marked on the wrapper. In spite of this card-makers continued to print the ace of spades in a more fanciful way than the other cards. In 1960 the duty was removed.

The process of making early cards was quite simple. First a wood-block designed for each card was made and then these blocks were assembled together in a printing press. The resulting prints were a black outline of the illustrations. Colouring was done by the use of stencils, one for each colour, and a large flat brush was used to apply the colours. Finally the sheet was pasted on to a suitable board with a layer of black between so that the card's identity could not be seen from its back. These sheets were cut up into individual cards. This procedure was used by L. Hewson, the card-making brother of 'cobler' Hewson (see Chapter Two, nine of hearts). Some packs appearing in 1765 were made from sheets that were waterproofed.

Finally mention must be made of the artist responsible for several of the packs dealt with in this book. Francis Barlow, 1626-1704, was the artist for the Rump, Popish Plot and Meal Tub packs, and probably for the Spanish Armada, All the Popish Plots, the Rye House Plot, Monmouth's Rebellion and the Reign of James II, the Revolution, packs. He was famous for his highly decorative canvasses of birds and animals and had illustrated *Aesop's Fables*. He was not an engraver and did not normally do political cartoons. But he seems to have served the Whigs well in their campaign to promote the credibility of Catholic plots. In his work he managed to avoid monotony, and he did not try to say too much on one card. His presentation of his subjects is unemotional but very effective. His Popish Plot pack was so popular that the copper plates had to be re-cut to cover publication demands. His Reign of James II, the Revolution, pack was an outstanding satire on the reign. Some of the original drawings he did for his cards are in the British Museum Department of Prints and Drawings today.

CHAPTER ONE

The Spanish Armada 1588

Nothing appears to be known about when this pack was marketed. It is possible that it was only a few years after the event, but it could equally well have been produced much later as they are in the style of Francis Barlow.

The Pope's participation in the Armada was a fundamental anti-Catholic point in this pack. The pope gave his help spiritually and financially (see also Chapter Three, ace, eight and queen of clubs).

The Spanish navy contained one squadron of 'Apostle' ships before the Armada and another squadron afterwards. Of the earlier squadron the St. Martin, St. Marcos, St. Felipe, St. Juan and St. Mateo were particularly mentioned in the Armada accounts. St. Martin was heavily damaged by Drake at the battle of Gravelines but succeeded in returning to Spain. St. Felipe was surrounded by 17 ships and had 200 casualties. St. Mateo went to her assistance and also suffered severely. Both drifted ashore between Nieuport and Dunkirk and were destroyed by the Dutch. St. Juan suffered heavy damage in the same battle. (See Chapter Three, five of hearts).

The strength of the Armada is given in detail on the ten of hearts. The figures given are near to those accepted as accurate today. Figures held by historians today are:

Knave of hearts

Nine of hearts

Ten of hearts

Ships	Soldiers	Sailors	Rowers	Others	Total man power
130	18,973	8,050	2,088	1,545	30,656

Of the 130 ships, 65 were galleons, 25 hulks (store ships), 32 small ships, 4 galleasses and 4 galleys.

There follows a number of cards giving a break-down of the Armada's strength. Emanuel van Meteran, a Flemish contemporary, drew up a list in similar fashion and it is interesting to compare his figures with those on the cards. He tended to overstress the Armada's might. He also listed 650,000 lbs (295,100 kg) bacon, 300,000 lbs (136,200 kg) cheese, 560,000 lbs (254,240kg) gunpowder, 7,000 muskets, 1,600 brass cannon, 1,000 iron cannon, and 'likewise they were provided of all instruments necessary on land to conveigh and transport their furniture from place to place; as namely of carts, wheeles, wagons, etc'.

Seven of hearts The Portuguese fleet is listed on the seven of hearts, namely 12 ships with 3,330 soldiers, 1,233 sailors and 200 cannons.

Six of hearts Meteran's list for the Biscay squadron gives 10 galleons, 4 pataches (dispatch vessels), 2,000 soldiers, 700 mariners and 260 'great pieces' (cannon). His description of the Armada's galleons reads:

> 'being of an huge bignesse, and very flately build, being of marvellous force also, and so high, that they resembled great castles, most fit to defend themselves and to withstand any assault, but in giving any other ships the encounter far inferior unto the English and Dutch ships, which can with dexteritie weild and turne themselves at all assayes. The upperworke of the said galleons was of thickness and strength sufficient to bear off musket-shot. The lower worke and the timbers thereof were out of measure strong, being framed of plankes and ribs foure or five foote in thicknesse, insomuch that no bullets could pierce them, but such as were discharged hard at hand; which afterward proved true, for a great number of bullets were found to stricke fast within the massie substance of those thicke plankes'.

Five of hearts For the Castile squadron he listed 14 galleons, 2 pataches, 2,400 soldiers, 1,700 mariners and 380 'great pieces' whereas the card has 14 galleons, 2 pinnaces, 2,485 soldiers, 1,719 mariners and 384 cannons. Diego Flores de Valdez, chief of staff, was the real commander of the expedition and after its failure was made the scapegoat. He was hated by his officers as he was a jealous, touchy man. His appointment as chief of staff was a bad one.

Four of hearts According to Meteran, the Andaluzian squadron consisted of 10 galleons, one patache, 2,400 soldiers, 800 mariners and 280 (the card has 260) 'great pieces'. Pedro de Valdez was a good navigator and a man of character and initiative. He was captured by Drake (see three of diamonds).

Three of hearts The spelling of the names on the three of hearts is wrong. The Guipuzcoan squadron was commanded by Miguel de Oquenda. Meteran listed it as 10 galleons, 4 pataches, 2,000 soldiers (the card has 2,800), 700 mariners (807), 310 (311) great pieces. Oquenda was known as 'the Glory of the Fleet' a flamboyant and rashly brave man.

Two of hearts Meteran gave the strength of John Lopez de Medina's squadron as 23 (the card has 25) 'great Flemish hulkes', 3,200 (3,221) soldiers,

Knave ♥ The Pope Consulting with his Cardinalls & Contributing a Million of Gold towards the Charge of the Armada.	 **IX ♥** The twelve Spanish Shipps Caled the 12 Apostles	 **X ♥** The Spanish Armada consisting of 130 Shipps whereof 72 were Galleasses and Galeons in w.ch were 19290 Souldiers, 8359 Mariners, 2080 Gally slaves & 2630 great Ordinance. y.e Navy was 3 whole yeares sparing
 **VII ♥** The Fleete of Portugall consisting of 12 Vessells, in w.ch were 3330 Souldiers, 1233 Mariners, 300 Canons	 **VI ♥** The Fleete of Biscay Comanded by Don Ioan Martinez de Recalde which Consisted of 14 Vessells, 2037 Souldiers, 863 Mariners, 200 Canons.	 **I ♥** Pinnaces and Zabra's Comanded by Don Antonio de Mendoza w.ch were 22, and had in y.m 479 Souldiers, 574 Mariners, and 193 Canons &c
 **X ♦** The 4 Galleasses of Naples Comanded by D: Vgo de Mencado carrying 800 Souldiers, 468 Mariners 1200 Slaves, 200 Canons	 **Knave ♣** Don Alphonso Duke of Medina, Cheife Comander of y.e Spanish Fleete & Iohn Martin Recalde a great Seaman.	 **VI ♦** Arthur L.d Grey, S.r Francis Knolles, S.r Iohn Norris, S.r Richard Bingham, S.r Rog Williams & others in a Councell of War, consulting how y.e land Service should be Ordered

	700 (708) mariners and 400 (110) 'great pieces'.
Ace of hearts	Don Antonio de Mendoza had 22 pataches and zabraes (pinnaces), 488 soldiers, 574 mariners and 193 'great pieces' on Meteran's list.
Ten of diamonds	Don Hugo de Moncado from Naples commanded 4 galleasses with 1,200 slaves, 870 soldiers, 460 mariners, 200 'great pieces'. The ten of diamonds fails to show the galleasses' oars.
Nine of diamonds	Don Diego de Mandrana had 4 Portuguese galleys with 888 slaves (card has 200), 360 (212 mariners and 20 (100) 'great pieces, and 'other requisite furniture', (card adds 220 soldiers) wrote Meteran. It is noticeable that these figures clash with those on the nine of diamonds. Meteran's lists included the squadrons of Medina Sidonia and Martin de Vertendona besides those already mentioned.
Knave of clubs	Medina Sidonia, Admiral of the Fleet, was a colourless, methodical man. He was extremely religious, free from pride and socially qualified for his high post. He was keen to equip his fleet with culverins as he felt large ship-smashing guns were better than smaller man-killers. He scoured Europe to get enough, but never found all he wanted. He made sure there were 50 cannon balls for every cannon aboard. Juan Martinez de Recalde had been a fleet commander for 16 years and had been Santa Cruz's vice-admiral. He was no longer young, but he was a skilled and valiant seaman, the most valuable sailor in the Fleet.
Eight of hearts	The eight of hearts gives the sailing date as May 20, but it is more generally taken as May 30 today. This pack uses the old style dating which works out as ten days earlier than the new style.
	The War Council in England which met in March, 1588, had considered where they expected the landings to be (Plymouth, Milford, Thames, Margate, etc.), the places to be fortified and the need to defend the north in case troops from Flanders landed in Scotland. They wanted to ensure a maximum degree of flexibility in their defence plans. They recommended that all cattle should be driven from the area invaded. Beacon signals which could transmit a warning nearly at the speed of light were set up. Three signals could be sent, a general coastal warning (one beacon), an alert to troops along the coast (two beacons) and an alert for inland
Six of diamonds	counties too (three beacons). 'Black' John Norris was in charge of the veteran mercenaries in Devon and Cornwall. Defences were
Seven of diamonds	particularly good between Plymouth and Exmouth. 3,000 men were stationed on the Isle of Wight. Essex reported a potential force of 13,062 infantry and 300 horses, and promised up to 4,000 men armed with muskets and pikes. The final figure mustered on
King of diamonds	paper was 100,000. Lord Hunsdon referred to on the king of diamonds was Lord Chamberlain. It was considered that 2,000 men were enough to defend the queen herself.
King of hearts	By July, 10,000 at the most were at Tilbury and when Essex's

4,000 arrived, the Earl of Leicester complained bitterly as they had come without beer or bread. He said he was more 'cook, caterer and huntsman' than captain-general. A royal proclamation fixed food, horse meat and lodging prices, etc., within a 20 mile radius of Tilbury. For example, qtr. (12.7 kg) of wheat £1; fat pig 14d (6½p); qt. (1.14 litres) of ale, ½d (¼p); a soldier's supper, which was to include on the menu boiled beef, mutton, veal or lamb, 3d (1p); a night's lodging on a feather bed, 1d (½p). A boom was fixed from Gravesend to Tilbury Fort at a cost of £2,087. It consisted of an anchored string of barges, reinforced by ship's masts used as stakes. It was to block the way to enemy ships and act as a bridge for the defenders. It is believed that it broke under its own weight at the first flood tide. (See queen of hearts, queen of clubs).

The nobility played a full part in checking the defence preparations as the five of clubs shows. — Five of clubs

The English fleet consisted of 195 ships, of which a large number were pinnaces. 14,385 sailors and 1,540 soldiers were ready to man them. The flagship was the *Ark Royal,* 800 tons. — King of clubs

On 21 July, 1588, at 9 am the first shot was fired when the Lord Admiral sent his 'defiance' to a pinnace he had sighted which he had wrongly thought to be Medina's *San Martin.* The 'Defiance' pinnace was in fact the 80 ton bark, *Disdain,* under Captain James Bradbury. She fired one shot and returned unscathed. It should be noticed that no card refers to Drake's game of bowls for there was no contemporary evidence of the game having taken place. (See Chapter Three, eight of hearts). — Five of diamonds

On that same Sunday Drake in the *Revenge,* Hawkins in the *Victory* and Frobisher in the *Triumph* attacked the Armada's rearguard under Recalde. Recalde's powerful galleon and one other ship swung round to take them on, but the rest kept on their course. For an hour Recalde withstood the English onslaught at 300 yards' (274m) range. It is not clear why the other Spanish ships failed to aid Recalde, but possible reasons are (a) the Spaniards panicked, (b) Recalde did not signal them properly, (c) he disobeyed instructions by turning to face his attackers. In the end four of the 'Apostles' rescued Recalde. — Four of diamonds

Drake was fortunate in capturing Pedro de Valdez's *Nuestra Senora del Rosario,* 46 gun, 1,150 ton flagship with 118 sailors, 300 soldiers and 55,000 gold ducats aboard. At 4 pm on July 31 *Nuestra* had collided with another Spanish ship and lost her bow-sprit. When Captain Fisher's *Margaret and John* found her at 8 pm she was wallowing helplessly. It is odd that she surrendered to Drake the next day as her high castles made her unboardable. Drake sent Captain Whiddon in the *Roebuck* to escort *Nuestra* to Dartmouth and get all the fighting gear out of her. But when she docked local people grabbed all the booty they could before magistrates could — Three of diamonds

VII ♦ The Army of 20000 Souldiers laid along ye Southern Coast of England.	 **King ♦** The Army appointed to guard the Queenes person consisting of 24000 Foot, and 2000 Horse, whereof the Lord Hunsdon was Generall	 **King ♥** The Army of 1000 horse, and 22000 Foot, which ye Earle of Leicester comanded when hee Pitched his Tents att Tilbury
 **V ♣** The Earle of Oxford Northumberland Cumberland, wth many more of the Nobility and Gentry going to visit the English Fleet.	 **V ♦** The English Pinnace caled ye Defiance sent from the Admirall, and by a great Shot Challinging the Spaniards to Fight. the 25 of July 1588.	 **IIII ♦** Drake, Hawkins, & Forbisher letting Fly agt ye utmost Squadron which Recalde Comanded and making him Fly to their main Navy for Succor.
 **III ♦** The Galleon of Don Pedro taken Prisoner by Sr Francis Drake, and sent to Dartmouth.	 **Queen ♦** The 2d Squadron ruled by Sr Francis Drake	 **VI ♣** The Ld Admirall Howard Knighting Thomas Howard, the Lord Sheffeild, Rogt Townsent Iohn Hawkins, and Martin Forbisher for their good service

stop them. Whiddon took 10 of the 13 good cannons then on board. (see Chapter Three, nine of hearts).

The English fleet continued on its way in pursuit of the enemy, picking off any that lagged behind.

Howard commanded a squadron of 38 merchant ships and coasters.

Drake had 34 ships in his squadron. Hawkins and Frobisher, veteran sailors, led their squadrons too.

On the morning of July 26, Howard knighted 3 seamen and 3 non-seamen on the deck of the *Ark Royal,* not on a jetty as shown on the six of clubs.

On July 27, Medina Sidonia arrived at Calais and sent a message to the Prince of Parma.

'I am anchored here, 2 leagues from Calais with the enemy fleet on my flank. They can cannonade me whenever they like, and I shall be unable to do them much harm in return. If you can send me forty or fifty fly boats of your fleet I can, with their help, defend myself here until you are ready to come out'.

The fly-boats were fast, shallow-draught ones, just the sort that Parma was short of. He only had a dozen of them. The rest were canal boats without masts, sails or guns, for they were normally used to transport cattle. Medina had no notion of Parma's position (See five of spades, and Chapter Three, seven of clubs).

Seymour had 40 English and Dutch ships to prevent the Prince of Parma's forces from embarking in the Netherlands.

The English fleet anchored only 2 miles away from the Spaniards on that Saturday afternoon. This was within range of long culverin shot. (See Chapter Three, ten of hearts).

On the Sunday it was decided to use fireships against the Spaniards. Drake contributed his own ship, *Thomas,* 200 tons, and Hawkins offered *Bark Bond,* 150 tons. Six more were forthcoming. Their guns were double-loaded with tar-soaked faggots. Just after midnight the eight ships set off. They passed the Spanish pinnace-defence line. When they saw the danger the Spaniards cut their anchor cables, each ship having two anchors out at the time. Thus the fireships' affect was more indirect than direct as they did not set fire to the enemy fleet. The majority of galleons had no spare anchors and drifted away. Off Gravelines Medina managed to get 15 ships together. The English tactics were to drive the Spaniards onto the banks, and two were run ashore and two sunk. Drake's ship received 40 hits and two went through his cabin. 'About the conclusion of the fight, the bed of a certaine gentleman lying weary thereupon, was taken quite from under him with the force of a bullet. Likewise, as the Earle of Northumberland and Sir Charles Blunt were at dinner upon a time, the bullet of a demi-culverin brake thorow the middest of their cabben, touched

Ace of diamonds

Queen of spades
Queen of diamonds
Ten & nine of clubs
Six of clubs

Seven of clubs

Eight of diamonds
Four of clubs

Three & two of clubs

VII ♣ — The Spaniards dispatching Messingers to the Prince of Parma requiring him forthwith to joyn himselfe with them.	 **III ♣** — 8 Fireships Sent by y͌ English Admirall towards y͌ Spanish Fleet in y͌ Middle of y͌ night Under the Conduct of Young and Prowse.	 **II ♣** — The Spaniards on sight of the Fireships weighing Ancors cutting Cables and betakeing themselves to flight w͌ a hideouse noise & in great Confusion.
 **II ♦** — The 2͌d Fight betweene y͌ English and Spanish Fleetes being the 23 of June 1588. wherein only Cock an Englishman being w͌ his little Vessell in y͌ Midst of y͌ Enimies died valiently. but y͌ Spaniards much worsted.	 **King ♠** — Drake and Fenez w͌ great Violence set upon the Spanish fleet gathering together before Graveling.	 **VI ♠** — More then halfe y͌ Spanish Fleet Taken and Sunck
 **VIII ♣** — The third Fight betweene y͌ Eng.͌ and Spanish Fleetes, being the 25͌th of June 1588. wherein the English had again y͌ better	 **V ♠** — The Prince of Parma coming to Dunkerk with his Army but too late is received by the Spaniards with reproach	 **X ♠** — The Spaniards Consulting and at last resolving to return into Spain by the north Ocean many of their Shipps being disabled

their feet, and strooke downe two of the standersby'. (See Chapter Three, knave of hearts).

Historians disagree over the date of the incident referred to on the two of diamonds. It seems unlikely that it was June 23, but more likely July 23 or 29. William Coxe of Limehouse had been master of the bark, *Bear*, twelve years earlier and had marooned his commanding officer in Honduras Bay. When he got back to England he was tried for murder as the Spaniards had killed the marooned man. After serving some years in prison, he was made, master of the *Golden Hind,* in Sir Humphrey Gilbert's Newfoundland expedition. In 1588, he commanded the pinnace, *Delight*, and was twice mentioned in dispatches. First in March when he brought tidings from Spain of the Armada's preparations. Secondly, for gallantry in the wild rush for the *San Lorenzo* galleass. On Monday July 29, during the fireship attack, the *San Lorenzo* become beached. On board her were 300 soldiers and 450 slaves. They put up a fierce fight until their captain was shot. Later that day Coxe was hit on the head by a cannon ball. He was often known as Cock or Cope.

Two of diamonds

The fight at Gravelines was on Monday, July 29, and started at dawn. Howard, Drake, Hawkins, Frobisher and Seymour went into the attack. Howard and Sheffield were the last to join in with their ships. The fight lasted all day and the Spaniard's ammunition ran out after they had fired 123,790 rounds. This made it possible for the English to get in closer and use their lighter guns, but still they could not smash the Spanish hulls. Consequently they concentrated on aiming at sailors and rigging. 600 Spaniards were killed, 800 wounded. One English ship was put out of action with the loss of 100. At 4 pm a sudden squall and heavy rain ended the fight.

King of spades

Ace of clubs

Six of spades

The eight of clubs presents something of a mystery due to the date on the card. It could be taken as being two days after the events referred to on the two of diamonds. As we have seen that card appears to be wrongly dated. If so, the eight of clubs refers to July 31. It seems unlikely that this mystery can be conclusively settled.

Eight of clubs

On Monday and Tuesday, July 29-30, Parma embarked his men at Dunkirk. The fly boats had taken a long time to construct and green wood and rotten timbers were intermixed with sound ones. During the embarkation one set of barges sank in a canal and the men were up to their necks in water. Many of these fly boats had no guns, some had defective rigging and others were uncaulked. It seems odd that Parma did not know that the Armada had been defeated by this time. Perhaps he was going through the motions of embarking for the sake of his record in the campaign. (See seven of clubs, also Chapter Three, seven of clubs).

Five of spades

The remaining Spanish ships had set out to return to Spain by way of sailing round the north of Scotland immediately after the battle of July 29.

Ten of spades

Eight of spades	As the Spaniards headed north they were forced to cut their rations to ½lb (227 g) bread, 1 pt (0.57 litres) water and ½ pt (0.28 litres) wine per man per day. Three Levant carracks were lost near the Shetlands. Howard had pursued the Spaniards to the Firth of Forth but shortage of powder had made this effort rather fruitless. In the south of England false reports came in of a battle on August 3 that had involved the loss of 15 English galleons. Drake was reported to have been taken prisoner on board the *San Martin* and to have lost a leg. Under these circumstances Elizabeth felt it wise to visit her troops at Tilbury on August 8.
Queen of hearts Queen of clubs	The Archbishop of Canterbury had been instructed to raise part of the queen's body-guard at Tilbury, and his circular to his bishops raised 560 cavalry. The queen came by barge from St. James's Palace preceeded by silver trumpeters. When she arrived at Camp Royal, which was 2 miles from the river on a hill at West Tilbury, she found it clean and gay with palisades at last in place. Only four men and two boys escorted her round at her own request. She was dressed in white velvet with a silver cuirass embossed with a mythological design, and carried a silver truncheon chased in gold; there were pearls and diamonds in her red wig and she smiled with her black teeth as she rode round on a white gelding. Her speech to her troops is too long to quote here. (See also king of hearts and Chapter Three, ace, queen and king of hearts).
Seven of spades	Meanwhile what remained of the Armada neared Ireland. Twenty-five ships were to be lost off the coast. 2,000 bodies were washed up in one Irish bay alone.
Nine of spades	Don Luis de Cordova, a marquis' brother, was taken from the *Falco Blanco*, which perished at Connemara, as he was worth a ransom. About fifty lesser Spanish nobles and gentlemen escaped drowning off Connaught. The English Lord Deputy of Ireland ordered the slaughter of all those captured save Cordova and his nephew, for fear of an Irish Catholic uprising. Don Alonso de Luzon, commander of *La Trinidad Valenceru*, which was wrecked on a reef near Lough Foyle, was seized and taken to Drogheda. From thence he was taken to London and probably ransomed. Only about six officers captured in Ireland ever saw Spain again.
Knave of diamonds	Those on board the *San Martin* had only the damp of their ragged shirts to drink for the last 12 days of the journey home. Notice a monk is pictured as the knave on the knave of diamonds.
Two of spades	In all the Armada lost 51 ships, namely 4 galleons, 8 flag or vice-flag ships, 10 auxiliary warships, 11 hulks (storeships), 15 small craft (pataches, zabras) 2 galleasses and 1 galley.
Ace of spades	The ace of spades presents something of a mystery as the weapons shown do not seem to warrant the description of 'strange weapons'.
Knave of spades	Twenty-one priests and ten laymen were executed at the time; four of them as the Aramada sailed up the Channel. The rest were

VIII ♠	**Queen ♥**	**Queen ♣**
The Spanish Ships lost on the Coast of Scotland and 700 Souldiers and Marriners cast a Shoare.	 Queen Eliz: visiting her Camp at Tilbury being mounted on Horseback with a Truncheon of an ordinary Captain in her hand	Queene Eliz: walking up and downe ye Camp at Tilbury and encouraging the Captaines an Souldiers.
 **VII ♠**	**Knaue ♦**	**I ♠**
Spanish ships cast away on the Irish Shoare with Marriners and Seamen	The Spanish fleet that remained, returned home disabled & with much dishonor	Severall strange Weapons taken from the Spaniard which were provid:d to destroy ye English
 **Knaue ♠**	**IIII ♠**	**III ♠**
Severall Iesuits hang'd for Treason against the Queene and for having a hand in the Invasion	Queene Eliz Riding in Triumph through London in a Chariot drawn by two Horses and all ye Companies attending her wth their Baners	Queene Eliz: wth Nobles and Gentry and a great number of people giving God humble thanks in St Pauls Church and having set upp the Ensignes taken from the Spaniards

executed from August 28 onwards. It had been known as early as March, 1588, that some Jesuits had been sent to England to rouse the Catholics when the Armada landed.

Four & three of spades

On September 8 the captured Spanish banners were taken to St. Paul's. On November 24 'the Queen, attended by her Privy Council, by the Nobility and other honourable Persons as well spiritual as temporal, in great number, the French Ambassador, the Judges, the Heralds and Trumpeters all on horse back, came in a chariot supported by four pillars and drawn by two white horses to St. Paul's Church, where alighting at the West Door, she fell on her knees, and audibly praised God for her own and the Nation's signal deliverance; and after a sermon suitable to the occasion, preached by Dr. Pierce, Bishop of Sarum, she exhorted the People in a most Royal and Christian manner, to a due Performance of the religious Duty of Thanksgiving, then going to the Bishop of London's Palace, where she dined, she returned in the same order as before, by Torch-light, to Somerset House'. (See also Chapter Three, ace of spades).

Chapter Two

The Knavery of the Rump 1647-1653

This pack is a particularly rare one, only three sets being known to exist earlier this century. One of the three has an additional title oval card. On this card is written, 'The Knavery of the Rump Lively represented in a Pack of Cards To be sold by R.T. near Stationers Hall, and at the Black Bull in Cornhill'. It has two figures on it, the devil and Oliver Cromwell, who is holding a scroll and saying 'Set us accord for a good old cause'.

The pack, designed by Francis Barlow in about 1681, forms a complete political satire of the Commonwealth period. It was produced from copper plates. The cards do not tell a continuous story, so that they do not have to be arranged in a set order. 'R.T.' was Randal Taylor.

Although there are so few of these packs today, the ace of hearts (and the three of hearts as well, as we shall see) are not the same in each pack. In one pack we have 'A Committee of Godwin, Nye, Peters, and Owen, discovering the Marks of Grace in Ministers'.

Ace of hearts

Hugh Peters (1598 — 1660) was a violent and celebrated preacher, a republican and a Leveller. Tall, thin and full faced, he had been whipped and expelled from Cambridge, and left England as he had committed adultery in 1641. Earlier in Salem, Massachusetts, he was the chief accuser at Old Ma Hutchinson's trial in 1637. As an army chaplain during the Civil War he had gread influence over the men. He also acted as a war correspondent and Fairfax's confidential agent. He referred to Charles I as Barabbas, and once called for the destruction of Stonehenge. He was keen on drastic social reform and thought that divorce should be permitted and that an Oxford college should be set aside for 'godly youths out of shops'. He was beheaded on 16 October, 1660. (See the knave of hearts).

John Owen, D.D. (1616-83) was Protector Cromwell's chaplain,

Dean of Christ Church and Vice Chancellor of Oxford University. He served on the Commission for approving public preachers in 1653. He was a tall, strong man with a slight scholar's stoop. A man of vast learning.

Thomas Goodwin (1600 — 80) was an Oxford D.D. and a Separatist preacher. In 1649 he was chaplain to the Council of State with a salary of £200 per annum, and, in the following year, he became President of Magdalen College. In 1653 he was on the commission for approving public preachers and the next year on the commission for removing scandalous ministers in Oxfordshire. His sermons were diffuse, but he appealed to the 'vulgar multitude' as he was against parentally fixed marriages, stressing that Eve was taken from Adam's side and not his foot. (See five of spades).

Philip Nye (1596—1672) was one of Cromwell's chaplains. He and Goodwin were in favour of the independency of each presbyterian congregation. In 1654 he was on both triers' and expurgators' commissions. He held the view that during sermons the preacher should wear a hat, but the congregation should not, but at communion the reverse should apply. (See five of spades and queen of diamonds).

On this card they are at work as commissioners. On the alternative ace of hearts are 'Cromwell, Ireton and Hudson all in ye same boate'. This refers to 1650 when Cromwell was commander-in-chief in Ireland, Ireton was his deputy and Hewson, or Huson (not Hudson as on the card) was governor of Dublin. They are shown sailing away from the sun of loyalty towards the night of treason. Cromwell is in the stern, Huson in the middle and Ireton in the bows.

Ace of clubs — The ace of clubs is an attempt to depict the Royalist opinion of the Long Parliament Roundheads.

Ace of spades — The ace of spades shows Bradshaw (1586-1659) was President of the 'court' which tried Charles I. No doubt this card is hinting at the illegality of the king's trial. 'Jaylor' means jailer. (See the king of spades).

Ace of diamonds — The ace of diamonds refers to the same trial. Possibly the signing of the death warrant is under discussion. (See the king of spades).

Two of hearts — Sir Richard Onslow (1601—64), a Roundhead colonel, was a member of the Protectorate's upper house, in spite of the fact that he was not a keen republican. His eldest son was Arthur Onslow, MP for Bramber in the Long Parliament. They were both in the Convention Parliament on Charles II's return.

Two of clubs — William Lenthall (d.1661) was MP for Woodstock and the Commons' Speaker who had refused to deliver up the Five Members to Charles I. In 1647 he fell under the army's displeasure but he was later restored to his Speakership. (See the nine of diamonds). He refused to take part in Charles I's trial. He was at times Master of the Rolls and Keeper of the Great Seal. He was a

I ♥ A Comittee of Godwin Nye Peters and Owen discouering the marks of Grace in Ministers.	 **I ♣** A Free state or a tolleration for all sort of Villany.	 **I ♠** Bradshā, the Taylor, and ye Hangman keepers of the Liberty of England.
 **I ♦** The High Court of Justice or Olivers slaughter house.	 **III ♥** Sr. Gilbert Gerard and his two sonns.	 **III ♣** Bulstrod and Whitlock present to Oliver the Instruments of Governmt.
 **III ♠** H. Martin defend Ralph who designd to kill the King.	 **III ♦** Simonias slandring ye High Preist to get his Place.	 **IIII ♥** The Rump roasted salt it well it stinks exceedingly.

member of the Convention Parliament and voted for Charles' return. His son, who is depicted hatless, was a Roundhead colonel and MP for Gloucester. He refused to take part in Charles' trial. He became governor of Windsor Castle and was made a Protectorate baronet.

Two of spades The two of spades probably refers to Edward Parry (d.1650) and his son, Benjamin (1634—78). Edward was bishop of Killaloe, although he would never have been safe there as there was a papal bishop there. He served on Wentworth's high commission for ecclesiastical causes in 1635-36. He died of the plague in Dublin. His son was precentor and dean of St. Patrick's Dublin and bishop of Ossory.

Two of diamonds Sir Henry Vane was one of the Secretaries of State deprived of his office when the Long Parliament took over. He was illiterate, revengeful and disliked. His son was an accomplished statesman and very religious. He had gone to New England when Laud began his church reforms. He returned to become Treasurer of the Navy. He was probably the author of the Solemn League and Covenant (See knave of spades). He was executed on 14 June, 1662, for having fought against Charles I.

Three of hearts The three of hearts has alternative pictures depending on the pack. One pack depicts 'Sir Gilbert Gerard and his two sons'. Gilbert, MP for Middlesex, is shown in the middle without a hat. He plotted to murder Protector Cromwell when he went to Hampton Court in 1654, but the 'Gerard Conspiracy' was discovered. It involved seizing the Tower of London, St. James's Palace and Whitehall. Twenty arrests were made and Gilbert was executed. It is not clear why the card refers to his sons as they were unimportant. His brother John was executed in 1654 too. The alternative three of hearts has the title, 'Cromwell pypeth unto Fairfax'. Cromwell is shown playing a pipe and tabor while Fairfax does a Morris dance.

Three of clubs The three of clubs is wrong in referring to Bulstrode and Whitlock as two people. Sir Bulstrode Whitlock (d.1675) was MP for Marlow in the Long Parliament and constable of Windsor Castle. He was a zealous and impartial man, who sought astrological advice at times. On 26 June, 1657, he put the purple velvet robe on Cromwell when he was installed as Protector. He was Richard Cromwell's ambassador for mediating peace between Sweden and Denmark.

Three of spades The three of spades shows Edmond Rolph holding a dagger and Henry Marten (1602—80) standing near him. The card refers to the outcome of Charles I's attempt to escape from Carisbrooke Castle on 28 May, 1648. Rolph, who had once been a shoemaker, was the major on duty when the king was confined there. Charles referred to him a 'a fellow of low extraction and very ordinary parts, who, from a common soldier, had been intrusted in all the intrigues of the army'. It was planned that Richard Osborne, one of the king's attendants, and Dowcett, the clerk of the kitchen, should help the king get out by means of a rope. When the king tried the first time he got stuck in the window bars so the plotters obtained nitric acid ('aqua fortis') to cut the bars. At the last minute two guards, who had been bribed, alerted Rolph, who decided to shoot the king as he emerged. When the plotters found Rolph there, they decided to accuse him of attempting to murder the king. While he was awaiting his trial, his wife, Alice Rolph, complained of his arrest, saying the warrant was illegal and Osborne and Dowcett should be held. Rolph was tried at Winchester on August 28 before John Wilde, who had been bribed with £1,000 to secure his acquittal. He was acquitted and the plotters were arrested. Marten was a regicide and known as a colonel of a regiment of horse and a regiment of whores. (See knave of diamonds).

Simonais may be Dr. Isaac Dorislaus, Professor of History at Cambridge. He was in charge of the London General Letter Office and opened suspicious mail. Being a foreigner, he was disliked by many. He was assassinated by twelve Scots, who surprised him at supper when he was at the Hague, in June 1649. John Evelyn called him 'the villain who managed the trial against his sacred majesty'. *Three of diamond*

The four of hearts refers to General Monck's intervention to restore the monarchy. Bonfires were lit in Cheapside and Bow bells were rung. 'There being rumps tied upon sticks and carried up and down. The butchers at the maypole in the Strand rang a peal with their knives when they were going to sacrifice their rumps'. The Rump was the name given to what remained of the Long Parliament after Pride's Purge. *Four of hearts*

No particular individuals are referred to on the four of clubs. The Covenanter's feet are entangled with thistles and the Independent's with brambles. Religious arguments were rife during the Commonwealth period. *Four of clubs*

Archibald Campbell, Marquis of Argyle, (1598-1661) was a zealous Covenanter as he found it in his interest to exploit that cause for his own aggrandisement. He dealt harshly with clans and families which were his enemies. In 1638 he advised the abolition of episcopacy in Scotland. On 1 January, 1651, he crowned Charles II at Scone, but this did not prevent his execution for treason in 1661. *Four of spades*

Sir Archibald Johnson, laird of Warreston (1610-63) was a strict Presbyterian. He devised a plan whereby whenever one of Charles I's proclamations was read out in Edinburgh, it should be followed by a protestation against it. He was a member of the Committee of Safety and was knighted by Cromwell. He was executed on 22ft high gibbet in Edinburgh in 1663. *Four of diamonds*

The Earl of Pembroke (d.1649) was originally a stout royalist, but switched sides. He was a passionate, undignified man. When the Lords was closed down in 1649, he became MP for Berkshire *Five of hearts*

♣ IIII — A Covenanting Scot & an English In:dependent differ about ỹ things of this world	 ♣ V — Sr H. Mildmay beaten by a foot:boy a great breach of Priviledg	 ♠ V — Nye and Godwin Olivers Confessors.
 ♥ VI — Worsley an Inckle Weaver a man of Personal Valor.	 ♠ VI — Skippon a Waggoner to Sr F. Vere one of Olivers Hectors.	 ♦ VI — Kelsey a sneaking Bodice maker a Gifted Brother
 ♥ VII — Nathaniel Fines whereby hangs a tale.	 ♣ VII — Harrison the Carpenter cutting down ỹ horne of ỹ Beast in Daniel	 ♦ VII — Marshall curseing Mevoz. (Cursed be Mevoz)

and the card shows him thanking the Speaker for his admission.

Sir Henry Mildmay (d.1664) was Master of the King's Jewel House and MP for Malden, Essex.(See king of diamonds). In 1642 he was involved in a brawl in Fleet Street and this may be the subject of the five of clubs. There is a curious reference to Mildmay and a footman in the Earl of Pembroke's will, which reads: 'Item. To the author of the libel against the ladies, called news from the Exchange, I give three pence, for inventing a more obscene way of scribbling than the world yet knew; but, since he throws what's rotten and false on divers names of unblemished honour, I leave this payment to the footman that paid Sir Henry Mildmay's arrears, to teach him the difference 'twixt wit and dirt, and to know ladies that are noble and chaste from downright roundheads'. People turned against Mildmay at the Restoration, and on 12 July, 1661, he was deprived of his title of knight, etc., and ordered to be drawn on a sledge from the Tower to Tyburn and back, and to stay in the Tower for the rest of his life.

Five of clubs

We have already met Nye and Goodwin on the ace of hearts (see also the queen of diamonds). In 1644 Nye had been offered a royal chaplaincy. They believed in the ultimate victory of good sense, and proposed to treat fanaticisms as follies and not crimes, but they were thorough-going independents all the same.

Five of spades

Sir William Waller was in charge of the Roundhead forces in Gloucestershire and Constable of Dover Castle. He was called 'William the Conqueror'. He was beaten by Lord Wilmot at Roundwaydown in 1643, when he lost all his cannon 600 dead and 900 taken prisoners, and at Cropredy Bridge in 1644. The card refers to these defeats.

Five of diamonds

The six of hearts probably refers to Col. Worsley (1622-56), who was one of the eleven major-generals appointed by Cromwell to run England. He was responsible for Lancashire, Cheshire and Staffordshire. He was MP for Manchester in 1654, and was particularly keen on suppressing alehouses. The word 'inckle' comes from Shakespeare's *Winter's Tale* and means tape.

Six of hearts

John Desborough (Desbrow), a major-general, depicted with a cannon in each pocket, married Oliver Cromwell's sister. He refused to take part in the trial of the king, although he was a staunch republican. He was chiefly responsible for Cromwell not taking the crown himself. Desborough did not think much of Richard Cromwell and worked to remove him.

Six of clubs

Philip Skippon had started life as a waggoner before becoming commander of Cromwell's cavalry in 1645 and then major-general of the London militia. He got on well with his men, speaking to them in a homely way before battles. He was wounded at Naseby. He refused to take part in the king's trial.

Six of spades

Colonel Kelsey was originally a button-maker of Birchin Lane London. In 1648 he detected a royalist plot to surprise Oxford, and

Six of diamonds

was awarded an M.A. degree. He became major-general of the Kent and Surrey militia in 1655, and served as MP for Sandwich (1654) and Dover (1656). Reference is made to him in a song called *The Gang:*

'Kelsey was a brave button maker;
  With a heydown, &c,
As ever sat mould upon a skewer;
And this wiseaker
Was a great painstaker,
T'make Lambert's nose look blewer'.
Kelsey is praying for the dole,
  With a heydown, &c,
Of the hospital that's Suttons;
He is out of the roll,
And hath ne'er a loophole,
And now he's making buttons'.

Seven of hearts — Nathaniel Fiennes (1608-69) was the son of Lord Say and Sele. He hated monarchy and episcopacy. As a Roundhead colonel he surrendered Bristol to Prince Rupert on 26 July, 1643. For this he was tried at St. Albans, 14-23 December, on a charge of treachery and cowardice and condemned. When Rupert was driven out equally easily, feeling turned in his favour, and Cromwell ordered his release. The whole incident may be the subject of the seven of hearts, or the card may refer to an incident on 31 July, 1643, when he reached Southampton at the head of 80 horsemen, each of whom had a woman riding behind him. He became the outspoken MP for Banbury and pressed Cromwell to accept the crown! At the Restoration he was pardoned.

Seven of clubs — Thomas Harrison was not a carpenter's son, but a butcher's son. He escorted Charles I from the Isle of Wight to St. James's. A fierce man, he was one of those who signed the king's death warrant. He was known for expounding the Bible, as the seven of clubs suggests. He turned Anabaptist, then became a Fifth Monarchist. On 13 October, 1660, he was executed, and Pepys said he was 'as cheerful a man as could be .... his head and heart shown to the people at which there was a great shout of joy'.

Seven of spades — Christopher Feake was an Anabaptist and Fifth Monarchist, who was imprisoned for denouncing Cromwell.

Seven of diamonds — 'Meroz Cursed' (not Mevoz, as on the seven of diamonds) was the title of a famous 1641 sermon, which was preached no less than sixty times by Stephen Marshall (1594-1655), a swarthy, broad-shouldered, celebrated preacher. He used to roll his eyes round when talking and his gait was 'shackling'. He was chaplain in chief to the Earl of Essex, and at Edgehill he went from tent to tent to encourage the troops before the battle. He was one of the seven morning lecturers at St. Margaret's, Westminster, which meant he had to preach a 6am sermon once a week. He had a salary of £300 p.a. for doing so. Fuller's *Worthies* says of him: 'He was their trumpet, by whom they sounded their solemn fasts .... In their sickness he was their confessor; in their disputations their champion. He was of supple a soul that he broke not a joint, yea, sprained not a sinew, in all the alteration of times'.

Major-General John Lambert, a skilled flower artist, was one of a group of officers who were cashiered for attempting to wrest power from Cromwell's parliament. Their badge was a yellow tulip. Lambert had been the second most powerful man in England at the age of 35, but his political career only lasted six years, and he then spend 23 years in gaol. He died in the Tower in 1683. *Eight of hearts*

Thomas Pride began life as a drayman before becoming a Roundhead colonel. He was a violent, unscrupulous republican. Cromwell found him a useful man as 'Pride's Purge' of the Long Parliament shows. Pride signed the king's death warrant. *Eight of clubs*

'Pride thee we shall not jeer,
Thou ever brought's good beer,
Measure thou didst allow
We'd liquor thee, I vow'.

Thomas Scot, MP for Aylesbury, referred to as Oliver's 'Clerk or Tallyman', was a zealous republican and regicide. He served on the Committee of Safety and Council of State and in 1649 was put in charge of the spy service with a salary of £800 p.a. He fled to Flanders in 1660, but returned to surrender himself. He was executed on 17 October, 1660. He was a radical thinker, who denounced all landowners as anti-Christians. *Eight of spades*

Sir Arthur Haselrigg was a violent opponent of the king. Charles had sought to impeach him in 1642. In 1657 he was a member of the Roundhead upper house, but later withdrew due to his strong republican feelings. He was a sour, morose and obstinate man. He was sent to the Tower in 1660, and died of fever there. The card calls him 'codled braine'. *Eight of diamonds*

The one-eyed Sir John Hewson was a cobbler before he became a soldier of fortune. He served as a Roundhead colonel and signed the king's death warrant. He was governor of Dublin. Later on 5 December, 1659, he became very unpopular when he suppressed the apprentices' demonstration in London. The apprentices were petitioning for a free parliament and when they saw him leading his men against them they shouted. 'A cobbler, a cobbler!' and kicked footballs at his men and threw missiles too. Two or three apprentices were killed and twenty wounded. *Nine of hearts*

'Lord Hewson, the cobbler's teeth greedily chatter
To carve up a'prentice head in a platter'.

The nine of clubs refers to the dramatic end to the apprentices' 'demo' in 1647. The London apprentices' demonstrations were the seventeenth century equivalent of student ones today. Their first demonstration in 1647 secured them a monthly holiday on every *Nine of clubs*

VIII ♥ Lambert K' of ye Golden Tulip.	 **VIII** ♣ Pride Oliver's. Drayman	 **IX** ♥ Huson the Cobler entring London.
 **IX** ♣ The Army entring the City persuing the Apprentices.	 **IX** ♠ A Comittee at Derby house to continue the Warr.	 **IX** ♦ Lenthall runns away With his Mace to the Army.
 **X** ♥ The Rump and dregs of the house of Com remaining after the good members were purged out.	 **X** ♣ Oliver seeking God while the K. is murthered by his order.	 **X** ♠ A Comitte at Haberdashers Hall to spoyle the Cavaleers, as the Iews did the Egyptians.

second Tuesday in the month, and some of them used the first holiday, July 13, to demand that parliament put a stop to the Presbyterians' take-over of the militia. The following day a rival group put on a counter 'demo'. On Friday, July 23, parliament decided to restore the militia to the Independents' control. The apprentices' reaction came on the Monday, when they started a 'sit-in' in the House of Lords. It was short-lived for the Lords agreed to their pro-Presbyterian demands. The Commons suffered a similar fate later in the day. (See nine of diamonds). But on August 6 the army invaded the city, as the nine of clubs shows, overthrew the 'Apprentices' Parliament' and restored the proper one. (See also Chapter Nine, ace of diamonds).

The Committee of Safety, consisting of a chairman and 14 members, was appointed by the Roundheads to raise companies of volunteers. Nine of spades

William Lenthall (See the two of clubs) was Speaker on Monday, 26 July, 1647, when the apprentices drove him out. (See nine of clubs). Three days later, taking the mace, he fled by night with 60 MPs to General Fairfax at Hounslow Camp. He returned on August 6, when the army overthrew the 'Apprentices' Parliament'. Nine of diamonds

On the army's orders Colonel Pride had purged parliament on 6-7 December, 1648, expelling 96 and arresting 45 MPs. This left 78 MPs, who became known as the Rump. One verse in a song of *The Resurrection of the Rump* goes: Ten of hearts

'A cat has a rump, and a cat has nine lives
Yet when her head's off, her rump never strives,
But our rump from the grave hath made two retrives
Which nobody can deny'.

The ten of clubs refers to the story that Cromwell spent the night of 29 January, 1647, in prayer after signing the king's death warrant. Ten of clubs

After the battle of Edgehill a committee was appointed by the Roundheads to meet at the Haberdashers' Hall to consider what fines should be imposed on the Cavaliers captured in the battle. The biblical reference is to *Exodus* 12 v 35-36. That the committee did far more than this is indicated in a song called, *Mr. Hampden's Speech against Peace at the Close Committee:* Ten of spades

'So many nights spent in the city
In that invisible committee;
The wheel that governs all;
From thence the charge in Church and State,
And all the mischiefs bear the date
From Haberdashers' Hall'.

Miles Corbet was chairman of the committee of plundered (or plundering) ministers set up on 1 January, 1642/3, to supply relief to ministers driven from their posts for adhering to parliament. Corbet, an MP and recorder of Yarmouth, was notorious as chairman of the committee for arbitrary, inquisitional procedure, a Ten of diamonds

'continual horse-fair'. Although he was appointed as one of the judges for the king's trial, he only appeared on the sentencing day and was the last to sign the death warrant. In 1662 he was executed and his head stuck on London Bridge.

Knave of hearts We have already met Hugh Peters on the ace of hearts. In a *Collection of Loyal Songs* comes these verses:

> 'And now for a fling at your thimble,
> Your bodkins, rings, and whistles,
> In truck for your toys,
> We'll fit you with boys:
> ('Tis the doctrine of Hugh's Epistles').

> 'To pull down their king
> Their plate they could bring
> And other precious things,
> So that Sedgewick and Peters
> Were no small getters
> By their bodkins, thimbles and rings!'

(Doomsday Sedgewick was a noted puritan preacher)

Knave of clubs Henry Ireton (1610-52) was Cromwell's son-in-law, and Lord-Deputy of Ireland. On 30 January, 1660, his body was dug up from Westminster Abbey and hung on the gallows from 9am to 6pm.

Knave of spades We have already met Sir Henry Vane on the two of diamonds, shown here distinguishing between a 'Legal and an Evangelical Conscience'. He was the principal mover of the Solemn League and Covenant.

Knave of diamonds Reference has been made to Henry Marten on the three of spades. He was a noted wit as MP for Berkshire, and, in spite of his graceful manner, he was a notorious profligate. In *Proper New Ballad on the Old Parliament* are these words:

> 'Sing hi, ho, Harry Martin, a burgess of the bench,
> 'There's nothing here is certain, you must back and
>   leave your wench'.

He had raised a cavalry regiment with the slogan 'for the people's freedom against all tyrants whatsoever', which led to Berkshire rustics joining in the hopes of levelling all sorts of people. He had signed the king's death warrant. He died in Chepstow Castle in 1681 after twenty years' imprisonment, aged 78.

Queen of hearts The queen of hearts refers to the Solemn League and Covenant made in September, 1643, between the Roundheads and the Scots in order to win the war and further church reform. (See the queen of diamonds).

Queen of clubs Oliver Cromwell's wife, Elizabeth, was also known as Joan. Oliver's godmother was Joan Cromwell, wife of Sir Henry Cromwell.

Queen of spades Lady Frances Lambert, a rigid puritan who constantly sang psalms, was reputed to be Oliver's mistress.

♦ X — A Comittee for Plundered Ministers Miles Corbet in the Chaire.	 ♥ Knave — Hugh Peters shews the bodkins and thimbles given by the wives of Wapping for the good old cause.	 ♣ Knave — Ireton holds that Saints may pass through all formes to obtaine his ends.
 ♦ Knave — H. Martin moves ye House that ye King may take the Covenant.	 ♠ Queen — The Lady Lambert and Oliver under a strong Conflict.	 ♦ Queen — The takeing of the Holy League and Covenant.
 ♥ King — The Saints think it meet that the Rump make a League wth. Oneale.	 ♣ King — Oliver declars himself and the Rebells to be the Godly Party.	♠ King — Bradshaw in ye High Court of Justice insulting of the King.

Queen of diamonds	The Solemn League and Covenant was agreed upon in September, 1643. By it the Scots agreed to send an army of 20,000 to help the Roundheads in return for £30,000 a month and a church reform in England. The queen of diamonds shows Philip Nye. (See the ace of hearts, five of spades) preaching on the scriptural authority for the Covenant at St. Margaret's, Westminster, on September 15. When he read the document out, the congregation rose and swore to uphold it. (See the queen of hearts).
King of hearts	The O'Neale referred to on the king of hearts was probably Owen Roe O' Neal (1590-1649), 'the Ruddy', who led those who sought an independent Catholic Ireland. In 1649 he bargained with General Monck. Owen wanted supplies and Monck wanted his hands free to deal with the Scots, so they made a three month truce on May 8. Later Sir Charles Coote saw Owen to make a peace treaty in order to preserve the Londonderry garrison and English interests in the area. Professor Kunzle says Daniel O' Neill is referred to.
King of clubs	Oliver Cromwell firmly believed that God directed his cause. The rebels referred to on the king of clubs are Roundheads.
King of spades	The king of spades refers to the trial of Charles I in Westminster Hall. Cromwell had been forced to nominate 'commissioners' as judges, headed by Bradshaw, who wore a shot-proof hat. The commissioners wore scarlet to suggest they were judges. It was the first trial to get full press coverage for nine papers covered the story. The words spoken on the card were the key words of the trial. Charles rightly pressed the court to prove its authority to try him, while Bradshaw endeavoured to silence him. Bradshaw was given £5,000 and the house of the dean of Westminster for his pains. 'Bradshaw the knave, sent the king to his grave. (See also the ace of spades).
King of diamonds	Sir Henry Mildmay was the subject of the five of clubs. He was married to Anne Hallyday, who is shown beating him for soliciting another's wife.

This is a song which connects the Cromwellians with a pack of cards, but unfortunately not the same pack. It is called, *Win at First and Lost at Last; or, a New Game at Cards*. It was sung to the tune of 'Ye Gallants that delight to play'.

> Ye merry hearts that love to play
> At Cards, see who hath won the day;
> You that once did sadly sing
> The Knave of Clubs hath won the King;
> Now more happy times we have,
>   The King hath overcome the Knave

> Not long ago a game was play'd,
> When three Crowns at the stakes were laid;
> England had no cause to boast,

Knaves won that which Kings had lost;
Coaches gave the way to carts,
   And Clubs were better cards than Hearts.

Old Noll was the Knave o' Clubs,   (Old Noll = Cromwell)
And Dad as such as preach in tubs,
Bradshaw, Ireton and Pride,
Were three other Knaves beside;
And they play'd with half the pack,
   Throwing out all cards but Black.

But the just Fates threw these four out,
Which made the loyal party shout;
The Pope would fain have had the stock,
And with these cards have whipt his dock;
But soon the Devil those cards snatches,
   To dip in Brimstone, and make matches.

But still the sport for to maintain,
Bold Lambert, Haslerigg, and Vane,
With one-eyed Hewson, took their places,
Knaves were better cards than Aces;
But Fleetwood he himself did save,
   Because he was more fool than Knave.

Cromwell, tho' he so much had won,
Yet he had an unlucky son;
He sits still, and not regards.
Whilst cunning gamesters set the Cards;
And thus, alas, poor silly Dick,
   He play'd awhile and lost his trick.

The Rumpers that had won whole Towns,
The spoils of martyrs and of Crowns,
   Were not contented, but grew rough,
As though they had not won enough;
They kept the cards still in their hands,
   To play the Tithes and College lands.

The Presbyters began to fret,
That they were like to lost the sett;
Upon the Rump they did appeal,
And said it was their turn to deal;
Then dealt the Presbyterians, but
   The Army swore that they would out.

The Foreign Lands began to wonder,
To see what gallants we liv'd under,
That they, which Christians did forswear,
Should follow gaming all the year —

Nay more, which was the strangest thing,
   To play so long without a King.

The bold Phanatics present were,
Like butlers with their boxes there;
Not doubting but that every game
Some profits would rebound to them;
Because they were the gamesters' minions,
   And ev'ry day broach'd new opinions.

But Cheshire mean (as stories say)
Began to shew them gamesters' play;
Brave Booth, and all his army, strives (Booth surprised
                    Chester in July '59 but was soon
                      defeated)
To save the stakes, or lose their lives;
But O sad fate! they were undone,
   By playing of their Cards too soon.

Thus all the while a Club was trump,
There's none could ever beat the Rump;
Until a noble General came,
And gave the cheaters a clear slam;
His finger did outwit their noddy,
   And screw'd up poor Jack Lambert's body.

Then Haslerig began to scowl,
And said the General play'd foul;
Look to him, partners, for I tell ye,
This Monk has got a King in's belly;
Not so, quoth Monk, but I believe,
   Sir Arthur has a Knave in's sleeve.

When General Monk did understand
The Rump were peeping into's hand,
He wisely kept his card from sight,
Which put the Rump into a fright;
He saw how many were betray'd,
   That shew'd their Cards before they play'd.

At length, quoth he, some cards we lack,
I will not play with half a pack;
What you cast out I will bring in,
And a new game we will begin;
With that the standers-by did say,
   That never yet saw fairer play.

But presently this game was past,
And for a second Knaves were cast:
All new cards, not stain'd with spots,

As was the Rumpers and the Scots —
Here good gamesters play'd their parts,
   And turn'd up the King of Hearts.

After this game was done, I think,
The standers-by had cause to drink,
And all loyal subjects sing,
Farewell Knaves, and welcome King;
For, till we saw the King return'd'
   We wish'd the Cards had all been burn'd.

CHAPTER THREE

All the Popish Plots 1588-1678

This pack is extremely rare and is probably the work of Francis Barlow. It deals with four plots, Dr. Parry's Plot (3 cards), the Armada (27 cards), the Gunpowder Plot (14 cards), and the Popish Plot (8 cards).

Two advertisements refer to the pack. The first is to be found in *Mercurius Domesticus,* On Friday, 19 December, 1679.

'A pack of cards containing an history of all the Popish plots that have been in England, beginning with those in Queen Elizabeth's time, and ending with this last damnable plot against his Majesty Charles II, excellently engraven, &c. The like not extant,. Sold by Randal Taylor, near Stationers' Hall, and Benjamin Harris, at the Stationers' Arms, under the Royal Exchange in Cornhill. Price One Shilling each pack'.

The second appeared in *Domestic Intelligencer* No. 31, 21 October 1679.

'There is newly published a Pack of Cards containing a History of all the Popish Plots that have been in England, beginning with those in Queen Elizabeth's time, and ending with this last damnable plot against his sacred majesty, King Charles the Second, whom God long preserve; wherein are an exact amount of the Spanish Invasion of 1588, the manner of their attempting England, and their being almost all burnt and taken by Sir Fancis Drake. The conspiracy of Dr. Parry to kill Queen Elizabeth, his confessing the design upon his Tryal, and his Papist-like denying it at his Execution. The History of the horrid Gundpowder plot to blow up the King, Lords and Commons, when they were all sitting in the Parliament House; the manner of its discovery by a letter sent to the Lord Monteagle, the Papists rebelling upon it, their being routed, and the Tryals and Executions of the several accomplices. And lastly, a true account of this present hellish plot against the life of his Present Majesty, the murdering of Sir Edmondbury Godfrey, the several meetings, Tryals and Executions of the Traytors, with all the material passages relating thereto. All of them so contrived that a child that can but read English will be acquainted with a chronicle for above 100 years past of all the bloody purposes and devilish designs of the Papists against the Protestant Religion and the true Professors of it, all excellently engraved on copper-plates, with very large descriptions under each card. The like not extant.

Some persons that care not what they say so they can get by it, lying being as essential to them as eating, for they can as soon live without the last as the first, have endeavoured to asperse this Pack by a malicious libel intimating that it did not answer what is proposed: the contrary is evident to any person that shall peruse them, there being not one material passage in any of the above mentioned plots, but is neatly engraven and exactly described in writing to the great satisfaction of all who have seen them. But malice must shew itself most where the least reason, the aspersors of this Pack do plainly show themselves Popishly Affected in that they would not have the English World know that the Papists have been always as well as now enemies to the Protestant Religion.

They are to be Sold by Randal Taylor near Stationers' Hall and at the Harrow in Fleet Street, at the Three Bibles on London Bridge, at the Feathers at Pope's Head Alley, and in Cornhill at the Ship in St. Paul's Churchyard, at the Three Flower-de-Luces in Little Brittain, and at the Bell in Duck lane and by most other Booksellers. The price of each Pack is one Shilling'.

Just how justified the criticism of the pack was will become apparent when we have studied its contents.

The pack opens with three cards, the two, three and four of spades, which record the essential facts of Dr. William Parry's plot, 1584-5. Born at Northop, Flintshire, Parry had had a legal training and been awarded the degree of D.C.L. He was an immoral person, and frequently in trouble with creditors. This problem had led to his working in Paris between 1579 and 1580 as a spy for Lord Burghley with the task of infiltrating Catholic circles. When he returned he was found guilty on doubtful evidence of having attempted to murder one of his creditors. The queen remitted the death sentence passed on him and he spent a year in prison. He was released on sureties towards the end of 1581. He returned to his spy works in Paris, Milan and Venice. He made contact with a Jesuit, Palmio, in Venice, saying he was prepared to help the Catholic cause. This information was passed to Cardinal Como on 12 March, 1583, and arrangements were made for him to travel to Rome. It was noted that he had worked for the queen for twelve years and, now that he had turned Catholic, was prepared to give important information about a design against the Catholic church known only to himself and the queen.

Parry, never went to Rome, saying it was now too late. Probably he had never intended going, but had shown his willingness in order to make direct contact with the pope. Instead he warned the queen not to trust the Scottish exiles, the Hamiltons, whom she was then sheltering, and also alerted her to trouble brewing in the north.

Two of spades

The question of killing the queen was discussed in Paris between Parry and two servants of Mary, Queen of Scots, named Thomas Morgan and Charles Paget. It seems clear to modern scholars that Parry never intended to carry out the murder, but to ensnare the men into plotting with him.

Morgan took him, muffled in a clerical coat, by night to see the Nuncio, who was very suspicious. The nuncio wrote to Cardinal Como on 10 December, 1583, voicing his suspicions. On January 1, Parry wrote to the pope saying he was prepared to free Mary, Queen of Scots, from her long sufferings in exchange for a plenary indulgence. He made no mention of the proposed murder.

Parry then returned to England, where he received a letter from Como instructing him to go ahead and saying the pope had granted his request. Parry persuaded the queen to see him in the presence of only one other on the pretext that he had something important to tell her. He told her how he had met Morgan in Paris and how he had pressed him to murder her. He even showed her his papal authority and plenary indulgence.

He had hoped for a reward in the form of the Mastership of St. Katherine's Hospital, and when this was not forthcoming, he contacted Edward Neville, another spy, who had lately fallen out with the English government. He proposed that they could better themselves by murdering the queen.

On Thursday, 17 December, 1584, Parry spoke strongly in the Commons against the third reading of a bill for penal measures against Catholics. He was then arrested, but he apologised for his comments and was released.

It was not until 8 February, 1585, that Neville reported Parry's murder suggestion. Parry denied it and pointed out that two witnesses were needed for a treason charge. But a few days later he made a full confession, and at the same time stressed that he had never intended to put the plan into operation.

Three of spades

He was tried on February 25. The prosecution assumed the existence of a papal plot, and claimed that Parry's earlier disclosure of the plot to the queen was made in order to make it easier for him to carry it out in the end. Parry insisted on his innocence, which conflicts with the caption on the three of spades.

Four of spades

He was executed on March 2 in Palace Yard, Westminster, being disembowelled while still alive.

II ♠ Dr. Parry consults some Persons to Poyson or Stab Q. Elizabeth.	**III ♠** Dr. Parry at his Tryal at Westminster Confesses himselfe Guilty and is Condemned.	**IIII ♠** Dr. Parry denyes the Fact at his Execution
VIII ♣ The Pope gives plenary Indulgence to all their sins who assist to the Conquest of England.	**Knave ♣** Cardinal Allen renews the Bull of Pope Pius to absolve ye Queen's Subjects from their Allegiance	**V ♣** Five Regiments of old Spanish Soldiers.
VI ♣ 124 Noblemen and others of the greatest houses of Spain Voluntiers.	**IX ♣** Sr. W. Stanley Capt. of 700 English Fugitives offers to serve the Spaniard against his own Country.	**X ♣** The Spaniards bring Torches Whips of Whipcord & Wire & Butcher Knives to Murther & torture the English

It would seem that he was an unstable character, who sought to work for those who paid him best. In the end he became ensnared in his own double-dealings and was made a scapegoat for anti-Catholic feeling.

Ace, eight, queen of clubs
Five of hearts

The Armada section opens with the ace of clubs depicting the pope's participation in the Armada's planning. Not only did he give a plenary indulgence to all concerned, but also financial aid. He blessed the ships involved too, naming twelve of them after the Apostles. (See also Chapter One, knave of hearts).

Two of clubs

The King of Spain saw the invasion not only as a crusade, but as an enlargement of his empire. Philip II asked the pope to make it plain that the Armada was putting Elizabeth's excommunication into effect.

Three of clubs

The commander-in-chief Don Balsano referred to on the three of clubs presents something of a mystery. Probably the man referred to was Don Alvaro de Bazan, better known as the Marquis of Santa Cruz. He had supplied an invasion plan in March, 1586, but Philip saw no hope of paying for the 60,000 soldiers, 30,000 sailors and 77,000 tons of shipping involved. He died in February, 1588, having worked himself to death preparing the Armada eventually agreed upon.

Four of clubs

A similar problem of identity exists over Vicar-General Don Alancorn and his 400 monks and friars on the four of clubs. Probably the reference is to Cardinal William Allen, ex-principal of St. Mary's Hall, Oxford, and co-founder of the English College at Rome. This tall, graceful and dignified man, saw his work in Rome as twofold. First the training of Catholic priests for missionary work in England, and, secondly, helping with plans to overthrow Elizabeth by force. He intended to make use of his missionaries to support the invasion.

Knave of clubs

In 1588 copies of his *An Admonition to the Nobility and People of England concerning the present war* were printed in Antwerp ready for distribution when the landing took place. Burghley got hold of a copy on June 12. In it Allen told Englishmen that the present pope had confirmed Pius V's declaration that Elizabeth was illegitimate and an usurper, and consequently excommunicated and deprived of the throne. He claimed that she was deposed by natural law as a tyrant and by divine law as an heretic. It was therefore the duty of Englishmen to aid the Spanish forces.

Five and six of clubs

Preparations went ahead with recruiting and drilling invasion forces.

Seven of clubs

Reference has already been made to the Duke of Parma's flat-bottomed boats in Chapter One, the five of spades. Each boat was to hold 30 horses.

Nine of clubs

The nine of clubs refers to Sir William Stanley (b.1548), who with Rowland York, had turned traitor on 28 January, 1587, and sold two posts on the Dutch defence line, Deventer and the Sconce (fortress) of Zutphen, to the Spaniards. The Earl of Leicester had put them in charge of these two important posts although the Dutch had pointed out that they were Catholics. In July 1589, Stanley was said to have planned a Spanish invasion of Ireland, which was to be followed up by an attack on Milford Haven. In 1593, Guido Fawkes served in Stanley's regiment in the Low Countries. Stanley lived on into the reign of Charles I.

The ten of clubs reflects the suspicion of Spaniards which was held by Englishmen. *Ten of clubs*

Philip had originally planned for his invasion to take place in the autumn of 1587, but, under pressure from Santa Cruz, he agreed to a postponement. In December, when war seemed certain, the English fleet was put on the alert. But no sooner had this been done than Elizabeth heard that Philip had agreed to a further postponement until March. She used the respite to try and strike a bargain. She fully appreciated the economic sufferings of her people as a result of the decline in woollen exports. Antwerp, Seville and the Rhine had been closed to England's major export trade. Peace was essential if the trade was to prosper again. She could not bring herself to make direct contact with Philip, but made use of the Duke of Parma and the Dutch mediators. Half way through January she ordered Howard to discharge half his men, but not to lay up his ships. A meeting was hastily arranged at Flushing between five commissioners, the Duke and representatives of the Dutch. Parma, ordered by Philip to prolong the negotiations, held preliminary discussions on where the conference should be held and then on what the agenda should be. The negotiations dragged on for six weeks until in March the queen realised their hopelessness. Philip had never slackened his preparations during that time, in fact he had gained by the cancellation of Drake's proposed winter raid on the Spanish ports. At least Elizabeth could claim she had kept the door to peace open. *Three and four of hearts*

The king of clubs refers to English preparations to counter the invasion. This subject has been dealt with in Chapter One on a number of cards. *King of clubs*

The defence preparations at Tilbury and the queen's visit there have been referred to in Chapter One, on the king and queen of hearts and the queen of clubs. *Ace, queen, king of hearts*

The coastal preparations in Kent and Sussex were all important as the king of diamonds in Chapter One showed and as the two of hearts in this pack underlines. *Two of hearts*

The invincibility of the Armada was believed in by many before it sailed and the ten of hearts draws attention to this. *Ten of hearts*

Shortly after sailing the Armada put into Corunna for water on Sunday, June 9. Nearly half the ships had anchored before nightfall, but the rest were still in open water. During the night a great storm blew up which was to last for the next day and a half. It *Six & seven of hearts*

I
An Army of Foot at Tilbury Camp, the Queen present .

Queen
Q. Elizabeth at Tilbury Camp with a leaders Truncheon en-couraging her Captains & Soldier

King
Q. Elizabeth makes an Oration to her Army upon the defeat of the Spanish Armado .

IX
Sr. F. Drake takes a great Gallion and in it Don Pedro with 40 Nobles of Spain and 55000 Duckets in Gold .

Knave
81 Ships of the Spaniards burnt and taken by the Queens Fireships & Men of War

I
Q. Elizabeth appoints a Thankesgiving for y Victory 11 Ensignes were hung up in St. Pauls

V
Catesby, Iohn Wright, Winter and Guy Faulkes consult to blow up the Parliament hous .

VI
a House taken adjoyning to the Parliament house to lay Powder in to blow up King and Parliament

VII
The Cellar under y Parliament house with 20 Barrels of Powder in it covered with 1000 Billets & Faggots

blew 70 ships out into the Atlantic. On June 11 it was calm enough for pinnaces to be sent to look for them. Three days later 2 galleasses and 28 large ships were still missing with 6,000 men aboard. A second start was made on July 12.

The story of the *Defiance's* opening of the battle has been told in Chapter One, five of diamonds. Once again the cards make no reference to Drake's famous game of bowls.   Eight of hearts

Similarly Drake's attack on Don Pedro's *Nuestra Senora del Rosario* is to be found in Chapter One, three of diamonds.   Nine of hearts

The famous fireships' incident has been dealt with in Chapter One, on the two and three of clubs.   Knave of hearts

The great thanksgiving in St. Paul's Cathedral has been described in Chapter One, three of spades.   Ace of spades

The story of the Gunpowder Plot is well known and this pack of cards does full justice to it.

The sequence opens with the conspirators making their plans to blow up James I and his parliament. Robert Catesby, aged 35, was a tall, handsome and charming man. He got on well with his girl-friends and lived above his income. He was a brilliant swordsman and had scenes from Christ's passion engraved on his sword. John Wright of Plowland Hall, Yorkshire, was a school-fellow of Guido Fawkes, both of them having attended the Royal Grammar School, York. Thomas Winter of Huddington Hall, Worcestershire, was a short, stocky man. He was also learned and a good linguist. Guido Fawkes, who used the name of John Johnson, was a tall, brown-haired Yorkshireman, who had fought in many parts of Europe. He was a mild, cheerful man, a faithful friend and not argumentative.   Five of spades

It was arranged that a house near the Palace of Westminster should be rented and a tunnel dug from it to beneath the Lords' chamber. Thomas Percy arranged the renting. He was a wild neurotic character, who supplied the plotters money by means of embezzlement. The fact the government spy-chief, Cecil, knew so much of the plot before Fawkes' arrest, indicates that Percy may have been party to a double-plot. The theory of the double plot is that certain conspirators, including Catesby, Thomas Winter and Fawkes, were employed by the government to assist Catholics in making the plans. This would enable the Catholic plotters to be arrested. In the end, it is argued, the government double-crossed its agents and silenced them.   Six of spades

The tunnelling went ahead slowly but surely until it was discovered that a cellar below the Lords' chamber had been vacated. Percy hired the cellar ostensively to keep fuel in. Although the seven of spades says 20 barrels of powder were put in there, in fact 36 were moved in. This was equivalent to 3 tons 4 cwts. The cost may have been £500, although there is doubt about this and the figure may have been only £250. The problem remains as to how   Seven of spades

they could have acquired so much powder, half a month's national supply in fact. It is curious that the man in charge of the government store was a relative of Lord Mounteagle (See eight and nine of spades) and that the official store records for 1605 are missing.

Eight of spades

On Saturday, 26 October, 1605, at 7pm Lord Mounteagle was sent a rather cryptic letter warning him to stay away from the opening of parliament. It read:

> 'My lord out of the loue i beare to some of youere frends
> i haue a caer of youer preseruacion therefo i would aduyse
> yowe as yowe tender youer lyf to deuys some exscuse to
> shift of youer attendance at this parleament for god and
> man hath concurred to punishe the wickednes of this
> tyme and thinke not slightlye of this aduertisment but
> retyere youre self into youre contri wheare yowe maye expect
> the euent in safti for thowghe theare be no apparance of
> anni stir yet i saye they shall receyue a terrible blowe
> this parleament and yet they shall not sei who hurts them
> this councel is not to be contemned because it maye do
> yowe good and can do yowe no hareme for the dangere is
> passed as soon as yowe have burnt the letter and i hope
> god will give yowe the grace to mak good use of it to
> whose holy proteccion i comend yowe'.

It seems strange that he asked one of those present when it arrived to read it for him as its writing was clear enough. Perhaps he wanted others to take careful note of what it said. It has been suggested that the letter might have been written by Cecil, so that the government could 'discover' the plot. Lord Mounteagle received a pension of £700 per annum afterwards, which is significant.

Nine of spades

Although it was dark, Mounteagle took the letter straight round to the Court at Whitehall and handed it over to Cecil. He showed it to the Lord Chamberlain and the Earls of Worcester and Northampton. The King was told when he returned on Friday, November 1, and he studied it carefully. He ordered a search to be made. On Saturday afternoon the search was carried out by the Lord Chamberlain, Mounteagle and others. They examined Percy's cellar full of faggots and coal, and even spotted Fawkes. They reported back to the king.

Knave of spades

James ordered a second and more thorough search, and a lame excuse about some missing robes and furniture was made. At midnight Sir Thomas Knivett, a Westminster JP and courtier, made a further search. He found Fawkes, booted and spurred, but 'this Johnson, being wondrously unwilling to be searched, violently gripped one Mr. Doubleday by his fingers of the left hand, who would have drawn his dagger, but bethought himself and did not; and in the heat he struck up the fellow's heels, fell upon him and

VIII
a Letter sent to ỹ L.d Monteagle to inform him of ỹ Plot in doubtful words & he comunicates it to ỹ King

IX
The Letter of the L.d Monteagle read in Council, and ỹ places about ỹ Parliam.t house ordered to be Search'd

Knave
Guy Faukes found at the Celler door with dark Lanthorn and Matches.

X
Guy Faukes brought to ỹ Council where he laments nothing but ỹ he had not Executed his designe

Queen
The Council gave order to the Lord Mayor for a strikt Watch at the City Gates

King
Bonfires are made in London for joy the Gunpowder Treason was discovered.

I
The Papists begin an open Rebellion, Catesby and Piercy fighting back to back k'ild with one Bullet.

II
The Papists design to Murther Faukes in S.t Georges fields if ỹ blow had been given & to lay ỹ Plot on the Protestants.

III
Guy Faukes in ỹ Tower hearing they intended to Murther him confesseth the Conspiracy

	searched him, and in his pockets found his garters, wherewith they bound him, together with some touchwood, a tinder box and a match'. They then discovered the gunpowder.
Ten of spades	Brought before the Council in the early hours of Tuesday, November 5, Fawkes insisted his name was Johnson, denied all knowledge of any other plotters and justified his intention to destroy the king. 'He is quick and careless in his answers unto all objections, fleering and scoffing all that mislike him, repenting only that the deed was not done'.
Queen of spades	The Lord Mayor was ordered to set a watch on all the city gates and an order was given for the arrest of Percy as he had hired the cellar.
King of spades	That night there were many bonfire celebrations to mark the failure of the plot. 'The Spanish Ambassador made bonfires and threw money amongst the people; and the like gladness is shown by the Ambassador of the Archduke, and by those of the French and Dutch churches'.
Ace of diamonds	When the conspirators, some thirty-six in all, realised things were going wrong, some of them set out for the Midlands on stolen horses. They reached Holbeach House, Staffordshire, where some of them were severely injured when the gunpowder which they were trying to dry blew up when a hot coal fell on it. They soon found themselves surrounded by the Sheriff of Worcestershire's posse, which arrived at noon on November 9. In the subsequent fight Thomas Winter was hit by a cross-bow bolt, and two Catesby and Percy, were shot dead by either a single bullet or two bullets fired from one musket. Ten were captured alive. Conveniently for the government Catesby and Percy, who were in the double-plot, were now dead.
Two of diamonds	A side twist of the plot is hinted at on the two of diamonds, which only serves to show that the plot was not so straight forward as it is often assumed to be.
Three of diamonds	Fawkes had been placed in a subterranean cellar under the White Tower, next to the torture chamber. It seems that stretching on the rack made him talk as much as news that the Catholics had intended to murder him. It is significant that the government was in a position to name the plotters on November 7, whereas Fawkes did not confess them until the following day. The government attributed its knowledge of the names to his confession.
Five of diamonds	On November 9 James addressed parliament. He stressed the 'cruelty of the plot itself', and said the discovery of it was not a 'little wonderful' as he had no suspicion of it before the Mounteagle letter. He went on to draw attention to the importance of king and parliament working together. Parliament was then prorogued until January 21.
Four of diamonds	The executions of the plotters took place on January 30 and 31. Four died on each of the two days. Probably the four of diamonds

V — King James Oration in Parliament upon the discovery of the Gunpowder Plot	**IIII** — The execution of y‍ᵉ Traitors for y‍ᵉ Gunpowder Treason	**VIII** — Pickerin attempts to kill y‍ᵉ king in S‍ᵗ Iames Park
IX — Coleman gives a Guiney to four Ruffians to Kill the King	**Knave** — The Irish Ruffians going to Windsor	**King** — D‍ʳ Oates discouereth y‍ᵉ Plot to the King and Councell
VI — S‍ʳ Edmondbury Godfree taking D‍ʳ Oates his depositions	**VII** — S‍ʳ Edmondbury Godfree Strangled Girald going to stab him	**Queen** — The execution of Coleman Grove Pickering and y‍ᵉ five Iesuits

refers to January 31 for on that day died Thomas Winter, Ambrose Rookwood, Robert Keyes and Guido Fawkes. They were drawn from the Tower to the Old Palace at Westminster.

'Winter was first brought to the scaffold where he made a little speech, in which he seemed sorry for his offence, protesting that he died a true Catholic. He went up the ladder with a very pale and dead colour and after a swing or two with the halter was drawn to the quartering block and there quickly despatched.

After him came Rookwood, who made a speech of some longer time, confessing his offence, and asking mercy of God, whom he besought to bless the King, the Queen and all his royal progeny and that they might long live to reign in peace and happiness over this kingdom; but he prayed also that God would make the King a Catholic. And so beseeching the King to be good to his wife and children, and protesting that he died a Catholic, he went up the ladder. He was left hanging until he was almost dead.

After him came Keyes, who made small show of repentance, but went stoutly up the ladder, where staying not the hangman's turn, he turned himself off with such a leap the he brake the halter. Whereupon he was drawn to the block and quickly divided into four parts.

And last of all came Fawkes, alias Johnson, that should have put the fire to the powder, who at his death was more penitent than any of the rest, beseeching all Catholics never to attempt any such bloody act, being a course which God did never favour nor prosper. His body being weak with torture and sickness, he was scarce able to go up the ladder, but yet with much ado by the help of the hangman went high enough to break his neck with the fall.

The quarters of these traitors are placed over London Gates and their heads upon the Bridge'.

The remaining cards in the pack deal with the Popish Plot of 1678. This plot is the subject of Chapter Four, so only brief comments are given on the cards in this pack.

Eight of diamonds

The Plot was to murder Charles II in favour of his Catholic brother, James, Duke of York. The eight of diamonds refers to the attempt of Thomas Pickering, a Benedictine, to shoot the king in St. James's Park in March, 1678. (See Chapter Four, knave of diamonds).

Nine of diamonds
Knave of diamonds

Edward Coleman, once James's secretary, was supposed to have bribed four Irish ruffians to come and shoot the king at Windsor. (See Chapter Four, four and knave of hearts).

King of diamonds
Six of diamonds

Details of the Popish Plot were supplied by that perjurer, Dr. Titus Oates, First he gave his evidence to the King's Council and then listed 43 Articles before the magistrate Sir Edmund Berry

Godrey (See Chapter Four, two and king of hearts).

The murder of Sir Edmund on October 12 has challenged historians over the centuries and is the subject of a number of cards in Chapter Four (spades, 4-queen).

Seven of diamonds

The trials of the conspirators took place in November, 1678. (See Chapter Four, seven of hearts).

Ten of diamonds

The queen of diamonds is inaccurate in showing them all being executed together. Coleman died on 3 December, 1678, Pickering on 9 May, 1679, and the five Jesuits on 20 June, 1679. (See Chapter Four, six of hearts, six of diamonds and the five of clubs).

Queen of diamonds

CHAPTER FOUR

The Horrid Popish Plot 1678

On 26 December 1679 the *True Domestick Intelligence,* No. 50, included this advertisement:
> There is lately published a new Pack of Cards neatly cut in copper, in which are represented to the life the several consults for killing the King and extirpating the Protestant Religion, the manner of the murthering Sir Edmondbury Godfrey, the Tryals and Executions of the Conspirators, and all other material designs relating to the contrivance and management of the said horrid Popish Plot, with their attempt to throw it on the Protestants. These have something more than the first have, and yet nothing left out that was in them nor any old impertinent things added. Printed and sold by Robert Walton at the Globe, on the north side of St. Paul's Churchyard, near the West end, where you may have a pack for eightpence of the very best, you may have them in sheets fit to adorn studies and houses.

In 1977 one of these packs was sold for £1,500 at a London auction.

The famous Popish Plot to murder Charles II had been disclosed to the King, his council and parliament in 1678, but the public had had little knowledge of it. The official newspaper, the *London Gazette,* had ignored the Plot, and citizens had only royal proclamations against Roman Catholics and execution notices to go on, together with the fact that 2,500 militia men patrolled the city during the mysterious crisis. During winter of 1678 to 1679 they became hysterical about the conspiracies which they suspected were going on, and it was not until the expiring of the Press Licensing Act in May 1679 that other newspapers, like the *Domestic Intelligence*, could appear, Londoners must have welcomed the appearance of broadsheets, commemorative medals (See my

"Commemorative Medals — a medallic history of England", David & Charles) and Robert Walton's pack of playing cards and a similar set by Jonathan Wilkins and Jacob Sampson, as a means of clarifying the confused events of the past year. The British Museum has one of the these packs in full colour.

These packs are a particularly good example of cashing in on a bewildered public as they not only offered them a clarification of what had been going on but also exploited the popular feelings of panic and patriotism which arose from those events. Truth and fiction based on perjured evidence are intermingled in these packs and were doubtless taken at face value until in 1685 the original informers were brought to trial.

The Popish Plot in its simplest terms was a largely fictitious series of Roman Catholic attempts to assassinate Charles II in favour of his Catholic brother, James, Duke of York. When the disclosures came panic arose in London due to a "vertical" Protestant versus Catholic struggle coinciding with a "horizontal" government versus the governed struggle. Lack of employment and underemployment, demarcation disputes between watermen and the up-and-coming hackney-coachmen, apprentices' fears of future unemployment, and a financial recession following the end of warfare joined together in the atmosphere of an unstable political situation to cause a panic reaction, which in turn was stimulated by rumours and scraps of information during the autumn and winter months. What explanation did Walton's pack of cards offer to its purchasers?

The first striking thing about this set of cards is that, apart from the cards dealing with the murder of Godfrey, there is no order based on the pack's suits. One wonders whether Walton was too ill-informed to construct a correct sequence, and, if so, to what extent his uncertainty reflected that of the population as a whole. But it may be that as the various informers who came forward added to their evidence over the months of interrogation and court hearings, it became impossible for Walton to decide what chronological system to work on, that of the supposed events, or that of the disclosures. Certainly I have found the task of bringing order out of the confusion of this set a very difficult one, and I do not think a perfect order can be arrived at. On the whole I have followed the order the events are said to have taken place, rather than when the informers disclosed their knowledge of them.

A patriotic set of cards could hardly begin without pointing firmly at the heart of the problem, the pope as the Plot's originator. There is no truth in this however much informers like Titus Oates would have his hearers believe. In fact a number of English Catholics took the oath of allegiance at this time, arguing that papal claims to depose princes had long since lapsed.

Ace of hearts

I have grouped together half a dozen cards which point to

♥ I — The Plot first hatcht at Rome by the Pope and Cardinalls.	 ♣ X — Capt. Bedlow carrying letters to Forraigne Parts.	 ♥ V — Dr. Oates receives letters from ye Fathers to carry beyond Sea
 ♥ VIII — Coleman writeing a declaration and letter to la Chess.	 ♣ VIII — The Conspirators Signeing ye Resolve for killing the King.	 ♦ Knave — Pickerin attempts to kill ye K. in St. Iames Park.
 ♦ I — The Consult at the white horse Taverne.	 ♦ VIII — The Consult at Wild House.	 ♠ I — The Consult att Somerset house.

general Catholic activity at the beginning. The nine of clubs shows Father Conyers denouncing oaths of allegiance and supremacy. George, or John, Conyers has been described as a Benedictine by some and as a Jesuit by others. It was said that he and a certain Keynes were planning to stab the king on his early morning walk over Newmarket heath. *(Nine of clubs)*

The ten of hearts shows Richard Langhorn (d.1679) was the Jesuits' lawyer, and named by the informer Oates as the ringleader of the Plot giving out officer's commissions. When Oates spoke to the Commons on 23 October, 1678, he told them that Langhorne had issued papal commissions signed by the Jesuit General appointing Catholics to ministerial posts in the forthcoming Catholic government. Edward Coleman, the Duchess of York's secretary, was to be a Secretary of State, Sir George Wakeman, the queen's physician, to be Surgeon General, while Langhorn would become Advocate General. *(Ten of hearts)*

Bedloe and Oates were the first of the informers to come forward. Captain William Bedlow had begun life as a Chepstow horse-thief and gradually built up his career as an international con man. Once when he appeared before the Commons he had said, *(Ten of clubs)*

'Mr. Speaker, I have binn a great rogue; but had I not been soe I could not have knowne these things I am now about to tell you'.

Titus Oates was a homosexual psychopath, the son of a Baptist preacher. He had been expelled from Merchant Taylors, a Jesuit training college, and a naval chaplaincy, but not from Cambridge. The Jesuit historian, John Warner, has described him as follows, *(Five of hearts)*

'the speech of the gutter, and a strident and sing-song voice, so that he seemed to wail rather than to speak. His brow was low, his eyes small and sunk deep in his head; his face was flat, compressed in the middle so as to look like a dish or discus; on each side were prominent ruddy cheeks, his nose was snub, his mouth in the very centre of his face, for his chin was almost equal in size to the rest of his face. His head scarcely protruded from his body, and was bowed towards his chest'.

Their part in creating the panic and securing the conviction of the so-called plotters will become clearer as we proceed.

If the Plot was to be seen as a truly popish one the more contacts with the Catholics abroad that could be pointed to the better. With this in mind Oates disclosed that Edward Coleman had been writing incriminating letters to La Chaise, Louis XIV's confessor, in Paris from September, 1675, to November, 1677. La Chaise had replied offering £10,000 for the murder, according to Oates. Coleman had originally been secretary to the Duke of York, but had then become the Duchess' secretary. He was a man of some administrative ability, great personal charm but no common sense. *(Eight of hearts)*

His excessive zeal and piety led him to have a narrow outlook. He figures on a number of cards in the pack.

Four of diamonds
Seven of clubs

Thomas Whitbread, alias Harcourt, became the Provincial of the Jesuits in England in December, 1677. In this capacity he dismissed Oates (known as Father Ambrose) from the Jesuits' St. Omer seminary in Flanders. It was said that Whitbread got twelve colleagues to sign a letter addressed to St. Omer saying that they would murder the Duke of York as well as Charles II if the duke did not come up to their expectations. It is possible that the Eight of Clubs depicts this signing.

Eight of clubs

Knave of diamonds

The first attempt on the king's life was made in March, 1678, by Thomas Pickering, a Benedictine, and Honest William Grove, a Jesuit lay brother, in St. James' Park. They were to shoot him with a silver bullet. Pickering was to have the reward of 30,000 masses at 1s (5p) each, and Grove, a sum of £1,500. Pickering failed as his pistol flint was loose, and he received thirty lashes for his feebleness.

Ace of Diamonds

It was at a Consult held at the White Horse Tavern by St. Clements in the Strand that co-ordinated conspiracy plan was laid on 24 April, 1678, said Oates. The meeting was called by Whitbread and constituted one of the triennial Jesuit business meetings. It lasted four days and some forty Catholics were present. The proprietress later argued in court that her room could only hold twelve, but several men present shouted it could hold thirty! Oates claimed to have been present, although at his own trial in 1685 twenty-one witnesses said he was at St. Omers as student at that time. According to Oates the meeting settled on stabbing, poisoning and shooting as the methods to be used to eliminate Charles II.

Eight of Diamonds

Ace of spades

The next day a subsection of the Consult was held at the Spanish ambassador's Wild House in Drury Lane, and Oates said that Coleman was informed of the Plot and so became deeply implicated. Another Consult was held at the queen's residence, Somerset House on 11 May, 1678. Here Bedloe maintained the queen met Coleman, Lord Belasyse, Lord Powis and Catholic priests and agreed to their plans. In addition to trying to incriminate the queen in the Plot, Bedloe also told the Commons on November 28th that he thought the Dukes of York and Norfolk may have been the two men whose backs he had seen there. Earlier, on November 13th, Oates had privately told the king that his wife had supplied the Jesuits with £5,000 to support the plan for her surgeon, Sir George Wakeman, to poison him. But, taken to Somerset House to point out where the meeting had taken place, Oates had to confess that he did not know one room from another!

Three of diamonds

In August Richard Ashby, alias Thimbleby, who was in charge of the Scottish Jesuits, received instructions from Whitbread to bribe Sir George Wakeman with £10,000 supplied by La Chaise to poison the king.

IIII — Coleman giveth a Guiny to Incourage ye 4 Ruffians.	 **Knave** — The Irish Ruffians going for Windsor.	 **King** — Dr Oates discovereth ye Plot to ye King and Councell.
 **II** — Sr E.B. Godfree takeing Dr Oates his depositions.	 **Queen** — The Club at ye Plow Alehouse for the murther of Sr E.B. Godfree.	 **Knave** — Sr E.B. Godfree dogg'd by St Clements Church.
 **X** — Sr E.B. Godfree is perswaded to goe down Somerset house Yard.	 **IX** — Sr E.B. Godfree Strangled Girald going to stab him.	 **VIII** — Sr E.B. Godfree Carrying up into a Roome.

Ace of clubs	On 22 August, 1678, an important Consult took place at the Savoy Palace, when the prior of the Benedictines promised £6,000 for the Plot, and Dr. W. Fogarty, Oates' doctor, explained his plan to hire four un-named Irish ruffians for £80 to stab the king at Windsor. When giving his evidence, Oates contradicted himself, saying first that the Jesuit George Conyers would stab the king, and second that the ruffians would do it. Robert Jenison (1649-1688), a
Queen of diamonds	lapsed Catholic lawyer, revealed the names of the ruffians to the authorities. Only one, Kearney, was arrested, and he was acquitted when Jenison failed to witness against him. (See Two of Diamonds, Meal Tub pack, Chapter 5.)
Four of hearts	Coleman's encouragement of the ruffians was simply part of Oates' perjured evidence. The Knave of Hearts shows the Irish
Knave of hearts	making their way to Windsor, though in fact nothing came of this plan. On the same day as the Savoy Consult, the Jesuit J. Fenwick
Nine of diamonds	(1628-79, true name, Caldwell) sent some students to St. Omers and made further arrangements overseas.
King & Ten of diamonds	At this point in the story, the pack includes two cards to show that Catholic activity was not solely concerned with assassination.

Staffordshire was one of a small number of counties where Catholic activity took place. The Catholics concerned met at Lord Aston's at Tixall where Stephen Dugdale (1640-1683) was the land agent. Dugdale had been cheating the estate workers out of their wages for some time and in April, 1678, he had been suspended for embezzlement and mis-conduct. Desire for revenge led him to turn King's Evidence, and as he had the status of a gentleman and appeared to be a decent, honest man, the government decided to make good use of him. He told the Privy Council's Committee for Examinations that Lord Stafford and the Jesuits, William Ireland (1636-1679 alias Ironmonger) and Francis Evers or Eure (Lord Aston's chaplain), had met him to discuss plans for shooting the king and the Duke of Monmouth. Dugdale said that he subsequently received incriminating letters from Paris addressed to Evers, and had helped to collect money. He claimed that he had been offered £500 to help with the murders, and maintained that in addition to this local plot there were Catholic peers' and Jesuit conspiracies. William Ireland was the master-mind behind the plan, aided by Lord Belasyse, Lord Arundell and the Duke of York's confessor, Bedingfield. When pressed to explain how the Staffordshire plan was to be achieved, he could only say that Ireland and Stafford had told him that they would give him the details in due course. But Oates had blown the plan skyhigh with his disclosures and he had heard no more. If this was a lame ending to his evidence, his superior intelligence and deportment had made the concept of a Plot sound much more credible than before. (See king of diamonds, queen of hearts, Meal Tub pack, Chapter 5).

Shortly after he had first given information to the king, Titus

Oates had drawn up 43 Articles listing the evidence he had produced. On 6 September, 1678, he had sworn to the truth of these Articles before a leading city magistrate, Sir Edmund Berry Godfrey. On September 27th and 28th, he saw Godfrey again to swear to the full set of 81 Articles which he had then compiled. Godfrey was an austere, melancholy but intelligent bachelor, who made his money as a wood and coal dealer. On Saturday, 12 October, 1678, Godfrey left his home and went to his death. That death has presented historians, doctors and writers with a challenge ever since.

King of hearts
Two of hearts

The pack of cards gave contemporaries the explanation which was based on the perjured evidence of informers. According to this evidence, the murderers met at the Plow Alehouse. They were Robert Green, a cushion-layer in Somerset House chapel, Lawrence Hill, servant to Dr. Gauden, the chapel's treasurer, Henry Berry, a Protestant palace porter, and a cleric named Kelly. They were under the direction of a priest called Girauld, who was employed by the Venetian envoy. They followed Godfrey when he left his house at about 10am on that Saturday, and trailed him until nearly 7pm. They tricked him into coming into the grounds of Somerset House to investigate a fight staged between Kelly and Berry. They grabbed him and strangled him. His body was carried to Hill's room in Dr. Gauden's Somerset House apartment. Two days later his body was moved to another room where Bedloe and Miles Prance saw it. Their part in the murder will be considered later.

Queen of spades

Knave of spades

Ten of spades

Nine of spades
Eight of spades
Seven of spades

On October 16th the body was removed in a sedan chair at midnight. They left it at the foot of Primrose Hill, having run Godfrey's own sword through it. They celebrated their achievement at the Queen's Head Inn at Bow with a barrel of oysters. Godfrey was buried on October 31st with great ceremonial. It is interesting to compare this sequence of cards with the collection of commemorative medals depicting the murder story. (cf my *Commemorative Medals — a medallic history of Britain,* p67). They present the same version of what had happened.

Six of spades

Five of spades
Four of spades
Two of spades

Bedloe said the reason for the murder was that the Jesuits wanted to get hold of Oates' original statement made to Godfrey in order to compare it with his later one, but this is ridiculous. Bedloe even said Godfrey had been smothered when he had clearly been strangled.

King of clubs

Miles Prance gave evidence too. He was Catholic silversmith of Prince St., Covent Garden, who had made religious emblems for the queen. His lodger lied and said Prance had been away during the days in question, and Prance was put in Newgate's 'Little Ease' cell. Bedloe managed to convey to him his notes on the murder and this made Prance realise that Bedloe wanted him to be a fellow informer. On Christmas Eve, Prance made a full confession, so

King of spades

VII — The body of Sr. E.B. Godfree is shewd to Capt. Bedlow & Mr. Prance.	**VI** — The dead body of Sr. E.B.G. Convey'd out of Sommerset house in a Sedan.	**V** — The body of Sr. E.B.G. carry'd to Primrose hill on a Horse.
IIII — The Murtherers of Sr. E.B. Godfre are diverting themselves at Bow after the murther.	**II** — The Funerall of Sr. E.B. Godfree.	**King** — Capt. Bedlow examin'd by ye secret Comitee of the House of Commons.
King — Mr. Prance discovers the murther of Sr. E.B. Godfree to the King and Councell.	**III** — The Execution of the murtherers of Sr. E.B. Godfree.	**VII** — Coleman examin'd in Newgate by severall Lords.

proving the government with its first real break in the case. Although his story did not tally with Bedloe's, his description of what had happened was a detailed one, and it is the basis of the story of the events described above. His evidence fitted most of the medical evidence, and he was able to show that he knew his way round Somerset House, unlike Bedloe. When he withdrew his confession he was promptly put in irons and left to die of cold. This was too much for him to bear, and when the murderers' trial took place he was there to give his evidence clearly and well. In spite of their innocence, Green and Hill were executed on 21 February, 1679, and Berry a week later.

Three of spades

What was the truth? One likely theory is that Godfrey committed suicide. He suffered from acute morbid depression and there was insanity in his family. If so, his body could have been found by several different groups of persons. Catholics could have found the body and feared that they would be blamed. Alternatively, Protestants could have seized the opportunity to put the blame on the Catholics. The Earl of Shaftesbury, a leading Protestant, tried to bribe a coachman Francis Corral with £500 to say he had dumped the body, at the same time threatening to have him rolled down hill in a barrel full of nails if he refused. The man refused, and he was chained up in Newgate.

Suicide has been ruled out by at least one pathologist on medical grounds, in that there were pre-death chest bruises on the body and the marks on the throat were too low down to have made self-strangulation possible.

The Catholics had nothing to gain by committing the murder, and a lot to lose in being blamed for it. An unlikely theory is that the Duke of York had Godfrey murdered for his having been told by Coleman that the Consult of April 24th was held in James' own palace.

One interesting theory was put forward by J.G. Muddiman in 1924 (*National Review,* vol. 84, p138f), namely that the twenty-five year old homicidal maniac, the Earl of Pembroke, was responsible. He had already made a number of unprovoked attacks on people, killing one, and was to kill another in 1680. But there is no evidence to prove this theory, and it is noticeable that no-one claimed the £500 reward by accusing him of Godfrey's murder.

It is doubtful if the truth will ever be known. The importance of Godfrey's death lies in the minds of the public, who reacted emotionally to the news at that time of tenseness. The complexities of the Godfrey case have taken us away from the chronological order of events and we must return to the so-called conspirators. A number of them had been arrested shortly after Godfrey's death.

Nine of hearts

Because of his position as one-time Secretary to the Duke of York, and subsequently secretary to the Duchess, Coleman was a key figure in the interrogations which took place. He was a man of

Seven of hearts

some administrative ability, but no common sense. His great personal charm was offset by his excessive piety and narrow Catholic outlook. Oates had certainly struck lucky when he suggested Coleman's papers should be searched. Old letters showed he had not done so in connection with the Plot. Coleman first appeared as a voluntary witness to refute Oates' accusations, but the letters led to his arrest.

His trial took place in Westminster Hall on 27 November, 1678, before Lord Chief Justice Scroggs and other judges. In those days judges played a greater role in the conduct of the cases and Scroggs gave Oates an unpleasant cross-questioning. Oates claimed he had taken a letter from Coleman to La Chaise, and returned with the reply offering £10,000 for the king's murder. He accused Coleman of being party to the Irish ruffian plan and the Wakeman poisoning one, but Scroggs challenged him as to why he had kept this evidence secret so long. In spite of Oates' bad showing, Coleman was found guilty of treason and went to his death on December 3rd.

Six of hearts

If we turn to Scotland during this period of crisis, we find that the Earl of Lauderdale had been carrying out a policy of religious conformity which particularly affected Presbyterians. In 1677 he made landowners enter into bonds for the good religious behaviour of all persons living on their lands. To enforce this he drafted a Highland army into the Lowlands in 1678. Belatedly the Plotters tried to extend their activities to Scotland. In December 1678, Edmund Everard made detailed accusations against the Scottish nobility to show that the Jesuits were planning a Presbyterian uprising. If there were any plans, they never materialized as no attempt was made in May and June 1679 to capitalize on the Coventers' Rebellion which took place then. Everard had been in the Tower for a supposed plot to poison the Duke of Monmouth some years earlier, before he turned informer.

Five of diamonds

Queen of hearts

Six of clubs

Attempts to present the Plot as a Protestant one did not succeed. Captain Berry and Alderman Brooks refused to be drawn in this respect when offered £500 to do so. Then on 17 December, 1679, the trials of five Jesuits took place. They were Whitbread, Ireland, Fenwick, Pickering and Grove, and they were charged with treason for the supposed Plot. Grove and Fenwick were forced to admit that they knew Oates, but Whitbread and Ireland insisted, quite rightly, that Oates had been at St. Omers when he had claimed to have been present at the Consult of April, 1678. In fact Ireland nearly wrecked the prosecution's case by pointing out that Oates had been found guilty of perjury in 1673. In the case of Pickering and Grove the story of their attempts to shoot the King in St. James' Park were told by Oates. Lord Chief Justice Scroggs directed the juries trying Whitbread and Fenwick to be discharged. They were sent back to prison to be re-tried six months later. The

VI ♥ — Coleman drawn to his execution.	 **II** ♦ — Ireland and Grove drawn to their execution.	 **Knave** ♣ — Reddin standing in y͛ Pillory.
 **VI** ♦ — Pickerin Executed.	 **V** ♣ — The Execution of the 5 Jesuits.	 **III** ♥ — Dr Oates discovereth Gavan in the Lobby.
 **IIII** ♣ — The Tryall of S͛ G. Wakeman & 3 Benedictine Monks.	 **VII** ♦ — S͛ William Waller burning Popish books, Images, and Reliques.	 **II** ♣ — London remember the 2.d of September 1666.

rest were found guilty and ordered to be hung, drawn and quartered, although the sentences were held up by the king until the Commons pressed him for their execution. On 24 January, 1679, Ireland and Grove were executed.

Two of diamonds

As the months of 1679 went by, panic in London continued partially due to the fact that half a dozen fires had broken out in the city. The Three of Clubs refers to a fire started in Fetter Lane by a servant girl, Elizabeth Oxley, on April 10th. Stubbs, a Catholic, was accused of persuading her to commit arson. When arrested, Stubbs put the blame on a Catholic priest, Guilford, who had told him the king would be murdered and 6,000 French troops would invade soon.

Three of clubs

The sensitiveness of MPs can be gauged from their reaction when Sir Henry Capel spotted a 'stranger' in the House on April 3rd. He was Nathaniel Reading, a lawyer often employed by Catholics. Bedloe, who was present, immediately accused him of suborning his evidence in earlier trials. At his subsequent trial on April 24th, Reading was found to have suggested to Bedloe that it might be profitable to reduce Bedloe's evidence against some of the accused Jesuits. As a result Bedloe had withdrawn his evidence against Whitbread and Fenwick, but he had told the government's Committee of Secrecy of Reading's move and they had told him to play along with Reading for the time being. Meanwhile Reading saw the Catholic lords in the Tower, who promised rewards for Bedloe if he would save them when their trials took place. On March 29th a meeting was held at the King's Head Tavern in Charing Cross to make the final arrangements. But, unknown to Reading, George Speke, MP, and another man were hidden in a room to overhear what took place. Reading told Bedloe that Lord Stafford had promised Bedloe an estate in Gloucestershire and Lord Powis, Lord Petre and Sir Henry Tichbourne had also promised rewards. At his trial, Reading said that Bedloe had suggested the whole idea and that the Gloucestershire estate was for himself and not Bedloe. Reading was found guilty and sentenced to stand in the pillory, pay £1,000 fine and serve a year in gaol.

Queen of clubs

Knave of clubs

Six of diamonds

Five of clubs

The executions continued with that of Thomas Pickering on 9 May, 1679. On the Six of Diamonds he can be seen being disembowelled. Then on June 20th, five Jesuits, Whitbread, Fenwick, Gavan, Harcourt and Turner, were hung, drawn and quartered. Dugdale had proved a good witness at their trial as he linked the Jesuits with Godfrey's murder. Oates was faced with sixteen witnesses who was mixing with the Jesuit plotters at their White Horse Consult. Judge Scroggs drew the jury's attention to this point. But in spite of this, and Oates' earlier failure to claim he had seen Gavan in January when he was active in Staffordshire, they were all found guilty.

Three of hearts

On 18 July, 1679, the trial of Sir George Wakeman, the queen's physician, and three Benedictines, William Marshall, William Rumley and James Corker, took place at the Old Bailey. What is not often realised is that the Old Bailey in those days was open to the air. Built in 1673 like a kind of theatre, it was not enclosed until 1737. The judges had a canopy over their section, but the prisoners were brought into the open-air Bail Dock at 6.30am and stayed there chained up until 9pm regardless of the weather.

Four of clubs

Wakeman had denied that he had agreed to poison the king as long ago as September, 1678, when he had voluntarily appeared before the King's Council. Oates appeared and claimed that an entry in a Jesuit ledger at Wild House recorded a payment of £5,000 to Wakeman, and named Corker as the President of the English Benedictines. Judge Scroggs thought little of Bedloe's evidence and directed the jury to acquit Rumley. They were all found not guilty. The popular fury which greeted this verdict forced the jury to flee, and a dead dog was flung into Scrogg's coach. Wakeman promptly left for Brussels. The acquittal marked turning point in the Plot saga, which was eventually to end in 1685 with the punishing of the informers, Oates and Prance, for perjury (See ace of diamonds, ten of hearts, Meal Tub pack, Chapter 5).

Two cards complete the pack. One depicts Sir William Waller (d.1699) burning popish books and relics. Throughout the crisis he had become well known for his ability to arrest Catholic priests and burn their vestments and books. He was a Westminster magistrate. When he stood for parliament in February, 1679, he failed to get in as the electors suspected that he had kept some of the property he had confiscated. Although he did become an MP in September, he was dismissed from his magistracy in April of the following year and fled to Holland to escape his creditors.

Seven of diamonds

The pack is completed with a reminder of the Great Fire of 1666. Accusations at the time of the Great Fire that it had been caused by Catholics had never been forgotten. As late as January, 1681, the Commons affirmed its belief that the Catholics had caused it. In the same year the city authorities added to the inscription on the Fire Monument the words, 'the treachery and malice of the popish faction'. These words were erased during the reign of James II and restored in that of William III. They were finally removed in 1830. The removal of the inscription is depicted on the Two of Clubs of the *Reign of James II, Revolution* set, in Chapter 9.

Two of clubs

Chapter Five

The Meal Tub Plot 1679-80

The Meal Tub Plot, also known as the Presbyterian Plot, came to light in the autumn of 1679. The set of cards for this plot are based on drawings probably done by Francis Barlow (1626-1704), who may have been designer of the Spanish Armada set too. The artist was once thought to have been Sir Andrew Fontaine.

The excitement created by the Popish Plot had begun to decline and the acquittals of Sir George Wakeman and others had undermined the credibility of that plot's witnesses when the news of this new plot broke. But first we must consider the introductory cards.

Knave of diamonds
Ace of clubs
Three of hearts
Nine of clubs
Ace of spades
Seven of diamonds
Knave of hearts

The set opens with a group of cards which point to the continued activity of Roman Catholic plotters. The devil is depicted as the driving force behind the pope, while Jesuits are taken as the instruments of their propaganda and plotting. Father Whitbread was probably seeking non-conformist support for the Catholics when he addressed a meeting of the Quakers.

Two cards in this set refer to Stephen Dugdale, Lord Aston's land agent, who was the subject of the king of diamonds in the Popish Plot set (See Chapter Four). On 26th March, 1679, he had told the House of Commons Committee for Examinations that the Duke of York had told Evers, Lord Aston's chaplain, that he intended to establish Catholicism when he became king. Dugdale had gone on to give evidence at the trial of the five Jesuits. But one night (17 December, 1679) before that trial, he had been approached by Mrs. Anne Price, a fellow-servant of Lord Aston's, who begged him not to give evidence against Father Harcourt, her confessor. Even after the trial she offered him £1,000 reward and the Duke of York's protection if he would recant what he had sworn. Dugdale was introduced to John Tasborough, a gentleman on the Duke's staff, who confirmed Mrs. Price's promises at

King of diamonds

Queen of hearts

♦ Knave — The Devill supplying the Pope with Plotters.	♣ I — The Pope gives out Fresh Comissions.	♣ IX — Father Connyers Preaching against ye Oathes of Alegance & Supremacy
♥ Knave — Whitebread holding forth at the Quaker meeting. "Freinds don't Idolize Poverty"	♦ King — Dugdale gives new depositions to the house of Commons	♥ Queen — Mrs Price cajoling Mr Dugdale to retract his evidence.
♥ X — L.C.J. declares no papist must live in England. S.G. Wakeman marches of.	♦ II — A Popish Zealot clamors at Mr Tennison for his discovery.	♥ II — Mrs Celleire & her dear Spaniard. "Thus the cause is carryd on"

meetings between them at the Green Lettice Tavern in Brownlow St. and the Pheasant Inn. Dugdale was to sign a declaration to the effect that all his evidence was false. But Dugdale had arranged for a person to listen into this conversation with the result that Tasborough and Mrs. Price were tried in January, 1680, for bribing a witness. Tasborough was fined £100 and Mrs. Price, £200, but no direct evidence was brought against the Duke of York.

    Three cards refer to the trial of Sir George Wakeman.(See the four of clubs, Popish Plot, Chapter Four). During the trial the Portuguese ambassador had sent a messenger to try and secure Wakeman's acquittal, but Lord Chief Justice Scroggs had rightly refused to see him. But on the evening of Wakeman's acquittal, 18 July, 1679, the ambassador came to see Scroggs to thank him for the verdict. Scroggs simply replied, 'I am placed to do justice and will not be curbed by the vulgar'. However Wakeman took Scrogg's hint that no papist should live in England and left the country. Robert Jennison, a witness at the Wakeman trial, was approached by a 'Popish Zealot' as he had disproved Ireland's alibi. She was probably Mrs. Cellier, the evil genius of the Meal Tub plot, to whom we must now turn.

Ace of diamonds

Ten of hearts

Two of diamonds

Queen of clubs

    Mrs. Elizabeth Cellier was popularly called the Popish Midwife. Her maiden name was Dormer and she had been brought up as a protestant. She married Peter Cellier, a French merchant who was a good deal older than her, and they settled in London. It is possible that they are the subject ('Rome's Friend') of the queen of clubs, and the ace and two of spades in the Reign of James II, the Revolution pack, described in Chapter Nine. She had a fashionable practice as a midwife, but she was also 'abandoned to lewdness' as she had 'an ungovernable passion for men'.

    At some point in her life she became an ardent Catholic and began visiting Catholics in prison. Whether she acted as a paid agent to care for their needs or simply out of good nature or from politico-religious enthusiasm is impossible to say. Lady Powis, whose husband was in the Tower, gave her money each week to distribute to imprisoned Catholics. Although sincere, she was also rash and excitable, showing a furious resentment for the way in which Catholics were treated in prison.

    About the end of March or the beginning of April, 1679, she met a twenty-five year old prisoner at Newgate imprisoned under the name of Willoughby. His real name was Thomas Dangerfield and he had been born at Waltham in Essex, in 1654. Thomas began his criminal career at the age of fourteen when his father turned him out of the house for illicitly courting a girl at nights. He forged his father's signature for a £50 cheque and went off to London. He travelled to Spain as a manservant, but lost his post and turned to begging and theft before joining the Spanish army. His soldiering days account for the caption on the two of hearts (notice the

Two of hearts

horned cleric muttering in the background). In the original sketch for this card Mrs. Cellier is seated at a table in her bedroom writing a letter to her Spaniard, while a man stands beside her waiting for her to finish it. He returned to England at the age of fifteen and became an apprentice barber before turning to robbery. He moved on to forgery and coining in Flanders and was condemned to death. It is said that he was reprieved when the halter was round his neck. He eventually returned to England at the age of eighteen to continue coining and theft, receiving numerous sentences between 1673 and 1678.

While in Newgate he gave away his associates in a break-out attempt and secured a pardon in January, 1679. But as he was unable to pay his prison fees, he was obliged to stay in prison until Mrs. Cellier paid them for him. It was his vulnerable position which left him at the mercy of Mrs. Cellier, who seems to have been on the look out for a man she could make use of for the Catholic cause. When she first met him, he said he had not eaten for two days and she gave him half-a-crown (12½p). Shortly afterwards she paid for his release. He was barely freed before he was back in a debtors' prison from which she got him moved to the King's Bench Prison. She promised him £1 a week allowance, and while he was under her care there he became a Catholic.

She got him to drug a fellow prisoner called Stroud, or Strode, who claimed that as an old associate of William Bedloe (See Chapter Four) he had come into possession of a letter by Bedloe admitting he knew nothing personally of the Popish Plot and had never seen Sir Edmund Godfrey in his life. Such evidence would help the Catholic cause and Mrs. Cellier was determined to have it. She got her son-in-law, Henry Blasedale, to supply six grains of odium dissolved in syrup of gilly flowers for the purpose. But as he supplied a milder dose than requested it had no effect on Stroud. Further attempts brought little success and Mrs. Cellier decided Dangerfield would be of more help to the cause out of prison, so she paid his debts, (£5 according to her and £70 according to him) and he was released. She installed him at the Goat Inn, Drury Lane, with an allowance of ten shillings (50p) per week. Wearing his old frieze coat lined with blue, blue stockings and breeches and a grey hat tucked up to prevent it flapping about his ears, he was sent round the coffee houses, such as Garraway's Jonathan's, Mann's, Farr's and the Rainbow, to pick up information against the Whigs and Presbyterians, and to aid the distribution of pamphlets he was engaged in helping to produce, such as *The Transforming of Traitors into Martyrs, The Presbyterian Unmasked,* and *The Ballad of the Popish Plot.* Mrs. Cellier was keen that he should spread the rumour that Shaftesbury was behind the murder of Godfrey. The significance of the seven of spades is not clear today unfortunately.

Five of diamonds

Seven of spades

During the summer of 1679 the Earl of Shaftesbury and the Whigs had to campaign hard to keep up the anti-Catholic hysteria of the Popish Plot. They had succeeded in securing the disgrace of the king's minister, Danby, and the execution of a number of Catholics, but they had not yet succeeded in their main object of destroying the Duke of York. In this atmosphere of plotting and counter-plotting, Dangerfield came to realise he could make his name and fortune if he could discover and expose such plots. The problem was that he could not obtain the evidence for the simple reason that it did not then exist in sufficient strength to be of value. There were no clear plot leaders or positive plans, so he decided to manufacture the evidence for the plot loosely called the Presbyterian Plot, and later known as the Meal Tub Plot.

Later on Dangerfield maintained that he had written down what Lady Powis had dictated to him. She was the wife of one of the five lords imprisoned in the Tower during the Popish Plot fever. It is highly unlikely that there is any truth in saying Lady Powis was involved at this stage. Dangerfield showed the documents to Mrs. Cellier, who encouraged him to find out more. It was then arranged that Lady Powis should introduce him to her son-in-law, the Earl of Peterborough, who in turn introduced him to the Duke of York, and through him to the king. Thus the Catholic came to expose a 'Presbyterian' or republican plot to the king. The Duke of York gave Dangerfield twenty guineas and the king gave him a further forty guineas. Dangerfield presented them with what he claimed were Shaftesbury's and Monmouth's plans, headed *The State of the Three Kingdoms,* a scheme for a revolutionary government.

The king sent Dangerfield to Secretary of State Henry Coventry. Coventry was a man with administrative ability, who already had a surfeit of false witnesses on his hands, and he was not impressed with the evidence Dangerfield produced. During his interrogation, Dangerfield mentioned that Col. Roderick Mansell was the quartermaster of the prospective army and had some treasonable papers in his rooms in the Axe Yard, Westminster. Mansell had a doubtful reputation in government circles and perhaps this is why Dangerfield picked on him. Coventry refused to grant him a search warrant for Mansell's room, and his attempts to get one from the Duke of York also failed. This was partially due to the suspicion he was now held in and partially to the fact that he was not prepared to swear to the truth of his story about Mansell.

At Lady Powis' suggestion, Dangerfield took a room in the same lodgings as Mansell, under the name of Thomas, and prepared forged papers to plant in Mansell's room. By pressure on the landlady, Mrs. Harris, he was able to get Mansell moved in his absence to the second floor, while he took over Mansell's first floor rooms. On October 20 or 22, when the landlady was out, he slipped into the room Mansell was to occupy and planted the papers behind the bed.

Four of hearts

Seven of hearts

V ♦ — Dangerfeild managing the sham Plot at the Coffee house.	**VII** ♠ — Dangerfeild takes a Iesuitt in the Court of Request.	**IIII** ♥ — Dangerfeild presents a book of y sham Presbyterian Plot.
VII ♥ — Dangerfeild hiding papers under Capt. Mansfeilds pillow.	**Knave** ♠ — Capt Tom examin'd before the Councell.	**VII** ♣ — The sham Plott discovered in the meal tubb.
VI ♣ — Dangerfeild offred mony to kill the King. "Heaven & this is y reward"	**III** ♠ — Dangerfeild offered the Sacrament to Kill y King.	**IX** ♥ — Dangerfeild is offerd 500ᵗᵇ to kill y Ld Shafts.

When Coventry again refused him a warrant, Dangerfield went to the Custom House and said Mansell had £2,000's worth of smuggled Flanders gold and silver lace concealed in his room. Shortly after 7am the following day, custom's officers Bostock and Stretch arrived to search the room. Naturally no contraband was found, and although they pulled the bed from the wall at Dangerfield's suggestion, they spotted nothing. This must have exasperated Dangerfield, who then looked himself and produced the packet of papers, shouting, 'Here's treason!', calling on them to secure Mansell. The two officers took the papers to their superiors and not to the Secretary of State, while Dangerfield hurried to the king to acquaint him with the discovery. Mrs. Harris found Mansell at the Cat in St. Paul's Churchyard and advised him to move his lodgings, but he refused as flight would only suggest guilt. He rushed to the Custom House to protest at the search, and all his papers, including the forged ones, were promptly returned to him. Having checked them through in front of Mr. Harris, his landlord, he went off to tell Mr. Justice Warcup of what had happened. Warcup knew something of Dangerfield's criminal background, and he in turn went to Mrs. Cellier's house to arrest him. Dangerfield tried to bluff it out, telling Warcup that the king knew all about Mansell's guilt. Unimpressed, Warcup ordered him to appear before the Privy Council the following morning, Tuesday, October 23.

While waiting in the lobby on Thursday morning, he met a Mr. D'Oyley, an officer of the Mint, who recognised him as a counterfeiter. While they argued the Lord Chief Justice passed, and D'Oyley told him of Dangerfield's past. The Lord Chief Justice said he would inform the Council. The outcome was Dangerfield's being held for coining.

Knave of spades

On the same afternoon Dangerfield, Mansell, Harris, Bostock and Stretch were brought before the Council. Unfortunately the account of the proceedings no longer exists. Surprisingly Dangerfield was released. On the Friday he went round to see Mrs. Cellier and gave her the papers which he said he had already shown to Coventry. She gave them to her maid, Anne Blake, who put them under a meal tub.

The Council continued its investigation into the matter and learnt of Dangerfield's forging and planting of the documents on Mansell. He was committed to Newgate on 27 October, 1679. Mrs. Cellier was imprisoned at 10 pm the following day on a charge of harbouring and corresponding with traitors. Sir William Waller

Seven of clubs

spent the night searching her house and so found the papers in the meal tub. Anne Blake confessed her employer had given her two packets to hide, one she had put behind the pewter in the kitchen and the other, wrapped in a sheet of white paper, and containing a paper book tied up with red ribbon, she had put in the tub. The papers were copies of those Dangerfield had put behind Mansell's bed to prove he was engaged in a 'Presbyterian' plot. Their presence in Mrs. Cellier's house helped to link her with Dangerfield in the intrigue. The documents included plans for risings in London, the north and in Scotland on the King's death. They referred to expected desertions from the horse and foot guards, and to the state of readiness of supporters in Dorset, Devon, Cornwall and particularly, York. Long lists of names were included, headed by the Duke of Monmouth as general. Other key figures were Lords Shaftesbury, Halifax, Grey, Essex, Buckingham and Wharton. Col. Blood's name was on the list as a major-general in the republican army, and it is possible that he was acting with Dangerfield and had intended to join in the exposure. But now, Blood hastened to insist on his innocence.

On October 31, Dangerfield was questioned from 8 pm to 2 am by the Lord Mayor, and switched his accusations from the 'Presbyterians' to the Catholics. He confessed that the 'Presbyterian' or 'Meal Tub' plot had been a sham invented by himself to cover Catholic intentions and ruin their adversaries. He claimed that Lady Powis had dictated the papers to him and that Mrs. Cellier and Lord Peterborough had approved of them. Dangerfield said he had rejected Lord Arundell's £2,000 bribe to kill the king, but that he had accepted Lord Powis' £500 bribe to murder Lord Shaftesbury. Twice he had gone to Shafestbury's Thanet House in Aldersgate St., taking Lady Powis' dagger with him, but had achieved nothing as his courage failed him. There is no evidence that he ever tried to kill Shaftesbury, and this story is pure fiction from start to finish. He went on to swear that Lord Peterborough, Lady Powis, Sir Robert Peyton and others met at the house of John Gadbury, the astrologer, who had upbraided Dangerfield for refusing to kill the king because he had 'calculated his nativity and found him to be a person fit for that enterprise'.

Six of clubs
Three of spades

Nine & Eight of hearts

Gadbury (1627-1704), whose mother was a Catholic, had written a book in 1659 entitled, *The Nativity of the late King Charles, Astrologically and Faithfully performed, with Reasons in Art of the various success and misfortune of His whole Life.* He was arrested on suspicion on 2 November, 1679, and held for two months, for which wrongful imprisonment he received £200 compensation in 1681.

Six of spades

The subsequent trials of the Earl of Castelmaine, who was arrested on October 31, and Mrs. Cellier were to depend on Dangerfield's evidence. He himself was released at the end of November and given £2 a week from the secret service funds, after the Council had carried out a thorough interrogation of all the accused. On November 17, the Green Ribbon Club put on a carnival procession which included a float in which protestants dressed up as the pope and the devil. The knave of clubs recalls this

Knave of clubs

♥ VIII — Dangerfeild doing penance for not killing ye E. of S.	 ♣ Knave — Protestants in Masquerade	 ♦ III — Sr. Thomas Gascoyns Tryall.
 ♥ V — Father Rushout gives ye Oath to Mr. Baldron to kill the King.	 ♣ V — Mowbery stab'd in Lei:cester Feilds.	 ♣ VIII — "the Dog is armed. Cut his throat." — Mr. Arnold assasinated.
 ♦ X — Giles in the Pillory.	 ♦ IX — Young Tongue swears against his Father and Dr. Oates.	 ♠ X — The Ld. North takeing Bedlows dying depositions.

float as a commentary of the events of the year.

1680 was to be a year of trials reflecting the fears and confusion that followed the accusations and counter-accusations of 1679. Anti-Catholic feeling was clearly demonstrated by the trial of half a dozen Catholic priests on January 17 on a charge of simply being Catholic priests under 27 Eliz cap 2, which had remained unenforced since Elizabeth I's death. One was a renegade called Father Munson, who went under the name of Lionel Anderson. He had signed the Remonstrance of Loyalty to the King, so denying all Rome's temporal powers, and so been allowed to stay quietly in England since 1671. Dangerfield said Anderson had heard his confession in Newgate and was therefore a practising priest, while Oates and Prance said that they had seen him celebrating mass. Bedloe insisted that Anderson came from a wealthy Oxfordshire family, which was untrue. The priests were all condemned to death, but they were not executed. Anderson was banished.

Four of clubs

The extent of the reaction to the Meal Tub scare can be gauged by the trial of a charitable and aged baronet, Sir Thomas Gascoigne (1596-1686), who was tried on a conspiracy charge on 11 February, 1680. Deaf, lame and half blind, this eighty-five year old man was forced to journey from his home at Barnbow Hall, West Riding, to London to stand his trial. At least he was tried by a jury of fellow Yorkshire men. Gascoigne had discharged one of his servants, Laurence Mowbray, on suspicion of theft and this led Mowbray to seek revenge. He ganged up with Robert Bolron, Gascoigne's coal pit manager, and they envisaged themselves as the Oates and Bedloe of the north. Mowbray laid evidence before the Lord Mayor that a group of Catholics had met at Gascoigne's house and resolved to kill the king, being prepared to pay £1,000 to whoever would do the deed. Bolron (Baldron) said that Father Rushton (Rushout) had administered the oath to him for that purpose. It was also alleged that London and York were to be burnt to the ground. Gascoigne's position was not helped by the fact that in 1678 he had started to give £90 p.a. to the Convent of the Blessed Virgin, which had been temporarily established by Mother Frances Bedingfield at Dolebank, near Fountains Abbey. Judge Scroggs walked out half way through the trial to hear another case, leaving three other judges to conclude the trial, which led to Gascoigne's acquittal. Later in the year other people accused of being present at the Barnbow Hall meeting were tried. Sir Miles Stapleton and Lady Tempest were acquitted in July, and Father Thwing was found guilty and executed on 23 October, 1680. Just before this, on October 15, Mowbray was stabbed as he crossed Leicester Fields, perhaps to prevent him giving evidence.

Three of diamonds

King of hearts

Five of hearts

Three of clubs

Five of clubs

Dangerfield was a leading witness at the trial of the Earl of Castlemaine on 23 June, 1680, for conspiring to kill the king. Among other points he said that Castlemaine had instructed the

Two of clubs	youths who had come from St. Omer's College to give evidence at the trial of the Popish Plot Jesuits as to what they should say. Castlemaine denied this. Dangerfield then accused him of making a
Eight of spades	compendium or account of his own and other Catholics' sufferings as a result of the Popish Plot, together with a list of Presbyterians whom the Catholics wanted condemned for treason. Castlemaine said that if such a list of Presbyterians existed they had written it themselves! The jury acquitted him after retiring for an hour, and he rewarded them with a dinner afterwards. The outcome was not surprising as he had shown considerable skill and calmness in defending himself. (See also Chapter Nine, king of clubs).
Eight of clubs	A certain Monmouthshire magistrate, Captain Arnold, was the attraction in April, 1680. He had a psychopathetic hatred of Catholics and, in addition to personally offering rewards of £200 for every Jesuit captured, he had led men on armed hunts for Jesuits, to the extent of assaulting strangers in London and accusing them of being papists. His efforts had led to the trial of a number of them, and on one occasion he had organized the beating up of witnesses. Between 10 and 11 pm on April 15, he claimed that he was sent on in Jackanapes Lane, or Bellyard, near Fleet St., a cloak being thrown over his head by three men who stabbed him in the head, chest and arm, but that his whale bone bodice had protected him. One of his attackers had shouted, 'Damme, he has armour on; cut his throat'. Arnold said that by the light of a woman's candle he recognised one of his attackers as John Giles, a friend of Thomas Herbert, a Catholic gentleman, whom Arnold was prosecuting for seditious libel against the king. Giles was tried for attempted murder and maintained that he had been on a pub
Ten of diamonds	crawl that night. The defence witnesses could not vouch for his movements after 10 pm and he was sentenced to a fine of £500 and three appearances in the pillory. When he was pilloried on July 26 at Lincoln's Inn Fields he was nearly pelted to death. At his subsequent pillorings he was given protection. In fact it seems certain that Arnold had inflicted the wounds on himself, and the assault story was pure fiction. He was still wearing his white hat and there was no dirt on his clothes, except where he sat. He had two small pricks on his arm, and there was no blood on the ground.
Nine of diamonds	In August, 1680, Simpson Tonge, appeared before the King's Council to testify that his father, Dr. Israel Tonge, and Titus Oates had invented the Popish Plot with the assistance of Lord Shaftesbury. He was not believed, and retracted the story two month laters. It seems that he had hoped to gain personally from the accusations.
Ten of clubs	Oates persuaded Simpson to make a false accusation that Sir Roger L'Estrange, the Tory publisher of the *News* and the *Intelligencer,* had given him a hundred guineas to defame Oates. L'Estrange had written *A further Discovery of the Plot, dedicated*

to Dr. *Titus Oates* in which he had said Oates was not to be believed, and in another pamphlet he had argued Godfrey had committed suicide by falling on his sword. Although he was acquitted L'Estrange became so unpopular that he went into exile in October when parliament met. On November 17 he was burnt in effigy by the London mob, who called him 'The Dog Towzer', which was a reference to his immorality. He was a good violinist and consequently suffered the nickname of 'Old Nol's Fidler'. In a mock edition of *Hue and Cry* appeared the following: 'He has a thousand dog tricks, viz, to fetch for the Papists, to carry for the Protestants, whine to the King, dance to Noll's Fiddle, fawn on the courtier, leap at their crusts, wag his tail at all latches, hunt and cring to the crucifix, but above all this he has a damn'd old trick of slipping the halter'. The poor man had a wife who gambled and a problem daughter too.

Four of diamonds

August was to witness the death of William Bedloe. He had ridden from London to Bristol, where his wife lay ill, and broken his gall bladder in the heat of the hard ride. Lord Chief Justice North, who was in Bristol for the assizes, visited him on August 16 and took down his dying deposition. North took care to have several witnesses present for he regarded Bedloe as an imposter. Bedloe declared that as he hoped for salvation all the evidence he had given about the Popish Plot was true. Pressed to reveal more he rambled on about danger to the king from Jesuits. It is possible that he was half delirious at the time, but he did make it plain that the queen was not involved in any plot to kill the king, only wishing to contribute funds to the Catholic religion.

Ten of spades

Bedlow died on Friday, August 20, at 2 pm, and he was given a handsome public funeral by the city of Bristol. His body lay in state, covered in black draperies, in the Merchant Taylors' Hall, and was then interred in the Lord Mayor's chapel. North reported Bedloe's deposition to the House of Commons on October 28 as the Whigs had claimed that he had tried to suppress sensational disclosures which Bedloe had made to him. The Whigs were most disheartened when they heard he had disclosed nothing new.

Six of diamonds

Ace of hearts

Although Mrs. Cellier had been acquitted on a charge of treason in June, she was found guilty of malicious libel on September 11, for *Malice Defeated: or a Brief Relation of the Accusation and Deliverance of Elizabeth Cellier* which she had written in July and sold at 18s (90p) a dozen copies, or 2s (10p) each. In it she claimed that Prance had been racked and Francis Corral (arrested in connection with Godfrey's death) had been tortured in Newgate, but Prance, Corral and the Keeper of Newgate all denied such accusations. She also exposed Dangerfield's character for what it was worth, drawing on herself his reply entitled, *An Answer to a Certain Scandalous late Pamphlet entitled 'Malice Defeated'*, which was followed by others. After first trying to claim she had

Queen of spades

VI ♦ — Capt. Bedlows Funerall.	**I** ♥ — L.C.I. North delivers Capt. Bedlows dying depositions to ye H. Com.	**Queen** ♠ — Celliers writeing her Narratiue. Jesuits dictateing.
VIII ♦ — "Oh horrid Cheat." Mrs Celliers adventure of the bloody bladder.	**Queen** ♦ — Mrs Celliers disgraceth the Pillory.	**VI** ♥ — Mrs Celleire consulting to burn the Kings Fleet.
IX ♠ — Dangerfeild gives his depositions to ye house of Comons.	**V** ♠ — The Tituler Arch-Bishop of Dublin committed to Newgate.	**IIII** ♠ — "I Abhor Petitions & Parliamts." The great Mouth with the huming Conscience.

written the truth, Mrs. Cellier changed her tactics and pleaded that she was a poor, deluded woman who deserved the court's mercy. The judge summed up the case strongly against her and she was found guilty. She was sentenced to be fined £1,000 and stand in the pillory three times between the hours of 12 am and 1 pm, and her books burnt by the hangman.

Terrified of appearing in the pillory she declared she was pregnant, but a midwife soon denounced that. The next day it took four women to dress her and two men to carry her downstairs. She threw herself on the floor shouting she was in labour. Some female Catholic friends rushed forward and it was agreed that the bellowing woman should be re-examined. The result was the discovery of a 'bladder of blood' which she had used to create the symptoms of labour.

Eight of diamonds

On September 18, she stood in the pillory at the Maypole in the Strand, wearing armour under her clothes and holding a kind of battledore in her hands. She was twice knocked down by the shower of stones, turnips and rotten eggs thrown at her. The sheriff's officers were wounded in trying to arrest her assailants. When she appeared at Covent Garden she was again knocked down, and stones were thrown when she made her final appearnace in Charing Cross.

Queen of diamonds

A year later William Lewis accused her of discussing with him a plot to burn the king's ships at Chatham. He claimed that she said the Duke of York would give her £300 to pass to Lewis to pay him for the dead. As Lewis was a known perjurer, it was decided not to pursue a charge against her. She was released from prison in November, 1683, and in 1687 and 1688 received sums from the secret service fund!

Six of hearts

In the meantime, on 26 October, 1680, Dangerfield had appeared before the Commons to make further charges against the Duke of York, Lady Powis and the Earl of Peterborough of being privy to the Meal Tub Plot. He maintained that the Duke had given twenty guineas towards his sham plot. The Whig leaders were still making frantic efforts to keep the plot alive to discredit the Duke and petitioned the king to give Dangerfield a pardon to include perjury. The king felt compelled to agree to a pardon but not to the extent of including coverage for perjury. Parliament did not pursue his accusations any further.

Nine of spades

Irish Catholic activities are to be found referred to on two cards in this pack. The king of spades refers to the activities of Thomas Sampson in March 1681, who tried to subborn four priests to invent a new plot against the Council of Ireland and to swear falsely that the Popish bishops and other clergy had met in Dublin a decade earlier to plan to bring in French assistance.

King of spades

The other card, the five of spades refers to the treason trial of Oliver Plunkett, titular Archbishop of Armagh, in 1681. He was

Five of spades

accused of agreeing to receive French troops in Ireland to wipe out the Protestants. It was said that he had visited seaports to see which were suitable for the landing and had chosen Carlingford, and raised 70,000 men. Brought to London in the autumn, he denied that he had collected money for the uprising, saying that he raised about £60 p.a. for his own upkeep in a small thatched cottage with one servant. He declared that he had never levied soldiers and that he had only been to Carlingford for half an hour in his life. He was executed and buried in St. Giles-in-the-Fields beside Coleman and Pickering.

King of clubs — Three odd cards conclude the pack. The king of clubs refers to John Smith, known as Narrative Smith, an apostate priest, who had become an anglican priest saying 'I hate ye bloudy Religion'. While a Catholic he had lived with the Jennison family, five of whom were Jesuits. He had then turned against the Jesuits and turned away any of them who came there, threatening to horse whip a relative of John Jennison's. He was subsequently tried out as a government witness only to be discarded before he reached the court room.

Four of spades — The four of spades presents something of a mystery as it would not be difficult to refer to a number of the characters of this period as the 'Great Mouth'.

Two of spades — Similarly the two of spades is open to a number of possible interpretations, the most likely of which is that the 'Knave', in the form of the fox-like Charles II, is calling for no parliament, intimidated by Shaftesbury's mob, and the 'Fool', in the form of the ass-like Duke of York, is calling for no petitions to exclude him from the throne.

There remains only the need to make a final comment on the Meal Tub Plot. Was it a Catholic plan to turn the plot into a Presbyterian conspiracy? The Catholics certainly tried to end or stifle the plot, but there is no proof that they tried to manufacture a plot on the part of the Presbyterians. Dangerfield's is the only evidence of this and it is quite likely that Lady Powis and the Earl of Peterborough knew nothing of his criminal character, but accepted him as a poor truthful debtor. We can thus dismiss the plot as a contrivance of Dangerfield's, and turn our attention in the next chapter to a real attempt at assassination.

CHAPTER SIX

The Rye House Plot 1683

Hardly had the Meal Tub affair subsided than the Rye House Plot of 1683 exploded to create added disturbance. The Earl of Shaftesbury who sought to curtail the king's power, had been outmanouvered by Charles II and left for Holland in the autumn of 1682. Opposition to the king now became centred in two groups.

    The first was the Council of Six, namely the Duke of Monmouth, Charles' illegitimate son, Lord Howard of Escrick, the Earl of Essex, Lord William Russell, Colonel Algernon Sydney, John Hampden, and later on, Lord Grey of Werke. They met to make plans to prevent James, Duke of York, from becoming king on Charles' death. The Earl of Essex and Algernon Sydney wanted a republic.

    It is impossible to say whether they knew of the existence of the second opposition group which was made up of conspirators who were destined to bring the Council of Six to their doom. This group of conspirators met at various inns, such as the Horse Shoe on Tower Hill, the King's Head in Atheist Alley and the Young Devil near the Temple, or in Mr. Sheppard's house in Lombard St. Their social status was well below that of the Council of Six, but they were more determined and united.

    The leading members among whom were ex-Rump officers, were Colonel J. Rumsey; Lt. Colonel Thomas Walcot; Richard Rumbold, an ex-Roundhead soldier and malster, known as Hannibal as he had only one eye; Richard Nelthorpe, a lawyer; Josiah Keeling, an anabaptist and oilman from St. Botolph-without-Aldgate; Robert West, a lawyer; and the Revd. Robert Ferguson, Shaftesbury's old chaplain and a troublesome pamphleteer. Ferguson had escaped with Shaftesbury to Holland, but returned in February, 1683, to take a leading part in the plot. When his arrest was ordered in August, he was described as 'A tall

King of clubs

Four of diamonds

Six of diamonds
Two of diamonds
Knave of diamonds
Ace & three of diamonds
Knave of clubs

IIII ♦ — The Counsell of Six sitting	VI ♠ — Rumsey sent to the Consult at Sheaphard by Shaftsbury	Knave ♣ — Ferguson the Independent Parson
IIII ♥ "I question not a Scott" — Ar. Smith sent into Scotland to invite Comissins	King ♦ — The places mentioned for Killing ye King	III ♥ "Wapping &c. is ours" — Conspirators veiwing the Citty and deviding it into 20 prts
V ♥ "they may be seized" — Mon. Arms. & Grey viewing ye Guards	Queen ♣ — A conspirator overturning a cart to stop the Kings coach	IX ♦ — Walcot &c other Conspirators ready to charge ye Kgs Guards

lean man, dark brown hair, a great Roman nose, thin jawed, heat in his face, speaks in the Scotch tone, a sharp piercing eye, stoops a little in the shoulders; he hath a shuffling gait that differs from all men; wears his periwig down almost over his eyes; about 45 or 46 years old'.

They referred to Charles II as the Black-Bird and to James, Duke of York, as the Gold Finch due to the colours of their hair. The conspirators set out to plan an insurrection, which they called the General Point, and the assassination of the king, codenamed the Lopping Point (Rumbold used the word 'lopping' for 'murder').

Early in 1683 the second group laid their plans. One of the first steps which had to be taken was to test the chances of Scottish support. Consequently Aaron Smith was sent in January to sound out the position. Smith was a Treasury Solicitor and friend of Titus Oates. He was No. 45 on Dangerfield's list of 48 members of the Green Ribbon Club, an active opposition group. He was given sixty guineas and told to invite several Scots to come to a consult. Sir John Cockran, Sir John and Sir Hugh Campbell and Alexander Monroe came south, pretending they were going to purchase land in California for colonization. Smith was arrested in the Axe Yard of the Tower on 4 July, 1683, and released in March, 1688.

Four of hearts

Any help from Scotland would be valueless if there was not a coup d'etat in London and uprising in England. In each county the conspirators appointed a leader, concentrating particularly on Taunton, Bristol, Exeter, Portsmouth, York, Chester and Newcastle. They hung a map of London up in Robert West's room, and Richard Goodenough, an ex-under-sheriff, divided the city up into twenty Divisions. A 'Principal Man of greatest trust' was put in charge of each Division, and these men were to collect ten assistants each and put them in charge of sub-divisions, called Underwalks. The assistants were to make lists of reliable supporters in their Underwalks. It was hoped that 8-10,000 names would be listed.

King of diamonds

Three of hearts

As we shall see the Council of Six found themselves arrested when the Plot came to light, but it is unlikely they would have involved themselves with the Rye House conspirators. Nevertheless this pack of cards contains a card which suggests that they were directly involved. On the five of hearts 'Mon' is the Duke of Monmouth, 'Arms', Sir Thomas Armstrong (also known as Henry Lawrence and described as 'a debauch'd Atheistical Bravo'), and 'Grey' Lord Forde Grey, who is the subject of three cards to be considered below.

Five of hearts

The Rye House conspirators considered a number of ways in which to kill the king and the Duke of York. Shooting them in St. James' Park, or sinking their barge by boarding it and shooting holes in it with blunderbusses, or shooting them at the Playhouse were all considered. Their final choice was to use Rumbold's Rye House, a moated castle-like building near Hoddesdon, Hertford-

The designe of Shooting the K.'s Postilian	The designe of Shooting into the K.'s Coach	Conspirators waiting for y.' K. coming by Rumbold's House
The fire at New-Markett.	West bying of Armes	Blunderbusses sent downe to Rumbolds House
Rumbolds Hous	Keeling troubled in mind.	Goodenough & Neltrop flying away in disguise

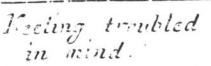

shire, as the hideout for an ambush when the king passed by on his return from the Newmarket races. The Newmarket-London road was reduced to a narrow lane, barely twenty-five feet wide, with high banks and hedges at this point and would be ideal for an ambush, although the cards do not show this. They knew that the king usually passed with only six guards around his coach, and that the horses would be tired as the next posting point was a little beyond Rye House.

Queen of diamonds

As soon as the king's approach was sighted some of the conspirators, dressed as farm labourers, were to overturn a cart in the narrowest point of the lane. Then the interception group under the leadership of Thomas Walcott, were to go into action. Each man had a task assigned to him, to shoot the guards or the postilion or the horses. The assassination group, led by Rumbold, using West's good blunderbuss consecrated by Ferguson, would attack the king's coach.

Queen of clubs

Nine & ten of diamonds

Queen of diamonds

While the conspirators waited at Rye House, the king watched the Newmarket races. On March 22, a serious fire broke out at Newmarket forcing the king to change his quarters, and then to return to London several days earlier than the plotters had expected. Faced with this disaster the conspirators instructed Robert West to get more arms for the uprising and the Revd. Robert Ferguson gave him £100 for them. West told the gunsmith, Daft of Sheer Lane, that he was buying arms for an American plantation and had them packed in sea chests. The purchases were stored in Rye House, and the 10 blunderbusses, 30 muskets, and 30 cases of pistols were referred to by the conspirators as swan-quills, goose-quills and crow-quills, and the powder as ink and the shot as sand.

Ten of hearts
Three of spades

King & Queen of spades
Seven of diamonds
Nine of hearts

They were not to find an opportunity for using them for the Plot was betrayed by Josiah Keeling on June 12th. Drawn into the group of conspirators because of his straightened circumstances, Keeling revealed the story to a courtier, Peckham, and in due course he was brought before the Secretary of State, Sir Leoline Jenkins. In order to produce a second witness, Josiah Keeling introduced his brother John, a Blackfriars turner, to the conspirator Goodenough. The unsuspecting Goodenough explained the Plot to John, and then Josiah took his brother to Jenkins as a witness! Josiah became a popular hero as a result of his disclosures and he received a pardon for his part in the Plot together with a gift of £500. In 1689, when the House of Lords carried out a post mortem into the conspiracy trials of 1683, Josiah was strongly criticised, and John gave evidence against him.

Ace and three of clubs

Four of clubs

On June 18, arrest warrants were issued and the conspirators met at Walcott's lodgings to decide what to do. Some wanted to stay put and deny everything, while others were for collecting a thousand supporters and fighting it out. In the end they split up

VII ♣ "I must discover all" — West writing a Letter to Sr G. J.	**VII ♠** Lord Russell apprehended	**II ♠** Hone and Rowse sent Prisoners to Newgate
VIII ♣ Lord Grey Apprehended.	**XI ♣** Lord Grey sent Prisoner to the Tower.	**IX ♣** Lord Grey making his Escape.
Queen ♥ Thompson one of ye Conspirators taken at Hamersmith	**VIII ♠** Ld Howard writing an account of the Plot	**Knave ♠** "the Jury is story" Goodenough.

and made a run for it. The majority were caught. On June 20th, the Temple chambers of the two lawyers, Richard Nelthorpe and Richard Goodenough, were searched but nothing found. They had escaped via Scarborough to Holland. When the States-General decided to arrest them, they fled to Vevay in Switzerland. They were to re-appear in the Monmouth Rebellion as we shall see in Chapter Seven.

On June 23rd, Robert West decided to turn King's Evidence, and surrendered himself to Sir George Jeffreys. He was taken to Hampton Court to appear before the King's Council, and later appeared as a crown witness in the subsequent trials.

On the evening of the following day, Colonel Rumsey surrendered himself and was brought before the Secretary of State. Rumsey and West had agreed beforehand on the stories which they would tell, and like West, he subsequently appeared as a crown witness.

On June 26th, Colonel Algernon Sydney and Lord Russell were arrested and sent to the Tower. The Council of Six had found themselves involved in the Plot whether they liked it or not. Three days later, a proclamation was issued for the arrest of the Duke of Monmouth, Lord Grey, Sir Thomas Armstrong and Robert Ferguson, announcing a £500 reward for each one captured.

On June 30th, William Hone, a joiner and Fifth Monarchy fanatic, was captured at Cambridge. A reward of £100 had been placed on his head a week earlier. He was eventually brought to Newgate with John Rouse, another conspirator, who had been captured on July 4th.

July 4th was to be an eventful day for on it Lord Grey was not only captured but escaped too. The captured noble was escorted to the Tower by Henry Deerham, or Deering, and when they found the gate shut, Grey seized the opportunity to get his escort drunk on wine at the Rummer tavern at Charing Cross. When Deerham fell asleep, Grey hailed a boat and got away. Another version of the event maintains that they both slept at the tavern and that on the following morning Deerham fell asleep in the coach en route for the Tower, so allowing Grey to step out at the Bulwark Gate and get a boat. Deerham was eventually fined £100 after admitting his carelessness.

Chancellor William Thompson's house in Essex St. had been searched on July 1st and 3rd, and Thompson was taken in Hammersmith. Lt. Colonel Walcot, described as a gentleman with an income of £1,000 pa from Ireland, was taken at Southwark on July 8th. He denied he had any intention of taking part in the actual killing of the king, maintaining that his sole task was to deal with the king's guards. He duly wrote this out for Sir Lionel Jenkins. On the same day Lord Howard of Escrick was taken at his Kensington house after a search had led to his discovery in 'a

Two of hearts	
Knave of hearts	
Two and seven of clubs	
Five and six of clubs	
Seven of spades	
Ace of spades	
Two of spades	
Eight, ten & nine of clubs	
Queen of hearts	
Four of spades	
Five of spades	

Eight of spades	cunning hole behind a hanging'. Howard decided to save himself by telling all, claiming that he had once hidden behind a curtain to learn what was being planned. He said that Lord Shaftesbury intended to rouse the city on 17 or 19 November, 1683.
	The next cards deal with some of the many trials which followed these arrests.
Knave of spades	The knave of spades poses a problem as Goodenough was in Europe and was not tried at this time. It is perhaps a reference to the fact that when he was under-sheriff, Shaftesbury had relied on him to choose juries who were pro-Wing. He had been tried on 16 February, 1683, for a pretended riot and assault on the Lord Mayor during the Sheriffs' elections on the previous mid-summer day. On that occasion he was fined 500 marks.
Nine of spades	The trials of Walcott and Hone took place on July 12th and 13th respectively. Keeling, West and Rumsey were prominent crown witnesses and the outcome of guilty of high treason was almost
Ten of spades	inevitable. Lord Russell's trial was held at the same time as Hone's. It lasted from 9am to 5pm, and Russell began by challenging thirty-two jurymen. Rumsey, Sheppard and Lord Howard, said
Six of spades	Russell, had attended several consults at Sheppard's house, although they could not produce any evidence that he had plotted the king's death. He defended himself by arguing that to 'imagine the levying of war' was not equivalent to planning to kill the king and consequently did not amount to treason, and secondly, the crown had failed to produce two witnesses who could swear to his making an 'overt act of compassing the king's death'. After an hour's deliberation the jury found him 'guilty generally' and he was sentenced to death.
King of hearts	Russell had been defending himself when news reached court that the Earl of Essex had died in the Tower. Russell asked for a moment to be allowed to shed a tear. The Earl of Essex had been arrested on July 10th and lodged in the Tower room from which his father had been led to execution. Not surprisingly he had suffered sleepless nights there, culminating in his cutting his own throat at 9 am on July 13th. He had asked his servant to get him a penknife to 'pare his nails', but as it was impossible to get one, Essex said that a razor would do. A razor was brought and the warder said that Essex walked up and down doing his nails. Later on his servant returned and went to look in the close-stool closet for him. Finding the door locked, he left, but soon returned and knocked on the door. When he noticed blood, he called the warder who forced the door to find the dead earl. Robert Andrews, a surgeon, said that there was a cut from one jugular to the other, through the windpipe and gullet and into the vertebrae of the neck. The argument that it was a case of murder is pursued by the eight, nine and ten of hearts and the two of spades in the Reign of James II, 1685-88 pack of cards described in Chapter Eight.

Walcot & Hone tryed at the Old Bayly (IX ♠)	Lord Russell Tryed at the Old Bayly (X ♠)	E. of Essex cutting his throat in ye Tower (King ♥)
Ld. Russell beheaded in Lincolne Inn Feilds (VI ♥)	Walcot going to be Executed (VIII ♥)	Hone & Rouse going to be Executed (VII ♥)
Walcot, Hone & Rouse Executed (VIII ♦)	Colliford Standing in the Pillory (V ♦)	Lord Shaftsbury going for Holland, Taking leave (♦)

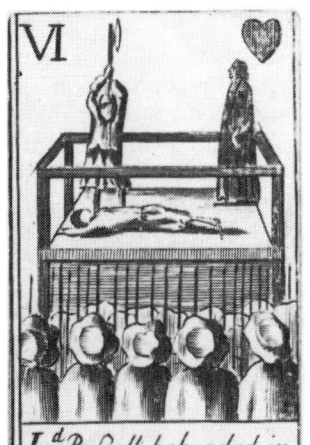

Six of hearts	On July 21st Lord Russell was hung, drawn and quartered. Before he left Newgate he had some tea and sherry and wound up his watch, remarking he had done with time as he was about to go to eternity. He was driven to Lincolns Inn Fields in his own coach with a 'most extraordinary guard of Watchmen and the trained bands'. He seemed to be unconcerned as he mounted the black lined scaffold. He said little but gave a paper to the sheriff. This was printed that evening and proclaimed his innocence. The executioner Ketch cut his head off with three strokes, 'very
Eight and seven of hearts	barbarously'.
	Walcott, Hone and Rouse were taken to their executions on July 22nd. Their quarters were buried, but their heads were displayed,
Eight of diamonds	Walcott's on Aldgate, Hone's on Aldersgate and Rouse's on the Guildhall.
Five of diamonds	On November 11th J. Calliford was charged by the Duke of York with libel for *The Growth of Popery*, which Calliford had printed.
Ace of hearts	The set is completed with the king's declaration of 9 September, 1683. This was a repeat announcement of the declaration of September 2nd explaining the Rye House Plot to the public. September 9th was observed as a thanksgiving day, with sermons, bells and bonfires.

Then on 29 October, 1683, the *London Gazette* carried this advertisement:

> The Late Horrid Fanatical Conspiracy, Lively represented in a Pack of Cards, Curiously Engraven in copper-plates is now Published, and are sold by Dan Brown at the Black Swan and Bible without Temple-Bar, Arthur Jones at the Flying Horse in Fleet-street and Walton Davies in Amen Corner. Price one shilling a Pack!

CHAPTER SEVEN

Monmouth's Rebellion, 1685

In the *London Gazette,* number 2085, of 9-12 November, 1685, appeared this advertisement:
> A New Pack of Cards Representing in curious lively Figures the Two late Rebellions throughout the whole course thereof in both Kingdoms, Price one shilling. Sold by D. Brown at the Black Swan and Bible without Temple Bar, and A. Jones at the Flying-horse in Fleet Street near St. Dunstan Church.

James, Duke of Monmouth, was the illegitimate son of Charles II and Lucy Waters. An unproduced black box was said to contain their marriage certificate. If Monmouth had been accepted as the legitimate son of Charles II, he would have been king on the death of his father, but as this was not done, his uncle, James had succeeded. Anti-catholics, encouraged by the Country (or Whig) party were keen to support a movement against the Catholic James II. In this situation an invasion was likely in the year that James came to the throne, 1685. This pack of cards is decidedly anti-Monmouth, and is probably the work of Francis Barlow.

The invasion was really a double one, for the Duke of Argyle led an attempt in Scotland, while Monmouth landed in the west country. The set opens with the former's attempt.

Archibald Campbell was the 9th Earl of Argyle. At a meeting of Scotsmen in Amsterdam on 17th April, 1685, he had planned his attempt. He was personally against Monmouth declaring himself king. A rich English widow in Amsterdam gave him £1,000 with which he bought a frigate and arms. He had been told by an astrologer that he had the ability to raise 15,000 men, but his followers thought they would not even raise 3,000.

At 7 pm on May 6, his three ships, the *Anna, Sophia* and *David* sailed from Vly with 300 men on board. They landed at Cariston in

Four of clubs

IV ♣ Argyle Landing in Ila with 5 Hundred Men	**IV ♦** Argyle persued by a Contry man into ye water.	**I ♠** Argyle receiving a wound on his Head
King ♦ Coll. Ayloff and 200 more brought in Prisoners to Glascow	**II ♠** Coll: Ayloff Desperately Wounded	**VI ♦** Rumbold the Malster and his man taken by five of the Earl of Arrons Militia,
X ♦ Rombold ye Malster Executed	**King ♥** Argyle Delivering a Canting paper to ye Dean of Edinborough	**III ♥** Argyle Executed & his head affixt on ye TALBOOTH

Orkney on May 6, and the alarm was given when his secretary Spence was seized at Kirkwall. His second landing was at Dunstafnage in Lorn to recruit 16-60 year old Campbells. His standard had 'Against Popery, Prelacy and Erastianism' on it (Erastus of Heidelberg had said in the 16th century that civil magistrates should have supreme power over the churches).

His ships then went through the Kyles of Bute and he occupied Ellengreg castle as a base. Although he took Greenock, he failed to take Inverary and shortly afterwards Sir Thomas Hamilton captured his ships, arms for 5,000 and 300 barrels of gunpowder without firing a shot. Argyle began to retreat towards Glasgow and his force decreased from 2,000 to 500.

After some skirmishes, Argyle was left with Major Fullarton as they all dispersed to make their escapes. Argyle disguised himself as a peasant and played the part of a guide to Fullarton. As they were fording the Caill at Inchinnan, a mile from Renfrew on June 18, they were stopped by a party of armed men. Fullarton talked to them while Argyle went deeper into the water. Just then two militiamen ordered Argyle to surrender his horse to them so they could use it to carry their baggage. When he refused there was a struggle and he fell from his mount. The two rode off as he drew a pistol, but two others shot at him and missed. Three men from a cottage then ran up. One, a drunken weaver, John Riddell, brandished a sword as he seized him. Argyle's pistol misfired as it had got wet, and before he could try another one, Riddell hit him on the head with his sword (not a pole as on the ace of spades). As Argyle fell into the water, he cried out, 'Unfortunate Argyle'. Riddell got the £50 reward for his capture.

Four of diamonds

Ace of spades

Col. John Ayloffe, one of Argyle's aides, was soon caught. He was a satirist and lawyer, and had left England for Holland when the Rye House Plot failed. While held a prisoner in Glasgow, he used a penknife, or some such instrument, to rip open his stomach. He did not die however, but was executed in Chancery Lane, London, at 10 am on October 30.

King of diamonds

Two of spades

The one-eyed malster Richard Rumbold of Rye House fame (See Chapter Six, seven of diamonds, nine of hearts) was also captured. He was hung on June 26. Forty of Argyle's men had a piece cut off their ears, while women supporters were burnt on the shoulder.

Six of diamonds

Ten of diamonds

Argyle was executed on Tuesday, June 30, for treasonable libel, for which he had been sentenced to death in 1681. He had escaped on that occasion. A long debate took place the night before his death as to whether he should be hung or axed. He walked to his death with the Dean of Edinburgh beside him. He said that his punishment was a just one for his sins. He then took out a ruler to measure the block, called the *Maiden,* and pointed out a defect. The carpenter duly rectified it, and Argyle was beheaded. His head was put on an iron pin on the west end of the Tolbooth.

King & three of hearts

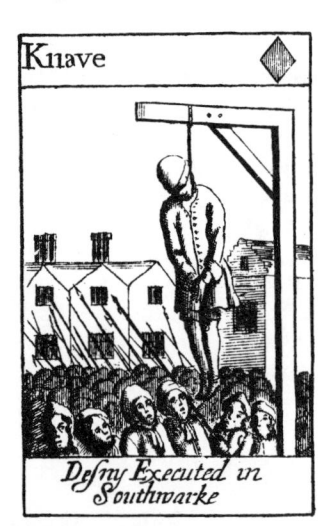

I ♣ The late D. of M. & other Rebells taking shipping for England	**VI ♣** The Late D. of M. entring Lime with 1500 Men	**V ♠** 7 Rebells kill'd in a fight at Bridport & 32 taken Prisoners
V ♥ The Rout of 1000 of the Rebells horse Comanded by ye Ld: Gray	**VI ♥** Libells thrown about the Citty concerning a Massacre yt was to be made by the Papists	**X ♣** The Late D. of M's. Declaration Burnt by Order of both Houses of Parliment
Knave ♦ Desny Executed in Southwarke	**II ♣** Two of ye Rebells Ships laden with Powder & Armes taken at Lime by Capt. Trevanion	**IV ♠** Severall Officers by Command of ye King going into ye West

Argyle's attempt was already doomed before Monmouth set sail on May 30 from Helderenburgh with a frigate, a fly boat and a ketch, and 82 men. £8,000 had been spent on obtaining the boats, 1,500 cuirasses, arms for foot soldiers, some grenadoes, shells, etc. On board commissions were given out for White, Yellow and Green regiments. *Ace of clubs*

They were off Lyme Regis at 8.15 pm on Wednesday, June 10, but delayed entering the port until the next day. It was at 5 pm on Thursday, bowling club day, that a newspaper was delivered to Lyme post-house announcing that three ships had left Holland with Monmouth on board. Mayor Alford became suspicious of the ships which had just arrived, and gave the order for the drums to be beat. But they had no powder available to fire the harbour gun, and before they could secure some Monmouth and his men had landed. Monmouth fell on his knees to thank God, then rose, drew his sword and led the eighty-two into the town. In the market place a declaration was read saying that he was the duke who had come to free England from the 'usurpation and tyranny of James, Duke of York'. His followers soon numbered 150, not 1,500 as on the six of clubs, and the next day they numbered 1,150. Having taken £400 from the Customs House, Monmouth stayed the night at the George Inn. *Six of clubs*

Monmouth's flag was green with the words 'Fear Nothing but God' on it, in gold. It was unfurled when he came ashore. *Queen of spades*

The Duke ordered an attack on Bridport on Sunday, June 14, to destroy the Dorsetshire Militia. Lord Grey was in command of the 440 men. His second in command, Andrew Fletcher, was ordered back to the ships after he had shot Heywood Dare who had refused to lend his horse to him! On their all night march they learnt that 1,200 infantry and 100 cavalry were in Bridport. In the thick dawn mist they took the militia completely by surprise. One militia officer hid himself in a plot of kidney beans! But the shock of a real fight made Grey's cavalry (not 1,000 as claimed on the five of hearts) turn and race for Lyme Regis. When they got there they told Monmouth that their foot soldiers were cut to pieces. This was quite untrue as Monmouth found out when he rushed reinforcements towards Bridport. He met them retreating in good order, having taken 30 horses and 2 prisoners (not 32 as claimed by the five of spades). Their commander said Grey and his men had run away! Not an inspiring encounter for the rebels to open their campaign with. *Five of spades / Five of hearts*

At this time Monmouth's Declaration was being distributed in London. It has been written by Robert Ferguson (See Chapter Six, ace and three of diamonds, knave of clubs, king of spades), and it declared that James II as Duke of York had started the Fire of London in 1666 and been behind the murder of Sir Edmund Berry Godfrey. On June 15, 5 complete and 750 half-printed copies were *Six of hearts / Ten of clubs*

found in the printing room of William Disney, when he was roused from his bed. The copies were burnt by the hangman before the Royal Exchange. One copy, 8 pages long, has survived and is now in the British Museum. Disney was executed on June 29 on Kennington Common and his quarters put on the city gates.

Knave of diamonds

Eight of spades

On the day of Disney's arrest, Monmouth's 3,000 men rose at 3 am and left Lyme Regis at 10 am, heading north.

Two of clubs

One of Monmouth's ships had already left Lyme Regis, when two days later Capt. Trevanion sailed into the harbour in the only English frigate with a Portuguese name, *Suadadoes* ('Good Luck', built in 1670 as a yacht for Queen Caroline), a sixth rater with 16 guns. He captured the rebels' two ships known as the *Pink* and the *Dogger,* together with 40 barrels of powder and 4-5,000 breast and back plates and helmets. The Mayor spent a lot on beer and cheese for Trevanion's crew, and this led to a protest in the borough council!

Four of spades

On June 19, James II concluded that Monmouth was heading for Bristol and ordered the Duke of Beaufort to secure it. In fact 6 companies of the Gloucestershire Militia had already arrived there to do so. He sent Lord Churchill to Bridgewater, the Earls of Gainsborough and Pembroke to command the Wiltshire Militia assembled at Salisbury, and the Duke of Norfolk and the Earl of Abingdon to Reading with the Berkshire and Oxfordshire Militias. The·Duke of Grafton left with the main forces, 3 battalions of Footguards to go to Bath.

Queen of diamonds

Monmouth reached Taunton on Thursday, June 18, and the following morning he was greeted by 27 'Maids of Taunton', aged 8-10 years old. Half of them were the pupils of Miss Blake and half those of Mrs. Susanna Musgrave. Miss Blake led the way, carrying a sword and a Bible, and the 'Maids' carried flags. Monmouth received the Bible from Miss Blake and a kiss from each girl. Mary Mead gave him a golden flag with a crown and the letters, 'J.R.' (Jacobus Rex-King James) on it. Monmouth then issued a warrant addressed to constables and tything men, which read:

'James R,
These are, in his Majesty's name, to will and require
you, on sight hereof, to search for, seize, and take
all such scythes as can be found in your tything, paying
a reasonable price for the same, and bring them to my
house to-morrow by one of the clock in the afternoon,
that they may be delivered in to the commission officers
that are appointed to receive them at Taunton by four of
the same day, and you shall be reimbursed by me what the
scythes are worth. And hereof fail not, as you will answer
to the contrary. Given under my hand this 20 day of June in
the first year of his Majesty's reign'.

Thus the famous scythemen of the Monmouth Rebellion came to

be equipped. The scythes were riveted to 8ft poles. Reluctant constables were threatened with having their houses burnt. After the collapse of the rebellion, the 'Maids' were to suffer for James II gave them as a Christmas present to the court Maids of Honour. The Maids of Honour demanded £7,000 to be paid for the 'Maids' ' pardon and safety. Finally terms were arranged by George Penn, pardon-broker and £50-£100 per 'Maid' was paid, amounting to less than half originally demanded. Miss Blake died of smallpox in Dorchester Gaol on November 25 and Mrs. Musgrave was traced to Arthur Case's house on Exmoor, but she was not arrested.

On June 17 a 'scandalous' nonconformist minister, John Vincent had led an attack on Magdalen Church, Taunton, to grab arms for Monmouth. The next day a newspaper arrived announcing James II's death and this led to more flocking to Monmouth, increasing his force from 3,000 to 7,000. Many clergy now called on him to proclaim himself king in order to show that it was not intended to start a republic. It would also have the effect of turning an insurrection into a legal advance. The proclamation was made at the Market Cross, and some magistrates were forced to attend in their gowns. *Ten of spades*

On June 20, Monmouth wrote to the Lord Lt. of Devon, the Duke of Albemarle, who was 7 miles away: *Nine of diamonds*

'My Lord,
Whereas we are credibly informed that there are some horse and foot in arms under your command for James, Duke of York, which are purposely raised in opposition to us and our royal authority; We thought fit to signify to you our resentment thereof, and do promise ourself that what you have transacted therein was through inadvertency and mistake; and that your Grace will take other means, when you have received information of our being proclaimed King, to succeed our royal father, lately deceased. We have therefore sent this messenger on purpose to intimate the same unto you; and it is our royal will and pleasure, and we do hereby strictly charge and command you, upon notice and receipt thereof, to cease all hostility, and force, and arms against us and all our loving subjects; and that your Grace would immediately repair to our camp, where you shall not fail of a very kind reception by us; or, in default of the premises, we shall be obliged to proclaim you, and all those in arms under your command, rebels and traitors, and shall proceed against you accordingly. Yet we assure ourself that your Grace will pay ready obedience to our command; wherefore we bid you hearty farewell.
James R'.

To which Albemarle replied as follows:
'For James Scott, the late Duke of Monmouth,

Qveen ♦ the godly Maids of Taunton prsenting their Colours upon their knees to ye D. of M.	**X** ♠ Ten Nonconformist Ministers Pressing ye late D of M to sett up for King.	**I** ♦ Two troopes of ye Rebells horse cutt of att Carsham Bridge by Coll: Ogilthorpe
VII ♣ The D. of Grafton &c. fighting their way through severll of ye Rebells horse in ye lane leading to Philips Norton	**Knave** ♥ The Constable of Froome putting up Ms treasonable Decl	**II** ♦ A Memorable accont: of ye Earl of Pembroks dispersing ye Rabble att Froome
VIII ♦ The Constable of Froome writing an abhorrence of Mon's Declaracon	**X** ♥ Rebells plundering the Loyall Gent: houses at Wells	**Knave** ♣ Ferguson Preaching to the Rebells ye Day before ye Defeat on Iosh. 22. v. 22.

I received your letter, and do not doubt that you would use
me kindly if you had me; and since you have given
yourself the trouble of invitation, this is to let you know
that I never was nor never will be a rebel to my lawful
King, who is James the Second. If you think I am in the
wrong, and you in the right, whenever we meet I do not
doubt but justness of my cause shall sufficiently convince
you that you had better have left this rebellion alone, and
not have put the nation to so much trouble.
                    Albemarle'.
The outcome was that on the following day Monmouth declared
Albemarle to be a traitor.

On Wednesday, June 24, Monmouth sent Capt. Tyler to take Keynsham (Cansham on the ace of diamonds) in preparation for a night attack on Bristol. During that night Tyler's men repaired the bridge over the River Avon, but on the following morning at 10 am they were surprised by Maj. Oglethorpe's Life Guards. Tyler lost 14 men and Oglethorpe 2 before Oglethorpe's men withdrew, leaving the rebels badly shaken. *(Ace of diamonds)*

On the following Saturday there was a sharp skirmish at Philip's Norton (Norton St. Philip), near Bath. The Duke of Grafton led his men down a long lane and found Monmouth had erected a barricade with Capt. Vincent's 50 musketeers at the far end. While they fought it out, Monmouth led his main force down a lane until they were behind Grafton's men, who only escaped by scrambling through a hedge. A fierce fight followed among the hedgerows, and was concluded with a 6 hour cannonade across a ploughed field. Grafton's men withdrew after losing 80 men to Monmouth's 18. The rebel Maj. Holmes had his arm shattered and later on cut it off himself with a carving knife! (See also, king of clubs). Joseph Winter of Ilchester, a surgeon, requested payment for the surgery he performed after the fight: *(Seven of clubs)*

'Itm. Robert Sandy of Cullington near Lime, at Norton was
wounded with some heavy cutting instrument on his head at
two places, on the hinder parte a piece of his scull was
cut off and left hanging by the flesh as bigg as a five
shilling piece and brayne left naked, only a thin skin
to keep it on, on the foreparte was a large wound out of
which I took several pieces of skull, but by my care he
is firmly cured and is transported and his wife and children
left very poore, this cure is honestly worth £5.
Itm. Joseph Phelps of White Church Canonicorum was at
Norton shot in his arme, the bullet went in at his elbow and
out by his shoulder, he was brought to prison in great
payne and a very sad wound it was, but with care and much
adoo I cured him, his friends are very poore and not able
to pay me, the cure is very well worth £3.'

Knave of hearts Two & eight of diamonds	Three cards are devoted to the events of Sunday, June 28, at Frome, where Monmouth's men went for a rest. The story was reported by the Earl of Pembroke to the *London Gazette*

'Being informed that the rabble at Frome, headed by the constable, had put up in the market-place the traitorous declaration of Monmouth, he marched thither on Thursday 25 June last, with 160 horse, and mounted behind some of them thirty-six musketeers. Being arrived near the town, he heard great shouting and beating of drums, and was informed that between 2,000 and 3,000, upon the notice of his coming, were assembled from Warminster and Westbury, some with muskets, some with pistols, some with pikes, and others with scythes. Notwithstanding the small number the Earl of Pembroke had with him, he marched into the town at the head of his muskets, followed by the horse. The assembled multitude seemed at first very resolute: and as the Earl came in at the gate, one fired at him, bidding the rest to fire, when his Lordship came to a particular spot; but in a moment they all threw down their arms, and fled out at the other end of the town. Lord Pembroke, having caused the Declaration to be pulled down, made the constable write, with his own hand, an abhorrence of the same, and a declaration that Monmouth was a traitor, and put it up in the same place, and then committed him to prison'.

Five of clubs	The five of clubs refers to 3 Scottish regiments, which had been sent to Holland, returning on Tuesday, June 30, on the orders of William of Orange to help put down the rebels.
Ten of hearts	On Wednesday, July 1, Monmouth, with 38 carriages, went to Wells and captured the king's baggage wagons. According to the *London Gazette,* 'They robbed and defaced the cathedral, drinking their villanous healths at the altar, plundered the town, ravished the women, and committed all manner of outrages'. The lower-most tiers of the west front were peppered with bullets and some of the roof lead was taken to make bullets. £500's worth of damage was done to the outside of the cathedral, and inside the furnishings were wrecked, the organ damaged, and horses stabled in the nave.
Knave of clubs	The Revd. Robert Ferguson, known as 'Ferguson the Plotter', was a hot-headed man who had been involved in the Rye House Plot, He had come with Monmouth as his secretary and army chaplain. At Taunton he had boasted, 'I am Ferguson, that famous Ferguson for whose head so many hundred pounds were offered; I am that man, I am that man'. The defeat referred to on the knave of clubs was that of Sedgemoor on July 6.
King of spades	It is possible that the king of spades refers to the failure of Monmouth's night march to Sedgemoor to surprise the enemy. Sedgemoor was 13,522 acres of peat-moor near Bridgewater, and Monmouth hoped to cross it in pitch darkness and surprise the

KING ♠ Devills in yͤ Ayre Bewitch: :ing Mͤ Army	**QUEEN ♣** The Defeat of the Rebells 2000 Slayn & their Canon taken	**IV ♥** The Battaile att Bridgwater
VII ♥ An Express sent by the Earl of Feversham of the Totall Rout of the Rebells	**V ♦** Severall of yͤ Rebells hang'd upon a Tree	**VII ♦** the Lᵈ Gray taken in Disguise
III ♠ The Late Duke of M: taken near the Lᵈ Grey	**I ♥** Williams yͤ D: of Mͤ Sarvant taken with his Coat &c	**VI ♠** The late D: of M: Lᵈ Grey & a German carried to yͤ Tower

king's infantry. His regiments were called Blue (600), White (400) Red (800), Green (600), Yellow, (500), together 600 horse, and 4 cannon. They faced 2,500 with 16 cannon. Any man making any noise and alerting the enemy was to be killed instantly.

Queen of clubs

Four of hearts

Things went wrong when their cavalry was faced with the Old Bussex Rhine, a drainage ditch of soft mud, and the enemy then opened fire on them. By the time the infantry were in position the cavalry had fled. Monmouth was experienced enough as a commander to realise that defeat was inevitable, and after a hard fight this proved to be so. He had made the mistake of thinking that a surprise night attack was possible, and his mistake was due to his ignorance of the existence of the ditch protecting the royal infantry's position. Moreover royalist spies had kept their commander posted on Monmouth's movements.

Battles are often described in great detail in history books, but rarely is sufficient attention given to the human aftermath problems. After this battle, James II authorised allowances for the wounded. For the Troops of Horse and Grenadiers, 36 'gentlemen' received £417.10.0 (£417.50) and for one 'gentleman' who was admitted to Chelsea Hospital, £16. One trumpeter and 14 privates of the Royal Regt. of Horse received £220.5.0 (£220.25), while in the two battalions of 1st Foot Guards, a colonel and a captain got £100, two captains and a lieutenant got £30; one lieutenant, £40, another, £80 and one sergeant, 2 drummers and 46 privates got £208.5.0 (£208.25), and 12 went to the Chelsea Hospital with £16.

Seven of hearts

Lord Feversham, the royalist commander, sent Oglethorpe post haste to tell the king of the victory. He was knighted when he delivered the message.

Five of diamonds

The remainder of the pack is devoted to the rounding up and punishing of the rebels. Feversham ordered the hanging of twenty-two immediately after the battle. Four of them were hung in gemmaces (chains) from a tree at Bussex.

Seven of diamonds

Lord Grey was the first important rebel to be caught. He was found at 5 am on July 7 when he and his guide, Richard Hollyday, were spotted near Holt Lodge in Dorset. £500 was given to the men who captured them. Grey asked for a pardon and appeared as witness against others. Before Christmas he was back at court.

Three of spades

On July 7 Lord Lumley and Sir William Portman were directed by Amy Farrant to the 'Island' in the middle of Shag's Heath, an enclosure of fields between roads leading to Ringwood and Fordingbridge. She was later to receive £50 from the secret service for funds for she had given the clue to Monmouth's whereabouts. At 5 am the following morning Monmouth's companion, Anthony Busse, a 30 year old Brandenburgh captain, was picked up. (See six of spades). To save himself he pointed to Monmouth's position and at 7 am Henry Parking (or Parkin) found him, unarmed and with a long grey beard, hiding in a ditch under an ash tree. The unit

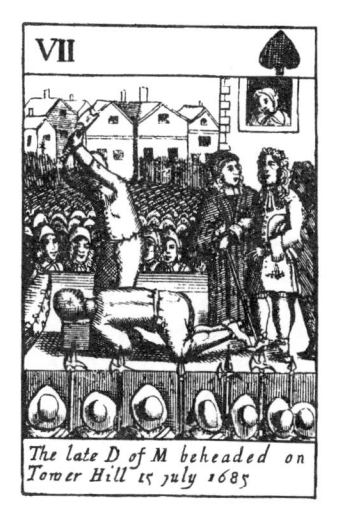

IX ♠ — Severall disaffected L^ds sent to y^e Tower	**VII ♠** — The late D of M beheaded on Tower Hill 15 July 1685	**VIII ♣** — Severall of y^e Kings Forces in search after Ferguson
III ♣ — Major Holmes and 2 other Rebells Hanged in Chaines	**VIII ♥** — Bonfires made the 26 of July att night being the thanksgiving for the Victory 1685	**IX ♥** — Nelthrope &c. taken att M^dm Lisle's house
Queen ♥ — M^dm Lisle Executed	**II ♥** — Severall Rebells tryed in the West	**IX ♣** — One Pitts is to be Whipt through every Town in Dorsetshire for Seaven Years togeather

Ace of hearts	responsible for his capture was given £5,000 in prize money.

William Williams, Monmouth's servant was caught with 300 guineas (£315) on him and hung at Chard.

Six, nine, & seven of spades

Monmouth arrived at the Tower with Busse at 8 pm on Monday, July 13, by barge from Whitehall. He was executed on Wednesday at 10 am. He wore a grey suit and was accompanied in the coach by the bishops of Ely and Bath and Wells, together with three officers with loaded pistols. He gave the executioner six guineas (£6.30). He felt the axe and said it was not sharp enough, and so it proved to be for the first stroke only wounded his neck. He made no sound, but turned and looked the executioner in the face. After the second blow he crossed his legs. After the third blow, Jack Ketch threw down the axe and cried, 'God damn me, I can do no more. My heart fails me'. The sheriffs told him to get on with it, and the crowd threatened to tear him to pieces for his bungling. He succeeded on the fifth stroke and then was escorted quickly away. Monmouth's head was sewn back on to his body, and he was buried in St. Peter ad Vincula.

Eight of clubs

It is not clear what happened to Ferguson, but he managed to get onto a boat. But when it was forced ashore by two frigates, he took to the woods. He got away to Holland and returned to England with William III.

Three of diamonds

Richard Goodenough (See Chapter Five, two of hearts, knave of spades) was taken near Ilfracombe. He had been made Eldest Captain during the voyage to Lyme Regis, and he had been in the White Regt. He was pardoned on turning king's evidence. Maj.

King of clubs

Abraham Holmes, a Fifth-monarchist and fanatical Anabaptist, had been on the fringe of the Rye House Plot. He served Monmouth as the Lt. Col. of the Green Regt. After being questioned in London at the end of June, he was sent back to the

Three of clubs

west country and executed at Lyme Regis on September 12. The horses refused to pull the sledge on which he was strapped, and when a fresh pair were harnessed they broke it to pieces.

Eight of hearts

James had announced that July 26 should be observed as a national day of thanksgiving, and he was taken at his word as the eight of hearts shows.

Nine & queen of hearts

On August 27 an old widow, Alice Lisle, was tried in Winchester Castle for harbouring two rebels on July 29 at Moyle's Court, near Ellingham, Hampshire. One was John Hicks, a fanatical dissenting minister and brother of the Dean of Worcester. He was eventually hung at Glastonbury. The other was Richard Nelthrop, described by the government as 'a blackman, high nose, pox holes in his face', who was to suffer death at Holborn. Hicks had taken Nelthrop to Moyle's Court as it was a centre of the non-conformist get-away underground system. A labourer, John Barter, had become suspicious when he was employed as a guide, and told Col. Penruddock who surrounded the house. He found Hicks under some rubbish in the malt house and Nelthorp in a recess in a wall. The jury were reluctant to convict the distinguished Mrs. Lisle and they had to retire three times before convicting her at midnight. She was sentenced to be burnt, but was beheaded at Wincester at 4 pm on September 2.

Much has been written about Judge Jeffrey's 'Bloody Assize' in the west country, and there is not space here to expand on the subject. Some statistics must suffice. A sick man, he had a vast job to do and results of it were: *Two of hearts*

Place	Executed	Transported	Fined or Whipped
Hampshire	1		6
Dorset	74	175	9
Devon	13	7	13
Taunton	144	284	5
Wells	99	383	—
Totals	331	849	33

Place	Monmouth's	Kings
In skirmishes (estimate)	100	100
At Philips Norton	18	80
At Sedgemoor	1,300	400
(to which are added those executed)		
Executed by martial law	61	
Executed after trial	331	
Totals	1,810	580

The tale behind the nine of clubs is a fascinating one. When arrested Thomas Pitts was at first acquitted for lack of evidence. It was then discovered that his real name was John Tutchin (1661-1707, see also Chapter Ten, card 51) a lying pamphleteer. He was then charged with raising men for Monmouth in Lymington and spreading false rumours that all Hampshire was for Monmouth and Argyle was within 60 miles of London. Jeffreys 'asserted that he was never so far outwitted by a young or old rogue in his life'. Failing to get sufficient information to hang him, Jeffreys sentenced him to 7 years' imprisonment, a fine, and an annual whipping through all the market towns of Dorsetshire. Tutchin petitioned to be hung instead, and, when this failed, he tried in vain to purchase a pardon. He caught smallpox two days before his first whipping, and Jeffreys reversed the sentence, probably on instructions. After the 1688 Revolution, Tutchin wrote a fictitious account of his sufferings. *Nine of clubs*

Knave of spades   The meaning of the knave of spades is obscure to-day. It shows five of Monmouth's men taking an oath not to 'discover who is ye Right?

Monmouth's rebellion had failed due to a number of factors, such as lack of leadership and equipment, and the military efficiency of the royal army, and finally to the poor military quality of Monmouth's supporters.

There remains the question of what place the rebellion has in the history of England. When William III invaded three years later he was not supported by the artisans who had supported Monmouth but by the men who had helped to suppress the 1685 rebellion. The reason is not difficult to find. The rebels of 1685 displayed a republicanism which those of 1688 feared and rejected. Both groups of rebels wanted to rid the country of James II but had different goals in view. Those of 1685 represented the Dissenter and republican elements of Whiggery while those of 1688 stood for the aristocratic and city financier elements of the same party. The latter looked to the former for numerical support, but when the former sought to rebel for their own ends the latter feared that they would lose control of them. The rebels of 1685 challenged the structure of society and so threatened the Whig aristocrats and financiers whose aim it was to overthrow the autocracy of James for their own oligarchical rule. James saw the threat to ordered society posed by Monmouth's men and so encouraged the Bloody Assize of Judge Jeffreys. The Monmouth rebels drew their republicanism from the Bible while the aristocratic Whigs, who had a leaning towards republicanism, visualized a kind of Roman republic in which the natural leaders of society ruled the rest. Thus Monmouth's rebellion posed a very real threat to the structure of society and its savage suppression underlines this.

CHAPTER EIGHT

The Reign of James II, 1685-1688

The first of two sets of cards on the reign of James II is of poor design and coarsely executed. Nevertheless from an historical point of view it is worthy of note.

Nine and eight of hearts

The set opens with a reference back to the aftermath of the Rye House Plot (See Chapter Six, king of hearts), namely the supposed murder of the Earl of Essex. The cards take up the story that the earl was murdered by means of a razor, and suggest that three men were involved. The trial of Mr. Brandon lasted from 7 February to 21 April, 1684. When a boy, who claimed he had seen the razor flung from the earl's window, denied his story in court, his sister went on to add that her brother was apt to lie. Judge Jeffreys commented, 'What an Age we live in that the report of every child should blow us up after this rate! It would make a body to think what a sort of people we live among'.

Two of spades, ten of hearts

One other card, the ace of spades, refers to the previous reign. As long ago as 1670 Charles II made a secret treaty of Dover by which the French agreed to pay £225,000 per annum and a further £150,000 if Charles declared himself a Roman Catholic. French support enabled Charles to keep parliamentary troublemakers at arms length.

Ace of spades

In 1686 the Court of Ecclesiastical Commissioners was set up consisting of the Archbishop of Canterbury, two bishops, three officers of state sitting under the presidency of Lord Chancellor Jeffreys. In fact Archbishop Sancroft refused to serve on the grounds of ill health. A Long Parliament act of 1641 had made such a court illegal, but James II argued that the High Commission Court then abolished affected both clergy and laity, whereas this new court affected clergy only. It had power to suspend, deprive and excommunicate clergy, and its first action was to suspend Bishop Compton of London as he refused to take action against a London

Ace of clubs

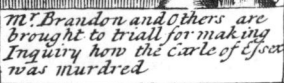

IX ♥ — The Earle of Essex is Murdered in the Tower.	 **VIII ♥** — a Rayſor is seen thrown out at window in the Tower where the Earle of Essex was.	 **II ♠** — Severall persons sent to Newgate for murdering the E. of Essex.
 **X ♥** — Mr. Brandon and Others are brought to triall for making Inquiry how the Earle of Essex was murdred.	 **I ♠** — 500 thousand pound from France Yearly to Charls the 2 to keep the sitting of the Parlement of.	 **IX ♣** — Judg Harbert writing a book in Defence of the Kings dispensing Power.
III ♣ — Mugdalens Coledg seized and ye fellows of ye Coledg routed for keeping to the Laws of the Coledg.	**II ♣** — The Chancelor sending commissions to regulat corperashons that the penall Laws might be taken of.	**X ♣** — Oxford and Winchester Declared to be Desolved from being a bodey politick.

rector who had publicly upheld the catholicity of Anglican orders. Thus its purpose was to direct the Church towards catholicism.

This was to be the theme of James's reign, and it led to his downfall three years after his succession. The superstitious might well have forecast this downfall, for on his coronation day three incidents had occurred. His crown had almost slipped from his head; the canopy, held over him by Samuel Pepys and others during part of the service, had collapsed on top of him; and finally, the royal standard had blown off its flagstaff.

If Roman Catholicism was to become the accepted form of Christianity in England, James would have to ensure that regiments were put under Catholic officers. But the Test Acts required officers to take Church of England communion to prove their patriotism. James's solution was to use his power of dispensing with the law for individuals by issuing a kind of exemption certificate. It was arranged to test this power before the courts and the Catholic Sir Edward Hales was challenged for accepting command of a regiment by his coachman, Godden. In his judgement in March, 1686, Lord Chief Justice Herbert said, 'There is no law whatsoever but maybe dispensed with by God himself'. Because of popular dissatisfaction with this decision, he published, *A Short Account of the Authorities in Law upon which judgement was given in Sir Edward Hale's case.* Herbert accepted the dispensing power, but not the suspending power which James was soon to use.

Nine of clubs

If the dispensing power could be used in the army, it could be used in the universities too with sinister implications. On 5 April, 1687, James ordered Magdalen College, Oxford, to elect Anthony Farmer, a Catholic and not a college fellow, as their president. The college reacted by electing Dr. J. Hough, a greatly respected man and chaplain to the Duke of Ormonde, on April 15. (See Chapter Nine, six and eight of clubs). This led to the appearance of the fellows before the Court of Ecclesiastical Commissioners on June 6. The fellows brought evidence to show that Farmer had been expelled from Trinity College, Cambridge, for misbehaving at a dancing class, and had disgraced Oxford by providing a naked woman for undergraduates, often coming in late and drunk, and throwing the Abingdon stocks into the river one night. Although the court declared Dr. Hough's election void, James was forced to drop Farmer's candidature. Instead he nominated the pluralist Bishop of Oxford, Dr. Samuel Parker. As the fellows refused to have him, James went to Magdalen at 3 pm on September 4 and met twenty-one of the fellows. He put the matter bluntly when he told them, 'Get you gone, know I am your King'. He expelled all twenty-five fellows and replaced them with papists. On the death of Parker, these fellows elected Bonaventura Gifford, titular bishop of Madaura, as president. Just before the Revolution in 1688,

Three of clubs

James restored the original fellows.

Two of clubs
King of clubs
If James could secure the repeal of the penal laws, then such confrontations would be avoidable. With this in mind he set out to secure a parliament favourable to their repeal. This would require the alteration of corporation charters so as to ensure that the electorate would support his aim. This attempt took place in 1687, when commissioners were sent out, but opposion to it was so strong that James had to abandon his plan for a new parliament.

Four of clubs
As he could not secure the election of a favourable parliament James's next step was to suspend the penal laws on his own authority as king. On 22 April, 1688, he ordered the Church of England clergy to read out his Second Declaration of Indulgence to give civil liberties to their professional rivals. Two hundred Durham clergy were expelled for their refusal to do so.

Ten of clubs
As the summer of 1688 went on the reaction against James intensified in the boroughs. Winchester had surrendered its liberties to the Crown in 1684, and on 6 June, 1688, Oxford corporation was dissolved and commissioners appointed to govern the city. But on 15 September, 1688, Winchester recovered its liberties, and on 22 October, Oxford's old charter was restored. James was forced to admit defeat.

Five of clubs
But it was the refusal of seven bishops to support James's suspension of the penal laws which was to provide the high light of the reaction. On Friday, May 18, they knelt before James with their petition against the Declaration of Indulgence, but only succeeded in making him lose his temper as he thought they had come to submit to his will. They were the Archbishop of Canterbury and the bishops of Ely, Peterborough, St. Asaph, Bath and Wells, Chichester and Bristol.

Six of clubs
On June 8 they were arrested and sent to the Tower, but the populace was behind them in marked contrast to the anti-episcopal demonstrations at the time of the Long Parliament. (See also Chapter Nine, nine of clubs). Their subsequent trial marked the point at which the principle of non-resistance to a divine-right king definitely broke down. It was not so much their resistance which was on trial as the king's suspending power.

Seven of clubs
The case was heard on June 29 and they were charged with publishing a seditious libel, namely their petition. The bishops argued that it was not seditious as it was presented privately, nor false as its matter was true, nor malicious as it was offered honestly. It was true, in their opinion, as they denied the king's dispensing and suspending powers. For the prosecution, it was said that it was libellous as it diminished the king's sovereignty and authority by accusing him of illegal acts; moreover Hale's case had established the legality of the dispensing power. Two of the judges summed up for the crown and two for the bishops. The jury brought in their verdict of 'not guilty' at 10 am on June 30, by a

V ♣ — The Arch Bishop of Canterbery with 6 more Bishops Deliver a petition to the King.	 **VI ♣** — The Bishops are Sent to the Tower by Watter.	 **VII ♣** — The Bishops are Cleared at their triall 2 of ye judges were after dis placed they giving for the Bishops
 **III ♠** — The Duches of Modena Presenting a wedge of Gold to the Lady of Loretta that ye Q: might Conceve a son	 **II ♦** — The Queen is brought to bed of a Boy. Reported so	 **I ♦** — Many Witnesses sworn before a great body of ye Peers that ye Child was a Lawfull Prince of Wales
 **VII ♠** — Sum of ye Nobillety of England are sending their memorialls of their Distreses to ye Prince of Oring	 **V ♠** — F. Peters brother preaching in Lime street & saying ye Bible is a lye, for which he hardly escaped	 **VIII ♠** — The Trained bands of London Compeled to gard ye Mass hous in Lime street

majority of seven to five. John Evelyn recorded that the verdict was unanimous after a brewer, Arnold, withdrew his objection to the bishops' acquittal. Holloway and Powell, the two judges who had supported the bishops, were dismissed by the king, but London was delighted with the verdict. (See also Chapter Nine, seven of clubs).

Three of spades

One of James's main desires was for a son to succeed him, and every effort was made to that end as the three of spades shows. (See also Chapter Nine, seven of spades). James's mother-in-law, the Duchess Laura of Modena, had made a pilgrimage to the shrine of Our Lady of Loretto just before she died in 1687.

Four of spades
Two of diamonds
Ace of diamonds

Early in 1688 Jesuits forecast that the queen should have a son, and they were suspected of taking measures to ensure this. James, Prince of Wales, was born at 10 am on Sunday, 10 June, 1688, in the presence of sixty-seven witnesses. (See also Chapter Nine, nine, ten and king of spades). Doubts as to the genuineness of the birth were raised at once, and in an effort to snub the rumours those who witnessed the birth were required to swear to the true fact of the birth. It was noticeable that the well-off midwife turned up plainly dressed and wearing an old scarf in order to suggest that she was an honest, humble woman. Other questions sprung to mind, such as why did the queen use a big enclosed bed rather than the low one provided, and why was a warming pan used in summer. The popular attitude to the birth is to be found reflected in the refusal of Gloucester churchwardens to ring the bells to greet the birth.

Six of spades
Seven & nine of spades

The birth meant an end to the hope that the Catholic movement would end with the death of James II. There was nothing to be gained by waiting for the king's death now, which left only one alternative, a revolution, so many nobles met to discuss the problem. The Protestant William of Orange, James's son-in-law, was the obvious man to turn to in the circumstances. A case could be made for his wife to become queen and his position as consort or king could then be settled. In July, 1688, Vice-Admiral Arthur Herbert delivered the invitation to William. At the end was a line of cypher conveying the names of those behind the invitation, all men of importance. William was only too willing to come provided he was accepted as king, and he was in a position to dictate his terms.

Five of spades

Meanwhile in London on October 1, Father Petre's Jesuit brother Charles denounced the English translation of the Bible and its use as the only rule of faith by the Church of England.(See also Chapter Nine, knave of spades). On October 7, John Evelyn noted in his diary that Dr. Tenison replied at St. Martins in the Field before a congregation of one thousand, taking 2 *Timothy* 3 v 16 as his text.

Eight of spades

Queen & king of spades

Anti-Catholic demonstrations directed against the Catholic chapels of foreign embassies now posed a problem for the authorities. (See also Chapter Nine, two, three and four of diamonds). The Lime St. Chapel was built in a house for the

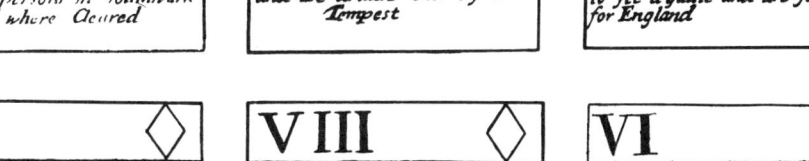

QUEEN ♠ Severall firebauls found on Severall persons in Southwark yet sum where Acured	**IIII** ♦ The Dutch flett put out to sea and are driven bak by a Tempest	**V** ♦ The Dutch Flet in 8 days put to see againe and are sailing for England
VI ♦ The King Expecting ye Dutch in the North sends forces yt way	**VIII** ♦ The prince of Oring with his Army landing in ye West at tor bay	**VI** ♥ The Prince of Orange going into Exeter.
♦ **QUEEN** The King going to Salisbury	♦ **KING** The Kings Artilary going to meet the Prince.	♦ **KNAVE** The King coming from Salisbury the Armie following in hast the Enemy not being near

Ten & knave of spades	Elector of Palantine's envoy in 1686. On October 29 it was wrecked. The authorities stepped up their vigilance and some terrorists were caught. James needed troops he could rely on in this time of crisis and so he turned to Ireland to obtain 3,000-4,000 Catholic troops. Tyrconnel promised them grants of land if they came, although he had no intention of keeping his promise.(See also Chapter Nine, knave of hearts). In fact they were of little military value as they were poorly trained and badly disciplined. Some of them robbed the mayor of Portsmouth as he was touring the sentry posts. As the kings of France and Spain and the Palatine Elector plotted to root
Queen of clubs	out Protestantism, Englishmen were quick to notice the comparison of the bringing in of these troops to the military measures taken to stamp out Protestantism in northern France. This fear
Knave of clubs	was justified for in August James asked Louis to have shiploads of troops ready at Brest should he have need of them. In fact the French fleet was at Toulon defending France's Mediterranean interests and could not be spared to sail to Brest. The only weapon Louis could use against the Dutch was bluff. (See also Chapter Nine, knave of diamonds).
Three of diamonds	The Dutch invasion fleet consisted of 200 transport ships, 3 squadrons of 13 warships each and 10 smaller warships and not 60 great and 500 small ships as the three of diamonds claimed. October 14, James's birthday, was the day of the battle of Senlac (or Hastings) when William I had won England. His coming had been heralded by a comet, and on this day in 1688 there was an eclipse of the sun and the wind changed to favour William's sailing.
Four of diamonds	When they set sail the first time they were hit by a storm on October 19. 1,300 horses were lost as a result. They set sail again in late
Five & six of diamonds	October, aiming for the NE coast of England where strong support for them had been organised by Danby and the local gentry. On
Seven of diamonds	November 4, John Evelyn noted that the Dutch were reported as being in the Channel and not the North Sea as expected. What had happened was that when they were off Essex a strong wind had forced them south, the 'Protestant Wind' as it became known as.
Eight of diamonds	November 5, that fatal day on several occasions in English history, witnessed the landing of William's army at Torbay. (See also Chapter Nine, nine of diamonds). His army of 11,000 foot and 4,000 cavalry was basically Dutch, but included Swedes and Swiss, and was joined by English supporters.
Six of hearts	By nightfall on November 8 Exeter had fallen. It was fair time and the town was full of country folk. William ordered the cathedral canons to cease their prayers for the baby Prince of Wales, and then took over the tax collecting administration which was centred there. From the first he acted as if he was the lawful sovereign rather than an invader. He had had royal seals made for his own use, and made full use of a portable printing press he had brought with him.

On November 16 James set out for Salisbury with his army, and reached there three days later. He stayed there five days, on two of which he suffered long nose bleeds. He expected another Sedgemoor to take place on Salisbury Plain, probably near Stonehenge, on Tuesday, November 20. Already it was clear that he could not count on the loyalty of his troops. *Queen, king & knave of diamonds*

The 'ould Oxford Regt. of Horse with 4 more' now joined William, but it is not clear which regiment is referred to on the king of hearts. On November 25, Captain Henry Bertie had left Oxford with 40 volunteers to join William. *King of hearts*

Under these circumstances it was decided to get the Prince of Wales safely out of the country. Lord and Lady Powis took him to Portsmouth on November 17. Lord Dartmouth, who was in charge of the fleet there and a longstanding supporter of James, refused to send the Prince across the Channel in the yacht *Mary* as he felt it would be treasonable to take the heir out of the country. He also feared that the fleet might hand the Prince over to William. Faced with Dartmouth's refusal there was no alternative but to take the Prince back to London, and at 5 am on December 8 he left Portsmouth. *Nine & ten of diamonds*

On the following day, December 9, William sent 150 foot and 500 dragoons to Reading under the Count of Nassau. They found the town in a state of defence with three companies of Irish dragoons and a regiment of Scottish horse holding the bridge. A skirmish took place in the narrow streets and James's men retreated leaving 20 dead and 40 taken prisoner. Then Nassau temporarily retreated when he heard this force was under a sergeant and two corporals and that they wanted to join William, he halted to greet them. He promoted the sergeant into a captain, and the two corporals into lieutenants, and told them to hold Reading for William. (See also Chapter Nine, seven of diamonds). *Queen of hearts*

Twenty-four hours later, on December 10, the Queen, the Prince of Wales and Father Petre succeeded in making their escape. At 2 am they crept down a secret staircase at Whitehall Palace which led to the rooms of Madame de Labadie, the Prince's nurse. They then passed six sentries and went by coach to Horseferry Stairs where they took a boat to Lambeth, and then transferred to a coach in the pouring rain. They rowed across the river at Gravesend to a hired packet-boat. They landed in France at 9 am on December 11. (See also Chapter Nine, queen of diamonds). *Knave of hearts*

At 1 am on December 11 James left Whitehall with Sir Edward Hales in a coach. They crossed the Thames at Horseferry, and the king dropped the Great Seal into the river. They continued on horseback, reaching Lambeth at 2 am. At 7 am they had refreshments at the Woolpack Inn, Aylesford Bridge, and by 10 am they were at Little Marston having done 50 miles in 8 hours. Near there they boarded a customs hoy, but when they found that they *Ace of hearts*

Two of hearts

IX ♦ — The yong Child going to Portsmouth garded by y` Lord Sallsboreys Trups of Papists	**X ♦** — The Lord Dartmouth refusing to carey y` Child over to France he returns to Whithalle	 **QUEEN ♥** — A fight at Raling wherin the Irish Souldiers suffred most the people fireing out at windows on them
 **KNAVE ♥** — The Queen and Child and father Peters going away in the night	 **I ♥** — The King leving London about three a clock in the Morning in his barge	 **II ♥** — The King and with 2 more are stoped by rude seamen being in an hoy by the Isle of Shipey
 **IIII ♥** — Barron Ienor is robed where besides money they took his Lordships pardon	 **V ♥** — The Chancellor going to the Tower and is followed by many more of Brethren	 **VII ♥** — The Prince of Orange coming to St Iameses is received with great Joy

needed ballast they turned back, only to be stranded on an ebb tide at Shellness, on the east end of the Isle of Sheppey. Just as they floated clear at 11 pm, forty men in three boats on the look out for Sir Edward Hales, detained them. They thought James was a Jesuit and stripped him, taking £200 in gold, a watch and a gold-hilted sword from him, but missed his coronation ring which he had concealed in his pants. They called him an 'ugly, lean-jawed, hatchet-faced Jesuit, popish dog'. His identity was discovered sometime after his arrest and he then had no option but to return to London, which he reached at 4 pm on Sunday, December 16.

James was not the only one to have his escape stopped short. Sir Thomas Jenner, Baron of the Exchequer (1637-1707), who had sided with the king in Godden v Hales case, had tried to join the king in his escape bid. However he had £400 and a 'general pardon' stolen from his chambers in Serjeants' Inn which delayed him. He was seized at Faversham and taken to the Tower, where he stayed until 1690. When he was charged with levying £3,000 fines from dissenters during James's reign, he pleaded the 'general pardon', and this plea was accepted. *Four of hearts*

Lord Justice Jeffreys was caught in the *Red Cow,* in Anchor and Hope Alley, Wapping, disguised as a seaman. He was spotted by a scrivener whom he had once bullied in court. He was taken to the Tower, where he suffered from acute inflammation of the kidneys in addition to his gall-bladder stone. He drank small quantities of sherry and weak brandy until he died in April, 1689, by which time he was reduced to almost a skeleton. (See also Chapter Nine, ace and two of hearts). *Three & five of hearts*

William insisted that the keys of the Tower were given to the Lord Mayor, Sir John Chapman. In fact he became so excited with the events that he died after several strokes! *Eight of clubs*

The pack is completed with the seven of hearts, showing the arrival of William at St. James's at 4 pm, Tuesday, December 18. On the previous night, James had been undressing as the Dutch infantry entered the Mall. William realised that the capture and imprisonment of James would not serve his purposes, and it was arranged that James should leave at midday. William drove down Piccadilly in triumph while the rain poured down on the dingy blue uniforms of his Dutch troops and the city bells rang out in greeting. (See also Chapter Nine, five of diamonds). *Seven of hearts*

In the next chapter the story is told in a pack which concentrates on the Glorious Revolution.

Chapter Nine

The Reign of James II
The Revolution

The second pack of cards concerned with the reign of James II is the work of Francis Barlow and has always been referred to as the Rebellion, or Revolution, pack. In fact it covers the events of James's reign, and prior to it, just as the pack we examined in Chapter Eight.

Ace of clubs

The set opens on the theme of pro-Catholic activities. Enough has already been said of the death of the Earl of Essex in Chapter Six, on the king of hearts, and in Chapter Eight, on the eight, nine and ten of hearts and the two of spades.

Two of clubs

Chapter Four's two of clubs referred to the blaming of the Catholics for causing the Fire of London. In this pack the two of clubs shows the removal of the anti-Catholic wording on the monument on 17 June, 1685. The monument had been erected not far from London Bridge. Its base was 40 ft high and 21 ft wide, while the column measured 15 ft in diameter; total height 202 ft. The Lord Mayor, Sir Patience Ward, had had these words put on it:

> 'This pillar was sett up in perpetuall remembrance of the most dreadful Burning of this Protestant City, began and carried out by the treachery and malice of the popish faction in the beginning of September in the year of Our Lord, 1666, in order to the effecting of their horrid plot for the extirpating the Protestant Religion and English Liberties, and to introduce popery and slavery'.

He had also had the following put up at the place where the fire started:

> 'Here by the Permission of Heaven, Hell broke loose upon this Protestant City from the malicious hearts of barbarous Papists, by the hands of their Agent Hubert, who confessed and on the Ruines of this place declared the Fact, for

♣ 2 I — The Earle of Essex.s Throat Cut.	♣ 3 II — The Inscription taken out of ye Monument	♣ 4 III — Oates Whipt from Algate to Tyburn.
♣ 6 V — Hanging Protestants in ye West.	♣ 7 VI — Two Brs and Iudge Ienner Speake rudely to Dr Huff ("Ile huff ye Dr Huff for all your huff")	♣ 8 VIII — Magdalen Colledge Scholars turned out.
♣ 10 IX — The Seaven Bishops going to the Tower.	♣ 9 VII — The Tryal of the Seaven Bishops.	♠ 16 III — Whiping Heresy Out of Windsor Chaple.

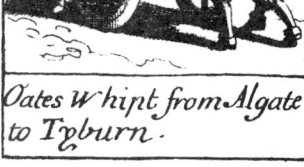

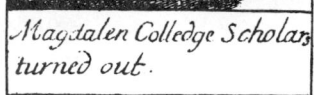

which he was hanged that here began that dreadful Fire, which is described and perpetuated on and by the neighbouring Pillar. Erected Anno 1681 in the Mayoraltie of Sir Patience Ward, Knight'.

Robert Hubert, a Calvinist from Rouen, was half paralysed and mentally defective. He had pleaded guilty to arson although the captain of the ship which brought him to England testified that they had not docked until two days after the fire had started.

Three of clubs

Titus Oates got his deserts on 20 and 22 May, 1685, when he was whipped 1½ miles from Aldgate to Newgate, and 2 miles from Newgate to Tyburn. This was part of a sentence for perjury, which also involved life imprisonment. In fact the verdict was reversed in 1689. Edmund Calamy wrote, 'I .... saw Dr. Oates whipped at the cart's tail the second time, while his back miserably swelled with his first whipping, looked as if it had been flayed'.

Knave of clubs

The knave of clubs shows the Lord Chancellor condemning Protestants in the west. This probably refers to the time when Jeffreys (Chancellor in 1685) was dealing with the aftermath of the Monmouth Rebellion in his capacity as Lord Chief Justice. (See also Chapter Seven, two of hearts, three and nine of clubs).

Four & five of clubs

Six & eight of clubs

The case of Dr. Hough's election to the presidency of Magdalen College, Oxford, has been dealt with in Chapter Eight, on the three of clubs and the four of hearts.

Nine & seven of clubs

Likewise the trial of the Seven Bishops is to be found in Chapter Eight on the five, six and seven of clubs.

King of clubs

James had set out to establish a firm relationship with the papacy at the outset of his reign. In November, 1685, an ardent Catholic, R. Palmer, Earl of Castlemaine, was sent as ambassador to the pope. He had faced trial in June, 1680, for his popish activities (see Chapter Five, two and eight of clubs), and owed his title to his wife's infidelity with the king. It is not surprising that the pope thought the choice of this man was an insult, and the situation was not improved when the earl insulted the pope. His task was to obtain cardinals' hats for the queen's uncle, Prince Rinaldo d'Este, and Father Petre. He succeeded so far as the Prince was concerned.

Ten of clubs

In due course the pope's nuncio, the Comte D'Adda, was publicly received in June, 1687. His procession to Windsor Castle consisted of 36 coaches, each drawn by 6 horses. The Duke of Somerset refused to escort him and was dismissed from his post as Gentleman of the Bedchamber as a result.

Three & four of spades

In the popular imagination James's policy of romanizing was now well under way as the three and four of spades show.

Five of spades

Who is doing a penance up a high hill with peas in his shoes is a mystery today unfortunately.

Six of spades

One of the main subjects of this pack is the birth of James's son, the Prince of Wales. James had longed for a son whom he could bring up as a Catholic, and prayers at shrines was one method tried

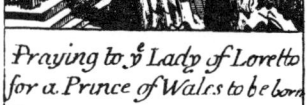

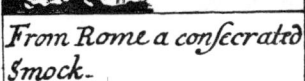

♠ 17 IIII — The Procession of ye Host through St. Iames's Park.	 ♠ 19 VI — A Lady going to S. Winifrids well for Penance.	 ♠ 22 VII — Praying to ye Lady of Loretto for a Prince of Wales to be born.
 ♠ 23 VIII — From Rome a consecrated Smock.	 ♠ 24 KING — My Lord Chancellor at the Beds Feet.	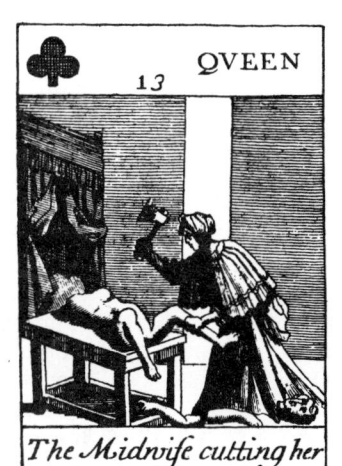 ♣ 13 QVEEN — The Midwife cutting her Husband to Peices.
 ♠ 14 I — The Popish Midwife putting his quarters in ye Privy	 ♠ 15 II — The Popish Midwife burning	 ♠ 21 QVEEN — Madam W—ks at Confession

to obtain divine assistance. James himself had gone to St. Winifred's Well in Flintshire in 1687. The well had been erected on the site of St. Winifred's martyrdom by Lady Margaret, mother of Henry VII.

Seven of spades

In the summer of 1687 James's mother-in-law, the Duchess of Modena, had prayed at the shrine of Our Lady of Loretto.(See also Chapter Eight, three of spades).

Eight of spades

Even a consecrated smock was sent from Rome.

King of spades

The birth of the Prince of Wales occurred on 10 June, 1688, as we have seen in Chapter Eight, two of diamonds.

Queen of clubs

Three cards, the queen of clubs, the ace and two of spades, present a fascinating mystery. Who was the Popish midwife and why should the murder of her husband and her own execution warrant three cards in this pack? As we have seen in Chapter Five Mrs. Cellier was known as the 'Popish Midwife', but apart from the fact that her husband died in 1689, there is no reason to connect her with these cards. So far as the birth of the Prince of Wales is concerned there were four midwives, but none were convicted of murder. Professor Kunzle has suggested the midwife was a Mary Aubrey.

Ace and two of spades

Queen of spades

The queen of spades refers to one of these midwives, Mrs. Judith Wilkes. Could she be confessing that she knew the true parents of the Prince of Wales, for there were many who doubted his parentage?

Nine of spades

The baby Prince was cared for carefully. Diet was an important consideration. The Prince rejected a wet-nurse until he took a robust brick-layer's wife, Mrs. Frances Smith. When appointed she wore a cloth-petticoat and waistcoat, a pair of old shoes and no stockings. She was given 200 guineas (£210) to improve herself. Doctors tried gruels, with oatmeal, barley, currants and wine, together with bread and milk. Dr. Goddard's Drops, described as 'liquid fire', were also used.

Ten of spades

He was baptised twice. First at a private ceremony on June 11, and then at a public one on October 15. The ten of spades refers to the latter, when the nuncio represented the pope, who was the Princes's godfather. The baby prince gave audiences according to the king of diamonds.

King of diamonds

Knave of hearts

The pack continues with the build up towards the Revolution. Tyrconnel's arming of Irish Catholics has already been dealt with in Chapter Eight (ten and knave of spades).

Eight of hearts

Lillybullero was an anti-papist doggerel written by the Marquis of Wharton to mark the appointment of General Talbot as Earl of Tyrconnel and Lord Lt. of Ireland in 1686. It was set to music by Henry Purcell as a quick step. It became a powerful weapon against James as everyone sang it.

> 'Ho! by Shaint Tyburn, it is de Talbote
> Lilli Burlero, bullen a-la.

26 ♠ X P. of Wales baptized ỹ Nuncio stands Godfather for ỹ Pope	**48 ♥ KNAVE** Tyrconel arming ỹ Papists in Ireland.	**43 ♥ QUEEN** Singing O brave popery delicate Popery Oh.
30 ♦ IX The Prince of Orange landing.	**31 ♦ KNAVE** Singing of Mass thinking that the French had landed.	**28 ♦ X** The Mass house at S.t Ione's pulling it down &c.t
35 ♦ IIII Bucklers Berry Popish Chaple burnt in the Stocks market	**37 ♦ III** Burning ỹ Popysh Chaple in Lincolns Inn Fields.	**38 ♦ II** Lime Street Chaple pulling down and burnt

And he will cut de Englishman's troate,
   Lilli, etc.
Ara! but why does he stay behind?
   Lilli, etc.
Ho! by my shoul 'tis a protestant wind
   Lilli, etc.
But see de Tyrconnel is now come ashore
   Lilli, etc.
And we shall have commissions gillore,
   Lilli, etc.
And now dis prophecy is come to pass,
   Lilli, etc.
For Talbot's de dog, and James is de ass.
   Lilli, etc.

Queen of hearts — Another song of the period is referred to on the queen of hearts.

Knave of spades — Father Charles Petre's sermon of 1 October, 1688, denouncing the English translation of the Bible, has been explained in Chapter Eight (five of spades).

Eight of diamonds — When the invasion threat began steps were taken to put the Tower of London into a state of readiness with mortars installed there.

Nine of diamonds — Then on November 5, William of Orange landed at Torbay. (See Chapter Eight, eight of diamonds).

Knave of diamonds — Hopes that the French had come to help in the hour of crisis, led to the offering of a mass.(See also Chapter Eight, knave of clubs).

Ten, four, three & two of diamonds — A wave of attacks on Catholic chapels in embassies now broke out. (See also Chapter Eight, eight of spades). The Lime Street Chapel of the Elector Palatine's envoy was attacked on October 29 and finished off in December. On November 11 and 12 attempts were made on chapels at Bucklersbury and St. John's, Clerkenwell, but the militia drove the mobs off. At Bucklersbury, a priest, clutching an altar candlestick, had his hand severed by a young hooligan. The seats and wainscot of Lincoln's Inn Fields' chapel of the Franciscan friars were burnt on December 10.

Nine of hearts — William had long planned for the time when the call would come for him to become king of England. He appreciated that not only was a military plan necessary, but also a propaganda programme too. He had arranged for thousands of copies of his Declaration to be printed and distributed to secret agents in various parts of England. When he landed it was to be published as widely as possible. In it he stressed that he would maintain the true laws, liberties and religion of England. This was likely to appeal to all except the most Jacobite of Catholics. Moreover, if he said that he would maintain the established laws, he could go on to claim that resistance to him would amount to resistance to the legally constituted authority in the land. No repeal of the Test Acts, the calling of a free parliament, removal of Catholics from office, were

♦ VII 36 — The Fight at Redding.	♦ VI 33 — Father Peters burning his Papers.	♦ QUEEN 32 — The Queen & Prince of Wales making their escape.
♥ VII 45 — A Preist selling of Relicks by Auction	♥ VI 46 — A Preist hard very hard at Work.	♥ III 50 — A Papist of quallity taken at Wapping
♥ II 51 — L. P. Taken in disguise going to Sea	♥ I 52 — My Lord Chancellor in the Tower.	♦ V 34 — The Prince of Orange coming to London.

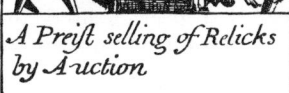

Banner on card 45: "Tho. A Beckets Old Stockins 5ˢ Once"

Ten of hearts

Seven of diamonds

Six of diamonds

Queen of diamonds

Seven, six & five of hearts

Four & three of hearts

Two and ace of hearts

King of hearts

Five of diamonds

Ace of diamonds

some of the other points he made. His aim was to appeal to the sentiments and convictions of Englishmen. He appreciated the need to subtly mould public opinion to recognise him as the king.

As William advanced towards London, more and more of James's army deserted. For example, on Friday, November 23, Lord Churchill's and the Duke of Grafton's men deserted to William. (See also Chapter Eight, king of hearts).

The fight at Reading has already been described in Chapter Eight (queen of hearts).

Faced with imminent disaster, James arranged for the escape of the Queen and the Prince of Wales. Father Petre was to accompany them, and he hurriedly burnt his papers before doing so.

The escape story has been told in Chapter Eight (knave of hearts).

Others planned their escapes at the same time. Catholic priests hurriedly sold relics, and destroyed the evidence of their trade before fleeing the country. Disguised papists who were caught were taken to the Tower.

Not all succeeded in getting away safely. Judge Jeffreys, the Lord Chancellor was wearing an old blue seaman's jacket and an old tarred hat when he was caught. He had shaved off his distinctive eyebrows too. (See also Chapter Eight, three and five of hearts).

As William advanced towards London, he was greeted by the Lord Mayor and Sheriffs at Windsor.

On 18 December, 1688, William reached London, entering it in a four-wheeled open coach. (See also Chapter Eight, seven of hearts).

A celebration drink at Ellis' in Grocers' Alley concludes this pack of cards. Thomas Ellis, a grocer, had been behind the apprentice riots on Monday, 26 July, 1647, when the 'Apprentices Parliament' was established. (See Chapter Two, nine of clubs and nine of diamonds). He was never prosecuted as his accuser 'was to go for the service of Ireland'.

Chapter Ten

The Reign of Queen Anne 1702-1704

The Post Man, number 1362, dated 30 December 2 January, 1704/5, contained an advertisement, which was also to be found in the *Daily Courant*, number 846 of 1 January, 1705. It read:
QUEEN ANNE'S CARDS: This day is published a new invented Pack of Cards, in which are described in Pictures done from Copper Plates, finely engraved the various Transactions of Her Majesty's most glorious Reign to the present, historically dispos'd according to the order of time in which they happen'd. Price 1s 6d a Pack. Sold by
H. Newman, at the Crown, in Little Brittain,
Mrs. Baldwin, in Warwick Lane, Mrs. Bond at the
Rising Sun at Charing Cross, Mr. Wotton in
Exchange Alley, Mr. Cook, at the corner of Row-lane (Bowlane), Stationers. And by Mr. Fullwood, at the Knave of Clubs, in Paternoster Row, Spittlefields, where are also to be had Fortune-telling Cards at 1s a Pack.

Mr. Fullwood was Samuel Fullwood, Master of the Company of Makers of Playing Cards in 1695 and 1696. The unusual thing about this pack is the fact that in addition to the normal card suit numbers, they are also numbered in chronological order. It is noticeable that the chronological order cuts right across the suits.

Anne was proclaimed queen on 8 March, 1702. It was the first sunny day there had been for weeks, and the ace of hearts depicts the traditional proclamation scene. Naturally parliament expressed its delight, particularly so as she was a true English queen in contrast to her Dutch predecessor, William III.

On Wednesday, March 11, she made her first appearance in the House of Lords, and in her speech she emphasized her desire to start a new era after the disturbance and problems of the previous twenty years.

1

2

3

♥ 1 I — Her M.ty Proclaim'd Q. of Eng. Scot. Fra & Ireland &c. March 8 1701	♥ 3 KING — Her M.tys first appearce in Parliam.t March 11 1701	 ♥ 6 QUEEN — Queen Anne Crown'd Apr. 23 1702
♥ 7 VII — Her Maj. Return from her Coronation to Westminster hall	♣ 8 KING — War Proclaim'd ag.t France. May 4. 1702	♠ 9 I — The Princess Sophia Ord.ed to be pray'd for in Church
♠ 10 KING — P. George at Portsmouth Viewing y.e Fleet & Army	♠ 12 X — The Queen Procla.md in y.e West Indies June 4 1702	♥ 13 VI — The Queen & Prince lay at Oxford in their way to Bath

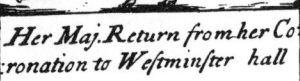

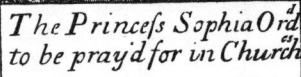

The True Concern I have for Our Religion for the
Laws and Liberties of England, for the Maintaining
the Succession to the Crown in the Protestant Line,
and the Government in Church and State, as by Law
Established, Encourages Me in this Great Undertaking;
which I Promise myself will be Successful, by the
Blessing of God, and the continuance of that Fidelity
and Affection, of which you have given Me so full
Assurance.

It was imperative to inform the Dutch of the death of their prince, William III, and to reassure them of England's continued friendship. To this end Marlborough was dispatched on March 10 with a letter which told how William had been seized by a fever on the previous Wednesday and had died at 8 am on the Sunday. The Dutch heard of William's death on March 25 and were dismayed at the news. When Marlborough arrived on March 28, he found that a French emissary was already there trying to renew old French connections with the anti-Orange party. The Dutch were delighted to hear that Anne proposed to stand by them in the future.

Anne was crowned on St. George's day, April 23. Aged thirty-seven, she was afflicted by gout and unable to walk, and had to be carried in a sedan chair to Westminster Hall, and for the rest of the way on an open chair. Medals commemorating the crowning were thrown to those present in the abbey. Mrs. Ducaila was paid £10.15.0d (£10.75) for 'doing the Queen's hair' and £12 for 'a head of hair with long locks & puffs' (a wig).

War was declared against Louis XIV on May 4 from in front of St. James' Palace. Louis had accepted the will of the late king of Spain which left the Spanish empire to the Duke of Anjou. This effectively tore up the agreement made with William III's help to divide the empire between the Duke of Anjou and the Archduke Charles when the king of Spain died. In throwing in her support with the Archduke at the very beginning of the Spanish Succession War, Enland was also demonstrating her alertness to the danger of a Jacobite invasion with French support.

This danger must have been in the back of Anne's mind when she ordered prayers for princess Sophia of Hanover. By the 1701 Act of Settlement, Sophia was to succeed Anne, all of whose children had died.

Prince George, Anne's consort, arrived at Portsmouth on the night of June 2. The following day he went to the Isle of Wight and commented favourably on the forces he reviewed there. He pardoned three deserters to show his pleasure at the drill. On the two following days he viewed Dutch and English ships before returning to London.

Anne's reign was to contain the Act of Union with Scotland in 1707, but in 1702 this was far from being a reality. Anne's speech

11 of March 11 contained an expression of her desire for a closer union with Scotland. But the Commons had divided on the subject in the debate which had followed the speech as those supporting the High Church viewpoint were not keen on dealings with Presbyterians. In Scotland it was felt that the High Church Anne would destroy William's new Presbyterian establishment although she had said that closer union would guarantee that establishment and destroy Jacobitism. In her letter to the Scottish Privy Council, Anne suggested that a closer relationship should be considered by their parliament. This led to the recall of the old convention parliament of 1689 as no elections had taken place for years in Scotland. The Country party and the Jacobites walked out of the parliament after stating their objections to closer union, leaving a 'rump' of 120 Whigs. Anne's reign had started inauspiciously so far as union was concerned.

12 The ten of spades records the proclamation of Anne as queen being read on June 4 in the West Indies. Col. Codrington, governor of the Leeward Islands, had taken the offensive against the French on that day as well as proclaiming her accession on board ship first at Nevis and then at St. Kitts.

13 In the autumn Anne and her husband went on a tour of the west country, which was to last from August until October. Prince George's asthma was troubling him and it was hoped that a visit to Bath would help him. They reached Oxford on August 26 to be met by the vice-chancellor, dons and others who rode out to greet them. They spent the night at Christ Church before attending a banquet in the Sheldonian on the following day. This demonstration of Anglican loyalty was crowned by the presentation of a Bible, Prayer Book and a pair of gloves for the queen. Presumably the

14 nine of hearts refers to touching for 'evil' which took place at Oxford. At Bath she was to touch thirty people. She had decided to revive this ancient royal custom.

   Meanwhile the war against France and Spain went on. Rota, at one end of the Bay of Bulls, was part of Cadiz. Secret information had come in about the lack of defences there and Admiral Rooke was given orders to take it with 10,000 English and 4,000 Dutch troops. The popular but useless Duke of Ormonde, who was in charge of the English troops, made the fatal decision to land the

15 troops between the Bay of Bulls and Fort St. Catherine. This was too far from Cadiz itself, but his aim was to seize the villages of Rota and Porta Santa Maria. The landing was easy and only twenty were drowned in the surf, but nothing was achieved by it. They

16 stayed for twenty-six days, plundering Santa Maria, sacking the churches, raping the women and the nuns. Ormonde proved a hopeless leader in the face of this outbreak. In fact his second-in-command, Sir Henry Belasys, led the plundering, placing guards in the streets to seize plunder from privates for his own

♥ 14 IX *Her Majesty touching for the Evil.*	 ♠ 16 KNAVE *Port St Marys Plunderd agst ye Generals Express Comand*	 ♥ 17 VIII *The Queen & Prince goe to Bristol from Bath.*
 ♣ 18 X *Landaw Besiegd & Taken Sep. 10 1702 And again 1704 No. 15*	 ♣ 19 KNAVE *The D. of Bavaria Traiterfly Declares for France & Seizes Ulme*	 ♥ 21 IIII *Her Maj. Entertaind by ye City of London on ye Lord Mayors Day Octo. 29 1702*
 ♦ 22 IIII *Vigo attacked at Sea by Sr Geo: Rook & at Land by his Grace the D. of Ormond*	 ♠ 23 VI *The Boom at Vigo forc'd by Vice Admll Hopson in the Torbay*	 ♦ 24 VI *The French & Spanish Fleets Attacqued in ye harbour of Vigo & 34 Men of War & Gallions destroyd & taken*

benefit. The government ordered Belasys' arrest on hearing of this.

17 In the meanwhile Anne and the Prince had reached Bath on August 28. On top of Lansdowne Hill they were met by two hundred virgins dressed in white as Amazons, carrying bows and arrows. When Anne's coach stopped on a steep street in the city, her weight proved too great for the horses and the brakes, and a dozen men had to prevent the whole equipage from slipping back down the hill! Bath was very crowded and Sarah Churchill described it as 'noisy and stinking', while Abigail Masham had trouble with her lodgings. Anne took the waters in the faint hope that they would help her to have another child, which was an accepted idea of their value. On September 3, she visited Bristol and was escorted through a triumphal arch at St. Nicholas Gate by the principal citizens on horseback, together with two hundred troops and naval captains. She knighted the mayor and then dined while all the ships in the docks fired their cannons incessantly and the church bells rang out. She returned to Bath and stayed there until October 8.

18 The war in Europe continued with the sieges of Landau, a fortress guarding the approaches to Strasbourg. The 1702 siege by the Allies lasted from June 18 to September 8. The magistrates begged the governor to surrender, and when the inhabitants flocked to the ramparts with white cloths and shouted, 'Mercy, Quarter', he agreed to do so. Count Tallard recaptured the city in November, 1703, but lost it again on 28 November, 1704.

19 However in the summer of 1702 the Duke of Bavaria opened negotiations with the Allies in order to frighten France into accepting his demand to Louis for a vast increase in his territories and the emperorship for himself, which he wanted re-sited in Bavaria. The resulting alliance of the Duke's 45,000 troops with France enabled Louis to take the offensive again. On September 8 Ulm, the Protestant outpost on the Upper Danube, was taken by Bavarian officers who entered it disguised as peasants. They overpowered the guard and opened the gates.

20 Marlborough's successes of 1702 are recorded on the ten of hearts. His 25,000 men took ninety days from September 29 to October 7 to wrest Ruremonde from the Prince of Hornes' 2,400. The Allies had 60 casualties and the enemy, 40. The siege of Liege took from October 12 to 26. Marlborough's 25,000 took on 7,200, but this time the Allied losses were 1,034. Liege's fortifications consisted of earthworks faced with brick, which did not prove much of a problem. Once the defences were breached it took only an hour to complete the capture. Huy, a fortress high up the Maas, near Namur, was taken after a siege from August 15 to 26. The Prince of Hesse-Cassel led 16,000 Allies to besiege Limburg from September 10 to 27. They only lost 100 and the enemy 60 before surrender came.

♥ 25 II Her Maty at St Pauls on ye Thanksgiving day for ye Action at Vigo Nov. 12. 1702	♠ 27 QUEEN The Speaker of ye H of Comons gives the thanks of ye House to Sr Geor. Rook	♥ 29 KNAVE Adal Bembo Cowardly betrd by some Capt in his Squadrn
♣ 30 II Adal Munden Tryed on board her Maty Shp Queen at Spithead	♦ 32 KNAVE Capts Kerby & Wade shot to Death on board of ye Bristol Ap: 16 1703	♣ 33 VI The Brave Camizars Routing their Enemies
♦ 35 VIII Marl Villeroy taken prisr in Cremona by Pr Eugen	♠ 37 VIII The Dredfull Storme Novber ye 26 1703	♦ 38 VII The K of Spains Arival at Windsor Decber ye 29 1703

21	On October 29, the Queen was entertained by the Lord Mayor, and when she reached the west end of St. Paul's Cathedral, she was greeted by a large number of workhouse children perched on the scaffolding. One of the children made a speech before she went on to watch a militia parade.
22-27	No less than six cards are devoted to the attack on Vigo and the celebrations which followed it. (See also Chapter Eleven, seven of hearts). The attack lasted from October 12 to 23, and it was made by the joint Anglo-Dutch fleet under Admiral Rooke and the Duke of Ormonde. Its object was to destroy or capture the Spanish treasure fleet and its escort of twenty-three French ships. When Vice-Admiral Hobson, or Hopsonn, in the *Torbay* broke the harbour boom of masts lashed together, the Allies were able to destroy plate and merchandise valued at 14 million pieces of eight, and capture that worth 7 million. The boom was over-shadowed by two batteries, one of which was a stone tower called Fort Randa containing 30 cannon. Leading his 2,000 men on foot, Ormonde approached it from the landward side. They had to march across 2 miles of ravines, vineyards and pine woods to get there. Using handgrenades they managed to silence the tower before the *Torbay* struck the boom. But an enemy fireship set the *Torbay* alight and her crew leapt overboard. When the fireship blew up it helped to put the *Torbay's* fire out! In all the Allies lost only 200 men. When the national celebrations took place on November 12, the Lord Mayor and aldermen conducted the Queen, Lords and Commons from Temple Bar to St. Paul's in a procession of coaches which took hours to pass by. The Tower guns fired a salute, and medals were struck to commemorate the event. (See my *Commemorative Medals*, p. 104).
28	On 23 December, 1702, an announcement was made, which read: It was her Majesty's pleasure that whenever there was occasion to embroider, depict, engrave, carve or paint her Majesty's arms, these words SEMPER EADEM should be used for a motto, it being the same that had been used by her predecessor Queen Elizabeth of glorious memory. John Evelyn did not forget this order when he wrote of Blenheim on 6 September, 1704, 'Semper Eadem — let her people take it to heart'.
29	Admiral Benbow intercepted the French fleet off Santa Martaz as it headed for Carthagena. With a superiority of more than 120 guns, Benbow should have won, but four of his seven captains failed to play their part in the six day running fight. On the sixth day, August 24, Benbow's right leg was shattered by chain shot.
32	(See Chapter Eleven, five of diamonds). Captains Kirby and Wade were tried by court-martial. Kirby's crew said he was scared, 'dodging behind the mizzen mast and falling down on the deck on

the noise of shot'. Both men were condemned and sent home in the *Bristol.* They were shot on deck in Plymouth Sound. (See Chapter Eleven, six of diamonds). An alehouse song of the period recalls the event:
    Says Kirby unto Wade: 'We will run; we will run'
    Says Kirby unto Wade: 'We will run'
    'For I value no disgrace, nor the losing of my place,
    But the enemy I won't face, nor his gun, nor his gun'.

    At a court-martial at Spithead on July 13, Rear-Admiral Sir John Munden had been acquitted on a charge of negligence. He had been sent to Corunna and told to cruise off Cape Prior to watch for French ships. On May 28, the French were spotted inshore of his ships after they had slipped past him into the harbour during the night. In spite of his acquittal, he was discharged due to popular pressure on the government to take action against him.   30

    Meanwhile Anne was faced with Scottish religious problems. Although the 1689 Revolution settlement had left the episcopalian church as the established church in England, in Scotland it had the opposite effect. The majority of Scottish Episcopalian clergy have been deprived of their livings. The fortunate ones had become chaplains to great families, but many were forced to live on alms. Bishop Burnet of Salisbury gave £200 for their relief. Anne's accession had led to Presbyterians producing pamphlets against their toleration, and the new abjuration oath of 1702 required them to deny divine right. It seemed that they had no alternative but to turn Jacobite and hope for a counter revolution. By 1707 only 165 out of 900 parishes were Episcopalian, but the Toleration Act of March, 1712, brought them relief by legalizing their services.   31

    The normal function of commissars as food supply officials seems to have temporarily changed in the case of the six of clubs. Their supply work was aided by private civilian traders, called sutlers, whose job it was to supply meat twice a week to troops.   33

    The purpose of fighting the Spanish Succession War was made plain on 12 September, 1702, when the Archduke Charles was declared to be the rightful king of Spain at a gathering held in Vienna.   34

    Marshall Villeroi (1644-1730), a brave but somewhat undistinguished French soldier, was captured at his headquarters at night when Prince Eugene mounted a special snatch raid.   35

    On 7 April, 1703, Marlborough began an eighteen day siege of Bonn. His force consisted of 40,000 men, 90 large mortars and 500 guns. A hard fight developed when the 3,600 strong garrison sallied out against them. The Allies lost 600 and the enemy 860 before this surrender of the last of the Rhine fortresses to the Allies. (See also Chapter Eleven, seven of diamonds).   36

    John Evelyn wrote of the terrible storm which raged from 1 am to 7 am on the night of 27 November, 1703:   37

> The effects of the hurricane and tempest of wind,
> rain and lightning, through all the nation, especially
> London, were very dismal. Many houses demolished,
> and people killed. As to my own losses, the subversion of
> woods and timber, both ornamental and valuable, through
> my whole estate and about my house, the woods crowning
> the garden-mount, and growing along the park-meadow,
> the damage to my own dwelling, farms, and outhouses, is
> almost tragical, not to be paralleled with anything
> happening in our own age. I am not able to describe it;
> but submit to the pleasure of Almighty God'.

Thus wrote a man who had lived through the fire of London. He lost 2,000 trees. The storm has been described as 'without rival in the recorded history of our island'. Brought by a WSW wind, it gave rise to an unfounded fear that the fleet was sunk. London Bridge was blocked by wrecked boats, and damage in the city was estimated at £1 million. The price of roof tiles went up from 21s (£1.5p) to £6 per 1,000. Bristol suffered badly when underground warehouses became swamped and £100,000's worth of property was lost. 3,000 trees in the Forest of Dean, and 4,000 in the New Forest were blown down. Ely cathedral's roof was left in shreds, and the Bishop of Bath and Wells and his wife were killed in bed when a chimney stack crashed on them.

38 & 39

The newly acclaimed King Charles III of Spain paid a state visit to England in December, 1703, before going on to Spain. Anne stood at the top of the staircase at Windsor Castle to greet him, and he touched the hem of her petticoat before they embraced and kissed each other on both cheeks. He then saluted forty court ladies with a kiss each. He was described as 'a very pretty gentleman, about nineteen years old, tall and slender' .... with 'very good eyes, very white teeth and a very becoming smile'. He was a great eater and his table manners were quite new to Anne's court. When he liked the look of a dish, he pointed at it with his fork! He treated his bread almost sacramentally, and at the end of one meal washed the tips of Anne's fingers for her.

40

He then proceeded on his journey and landed at Lisbon to take possession of his kingdom in the midst of the war.

41

The two of spades is the first of two cards which refer to political trouble makers in England. William Fuller had made a name for himself in the reign of James II when he wrote a pamphlet claiming that Mrs. Mary Grey and Lord Tyrconnel were the parents of the Old Pretender who was born in 1688. He was sentenced to stand in the pillory three times with a paper in his hat denouncing his crime, and then to receive thirty-nine lashes at Bridewell and six months hard labour there. He was not to be released until he had paid 1,000 marks, about £650. In spite of this episode, James II used him as a secret agent after the Glorious Revolution. Fuller concealed letters

41 — II — Will. Fuller beating hemp in Bridewell	42 — V — The Author of ye Shortest way wth Dissenters Pillor'd	43 — IIII — Namure Bombarded
44 — III — The D. of Marl: famous Mar.ch Into Germany to Reduce the El. of Bavaria	45 — VIII — The Glorious Victory at Hochstet wher ye French and Bavarians lost 40000 Men.	46 — VII — Marshal Tallard taken Prisoner
47 — IX — The Taking Gibralter by Sr Geo. Rook 24 July 1704	51 — III — Mr Tutchin Author of ye Observator on his Tryall at the Queens Bench Bar	52 — IIII — Maresh.l Tallard & other French Gen.ls bro.t Prisoners to England

by sewing them up in the form of coat buttons covered with silk on silver. This was never detected until he became a double-agent by working for William III as well. He used invisible ink made of milk or onion juice.

42 The five of spades refers to Daniel Defoe's pamphlet, *The Shortest Way with Dissenters*, of July, 1703. It was a parody on the violence of the High Church writers of the day. 'It is cruelty to kill a snake or a toad in cold blood, but the poison of their nature makes it a charity to our neighbours to destroy these creatures', wrote Defoe. His irony was taken in earnest, and as it was an anonymous publication, it was believed that some new unknown church champion had appeared. When the author's identity became known and the hoax exposed, the High Church leaders became very angry and secured a sentence of three periods in the pillory and a prison sentence for Defoe. This rebounded on them as Londoners seized the occasion to turn the pilloryings into an ovation, throwing flowers to the author.

43 The bombardment of Namur on the four of spades presents something of a mystery. Fighting occurred there in William III's reign, but not in Anne's.

44,45,46 Marlborough's famous march to Blenheim and its outcome is recorded on three cards in this set and three in the set on Marlborough's victories.(See Chapter Eleven, two three and ten of hearts). It is interesting to notice that both sets refer to the battle as being at Hochstadt rather than at Blenheim. The villages were only three miles apart.

Exasperated by the siege warfare of the Low Countries, Marlborough saw his chance to achieve a decisive breakthrough in the deadlock when he heard that the French were heading for Vienna. To stop them a 400 mile march would be essential. It was an unique event as military marches went as he saw to it that each stopping place was prepared by the time his men arrived. Food was paid for in cash so that civilians had no cause to grumble. At one point he arranged for 1,000 pairs of shoes, costing £97.18s.4d (£97.91½) to be supplied to replace worn out ones.

The battle is too well known to need re-telling here. What is perhaps less well known is the fact that there were seventeen doctors in the Allied army, one for every 600 men, and Marlborough saw to it that they went on to the battlefield during the battle rather than waiting until it was over as traditionally happened. The booty included 3,600 tents, 34 coaches and 24 barrels and 8 casks of silver, and for this battle and that at Oudenarde, £64,013 was given out as bounties to the English troops and their dependents. Marlborough got £717, and the men got the equivalent of a month's pay each. £4,000 was distributed among the disabled men, and £3,013 among widows. The capture of Marshal Tallard (1652-1728) was a bonus to the victory.

News arrived about this time of the capture of Gibraltar after a two-day attack by Sir George Rooke and Prince of Hesse Darmstadt. It was an easy task as the garrison numbered only 470 and the new defences, recently planned, were in the early stages of construction. 47,48

On October 26, Triers on the R. Moselle was captured by Marlborough in a surprise attack on his return from Bleneheim. 49

This event was followed by the successful siege of Traebach by the Prince of Hesse-Cassel, which lasted from November 4 to December 20. 50

The three of spades refers to John Tutchin, whom we have already met in Chapter Seven on the Monmouth Rebellion (See nine of clubs). The first number of his *Observator* came out on 1 April, 1702. It began as a weekly, but soon came out twice a week. His attack on the administration of the navy led to his trial on 4 November, 1704, at the Guildhall. He was found guilty but before the judges of the Queen's Bench had sentenced him, he made an appeal on a technical legal point. This led to the verdict being put aside. 51

The set was brought to a triumphal completion with the four of clubs. Marlborough was in fact criticised for burdening Allied resources by taking 11,000 prisoners at Blenheim. 5,678 of them were brought to England. Their ration scale was fixed as: 52

Sundays, Tuesday, Thursdays
Bread 1d
Beer ½d
Meat 2½d
Vegetables 1d

Mondays, Fridays
Bread 1d
Beer ½d
Peas ¾d
Butter 1¼d
Cheese ½d
Vegetables 1d

Wednesdays, Saturdays
Bread 1½d
Beer ¾d
Cheese 1d
Butter 1¼d
Vegetables ½d

One shilling (5p) a day was spent on those in hospital. At Southampton the jailer was accused of giving them half baked bread as it weighed more. Challenged with this, he produced a long list of signatures to say the food was satisfactory. It turned out that none of the signatories was in the prison. However the French prisoners lived in luxury compared with the English prisoners at Dinan. Prisoners were exchanged on the Channel Islands, and a rate of so many men per officer was fixed according to the ranks concerned.

Chapter Eleven

Marlborough's Victories 1702-07

Although many of Marlborough's victories were pictured in the set of cards on Queen Anne's reign described in the previous chapter, one set was devoted to the Spanish Succession War and his victories. The *Observer,* volume VI, number 72 of Wednesday, November 5 to Saturday, November 8, 1707, bore an advertisement which was repeated several times in that paper and also in the *Daily Courant,* the *Post Boy* and the *Weekly Comedy.* It read:

> Just Published
> Victory Cards representing in lively Figures on curious Copper-Plates the most memorable Battles, Sieges, Skirmishes, and Sea-fights, etc, also the Effiges of the chief confederates drawn to the life; together with Variety of Hieroglyphicks drawn from the present Constitution of France and its Monarch. The whole Contriv'd not only to divert the Ingenious, but to hand down to Posterity the stupendous Victories obtained by the Arms of her Majesty and her Allies, under his Grace John Duke and Prince of Marlborough, price 1s. is sold by B. Bragge and J. Broomhead in Pater-Noster Row, J. How in Talbot-Court in Gracechurch-street, and J. Morphew near Stationers Hall.

The set opened with a collection of the portraits of the key figures in the War of the Spanish Succession, which began in 1702. These are followed by the battle cards and concluded by the suit of spades denouncing Louis XIV and the French.

Queen of clubs

Queen Anne is depicted on the queen of clubs. She ruled from 1702 - 1714 in spite of predictions that her overweight and constant child-bearing would end her reign quite soon. A conscientious ruler, she chaired more cabinet meetings than any other monarch, although her mind has been described as being as slow as a lowland

QUEEN ♣ ANNE by ye Grace of God of Great Britain France and Irel. Queen Defender of ye Faith	 **QUEEN ♥** The most Illustrious ANNA Sophia of Hannover Born 1630	 **KING ♦** Victor Amadeus D. of Savoy born Octob. 18. 1663
 **X ♣** Prince Eugene of Savoy born October 18. 1663.	 **KING ♣** Charles III. King of Spain born October 1st 1685.	 **III ♠** The Royal Outcry: or ye Dauphine selling by Auction ye Reversion of his fathers Crown
 **II ♠** The Duke of Anjou Whipping Cardin. Portocarero for forging a Will of the Late King of Spain.	 **KING ♠** All Europ's Riveted in this Belief. My Grandfather before me was a Thief I'll steal Spains Crown & Jewels wth its pelf And be at last a Nominal king my self	 **KNAVE ♣** the just reward of Treachery Knaves are Fools

King of hearts	river. She married George, Prince of Denmark, in 1683, and in 1702 he was Generalissimo and Lord High Admiral.
Queen of hearts	After the death of her last surviving child, the Duke of Gloucester, Anne's successor became Sophia of Hanover under the terms of the Act of Settlement, 1701. She never succeeded to the throne as she died two months before Anne.
Queen of diamonds	The connection between the Princess Royal of Prussia and the Spanish Succession War is obscure. Joseph I, Emperor of Germany
Ace of clubs	from 1705 to 1711, is depicted as riding over two fallen persons, one of whom is crying out 'Libertie'. Victor, Duke of Savoy, had
King of diamonds	married Louis XIV's niece in 1684. In 1690 he had joined the first Grand Alliance against France, but withdrew from the war in 1696 after a series of heavy defeats. In 1701 he allied with France, but switched to the Allies' side in 1703. In 1713 he became king of Sicily, but exchanged this kingdom for that of Savoy in 1720, which he ruled as king until 1730.
Ten of clubs	Prince Eugene of Savoy (1663-1736) was an outstanding general, who fought with Marlborough at Blenheim.
King of clubs	Charles III of Spain was the Archduke Charles of Austria, who was to have been king of Spain on the death of his relative the Spanish Charles II under the Second Partition Treaty, 1700. This treaty sought to divide the huge Spanish empire up between the Archduke and the Dauphin of France. It was France's rejection of this agreement which led to the War of Spanish Succession. France accepted Charles II's will referred to on the two of spades.
Three of spades	Clement XI sided with France over the claim to the Spanish throne. The reference to the kingdom of Jerusalem on the three of spades may be to Frederick II crowning himself its king in 1229. The point being that Anjou crowned himself Spanish king.
Two of spades	The two of spades shows Philip, Duke of Anjou, whipping Cardinal Porto Carrero, Archbishop of Toledo, into forging the will of the king of Spain, Charles II. The cardinal had decided to support the Duke's claim to the Spanish throne as he was the Dauphin's son, and so he drove Charles to make a will in Anjou's favour. When Charles died in 1700, Louis XIV was tempted to accept the will in favour of his grandson instead of keeping to the Second Partition Treaty which had divided the empire up, giving the major part to the Archduke Charles.
King of spades	The Duke of Anjou's acceptance of the will is alluded to in the king of spades, where he mutters that as his grandfather Louis XIV had taken what he wanted, so now he would take the crown of Spain. In so doing, he precipitated the War of Spanish Succession.
Four of diamonds	But according to the four of diamonds France, the 'Gallic tyrant', tried in vain to separate angels labelled 'Peace' and 'Unity' as a crowned angel (Anne?) flew in to stop him.
Knave of clubs	At the outset of the war the Duke of Savoy was an ally of France

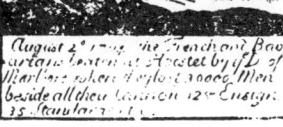

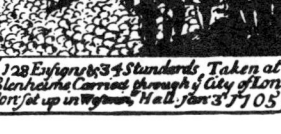

V♦ Aug 29th 1702 Adm'l Benbow engages w'th y'e French Squadron under Du Casse but is deserted by Kirby & Wade in which Action he Received a Wound of w'ch he Dyed December 4. 1702	 **VI♦** April 14. 1703. Kirby and Wade deservedly Shott on Board y'e Bristol man of war at Plymouth for Treachery & Cowardice in y'e Fight between (Benbow & Du Casse)	 **VI♥** Fort S't Michael Storm'd by y'e Lord Culls Sep't 3. 1702. Kill'd & th' enymie 600 men & took 200 prisoners in les y'n an Hours time
 **VII♦** Bonn Invested April 24. 1703 by the D'e of Marlborough Obliged y'e 14. of May following to Surrender	 **X♥** August 4'th 1704 the French and Bavarians beaten at Hostet by y'e D. of Marlb'ro where he lost 20000 Men beside all their Cannon 125 Ensigns 35 Standards &c.	 **II♥** The Pillar Set up at Hogsted by M'r Steepn in Memory of y'e Famous Victory Obtained by the Duke of Marlborough.
 **III♣** 128 Ensigns & 34 Standards, Taken at Blenheims Carried through y'e City of London set up in Westm'r Hall, Jan'y 3'd 1705	Had you my Post pray wou'd not you Tell mony over as I do. *I am not the first*	 **VIII♣** The D. of Marlboro obliges Limburg to surrender at discretion. Sept 28. 1705.

and gloated to see Bavaria invaded in 1702. The Bishop of Cologne allowed French troops through his country to spur his brother Maximilian Emanuel of Bavaria to make up his mind to swing the 4,500 Bavarians on to France's side. Although Maximilian did join France, he was not trusted as he continued to negotiate with England. In the spring of 1703, he let down the French march on Vienna.

Knave of spades — The knave of spades alludes to the intrigues at the outset of the war to enable France to secure all she could of the Spanish empire and central Europe by showing a priest attempting to alter the dying Spanish king's will to include Cologne and Bavaria.

Five & six of diamonds — The first incident in the war referred to is Admiral Benbow's valiant fight against the French which failed due to the lack of support from Captains Kirby and Wade. The details of the case have been dealt with in Chapter Ten in cards twenty-nine and thirty two. On the sixth day of the fight, Benbow's right leg was badly broken by chain shot. He told the ship's carpenter to make him a cradle on the quarter-deck so that he could continue to direct operations.

Six of hearts — The first land fight of the set portrays the storming of Fort St. Michael by Lord Cutts on 31 September, 1702. This was a key fortress guarding the approach to Venloo on the River Maas. It consisted of an elaborate earthwork fortress surrounded by a 10 ft moat, and not the structure shown on the card. At 4 pm Cutts' men attacked and crossed the 120 ft wooden bridge and scrambled up the fortifications by gripping the long grass and so forced the garrison to surrender.

Seven of hearts
Seven of diamonds — The taking of Vigo on 12 October, 1702, depicted on the seven of hearts has already been dealt with in Chapter Ten, on cards twenty-two to twenty-seven. Similarly the taking of Bonn on the seven of diamonds is to be found on card thirty-six.

Ten of hearts — Marlborough's first appearance in this set is on the ten of hearts, which refers to the battle of Hoistet (Hochstadt), better known as Blenheim, on 2 August, 1704. Hochstadt was a village three miles west of Blenheim, and the story of his achievement is told in Chapter Ten, cards forty-four to forty-six. Shortly after the battle, **Two of hearts** — George Stepney, (1663-1707), our ambassador at Vienna, had a marble pillar erected at Hochstadt. A contemporary pamphlet in the British Museum gives the Latin inscription written by Mr. Stepney, and it is 'English'd by a gentleman of Oxford'. It reads as follows:

> A Monument Sacred to Eternal Memory. On the 13th Day of August 1704 In, and near this Place were put to Flight after an incredible Slaughter The French and Bavarian Armies Under the Command of Emanuel the Elector And the two Counts of Tallard and Marsin. The Second of which Generals was taken Prisoner in the Battle; with XL others

of the First Rank, CIX Officers of Lesser Note And
12000 Common Soldiers, Besides 14000 put to the
Sword in the Field of Battle and 4000 Push'd into
the Danube. On the one Part Prince Eugene of Savoy
commanded the Victorious Army for Leopold the
Roman Emperor with Immortal Glory, On the other John,
Duke of Marlborough, an Englishman, who under the Happy
Influence of his Mistress Queen Anne, March'd at the Head
of Her Brave Troops, which he led from the Rhine to
the Danube To succour Germany, that was reduced
to the last Extremity which He began to Accomplish
with greatest Courage In conjunction with Lewis, the Prince
of Baden's Army By taking the strong Pass and Mountain of
Donawaert, That seemed Impregnable through its deep
Intrenchments, And afterwards brought to Perfection with the
same constancy of Mind, and success In the Battle that was
Fought here between Blenheim and Hochstadt. The
Enemies' Army Had the Advantages of Numbers, and the
Ground on their side; Nor was there any other Passage
to Victory For the Confederates, than through Rivers and
Morasses. From hence the Princes of the Grand Alliance may
know No Difficulty is unsurmountable to a Resolute and
couragious Mind. Rebellious Electors may lean
Conspiracies with the Enemies of their Native Country
go seldom unpunished And after all his boasted conquests,
Lewis XIV must at last confess That no Prince whatsoever
ought to be cry'd up for being Great and Happy Before
Death removes him beyond the Reach of Human Misfortunes.

On 3 January, 1705, the thirty-four standards and one hundred and twenty-eight colours captured at Blenheim were paraded in London from the Tower to Westminster Hall, while a forty gun salute was fired. — Three of hearts

The knave of hearts probably referred to Marlborough, who certainly benefited from the gratitude of the nation as Blenheim Palace constantly reminds us. — Knave of hearts

Then in July, 1705, Marlborough captured Brabant and received a tun of wine in gratitude for its relief. He himself was involved in the melee; an enemy soldier took a swipe at him, missed and fell off his horse. Three thousand prisoners were taken in the action in which the French cuirassiers in their amour were unable to stand up to the swords of the Duke's cavalry. — Five of hearts

Limburg's capture, depicted on the eight of clubs, raised problems. As it was in the Spanish Netherlands, the Dutch intended to keep it, but the emperor insisted the town was legally his. Marlborough stood in the middle of this argument, knowing that the town must not be seized as booty if the Grand Alliance was to hold together. His solution was to let the Dutch garrison it while — Eight of clubs

Eight of hearts	the imperial ambassador was put in charge of its administration.

The eight of hearts portrays another relief, that of Barcelona by Admiral Leake on 8 May, 1706. England had captured Barcelona in the previous year and it was now besieged by the French marshal Tesse. As the English fleet approached, the French warships suddenly left the bay. This enabled Leake to land 5,000 troops on the quay, who then marched to a breach made in the previous year's siege. Tesse, alarmed by the departure of the French fleet, decamped two days later after losing a quarter (7,000) of his force and abandoning 200 cannon, 10,000 sacks of meal and 3,000 barrels of powder. The day was marked by a total eclipse of the sun at midday, which accounts for the sale of medals and prints showing the symbolic eclipse of Louis XIV being on sale in London shortly afterwards.

Ten of diamonds

The battle of Ramillies, 23 May, 1706, is marked by four cards. This victory of Marlborough's drove the French out of Flanders. The mist cleared at 8 am on that Whitsunday morning to reveal the armies to each other. The forces were evenly matched, although Marlborough had more cannons. A 3 pm he ordered a feint attack, but to ensure his men fought well he did not tell them that it was only a feint. When it had achieved its object of deceiving the enemy he sent two messengers to convince his men that they were to hold back. Having put the real attack in motion, he found himself surrounded. He was thrown from his horse and was saved by the offer of a horse from a colonel, whose head was shot off a moment later. Marlborough saw to it that he got a memorial in Westminster Abbey and that his widow and children were cared for. By 6.30 pm the French were in chaotic retreat.

Six & seven of clubs

The medals referred to in two of the cards shown Anne as Minerva overthrowing Louis XIV, who is armed as a Roman warrior. 'Louis the Great', 'Anne the Greater' reads the Latin inscription. On the reverse Abimelech is shown being killed by a stone thrown by a woman, and he calls to a soldier to finish him off as he does not want it said that he died at a woman's hand (Judges 9 v 54). The medal is a rare one, and on its edge is inscribed in Latin, 'The Almighty Lord hath delivered him into the hands of a woman; *Judith* 16 v 6'. This means that Anne is seen as Judith who destroyed Holofernes.

Four of hearts

The fourth card shows the procession which took the captured standards to the Guildhall on June 27. A service was held in St. Paul's cathedral, which lasted from 1.30 pm until 4.15 pm and included Purcell's *Te Deum*.

Four of clubs

On 3 June, 1706, the magistrates of Oudenarde sought Marlborough's protection and recognized Charles III ('K C ye III') as king of Spain. Marlborough commented, 'There is so great a panic in the French army as is not to be expressed. Every place we take declares for King Charles .... I am so persuaded that this

The Battlel of Ramillias where ye D. of Marlbo-
rough &c. took 26. Standards & 63. Ensigns the
French lossing 20000 men all their Baggage
Amunition &c.

The Medal Struck at Utrecht
upon ye Victorie obtain'd at
Ramelies.

The Reverse of ye Medal Struck at
Utrecht upon ye Victory obtain'd
at Ramelies.

The 26. Standards & 63 Ens[illegible] taken
at Ramellies brought from St. James's thro' the
City of London & put up in Guild Hall

The Magistrates of Oudenard wait
upon the D. of Marlboro desire his
protection & swear fidelity to K.C. ye 3d
June the 3. 1706.

Ostend Taken by Monseu.
Overkerk. ye 6th of July. 1706.

Menin taken by ye D. of Marlborough
August. 25 · 1706.

Sept. ye 5. 1706. Dendermond Sur=
renders to General Churchill his
Grace ye Prince & D. of Marlboro's
Brother.

Sept 7. 1706. ye D. of Savoy & P. Eugene
raise ye seige of Turin rout ye French
kill & take 15000 men 40 Standards
1000 horse & all their Cannon. et c.

campaign will bring us a good peace'.

Five of clubs — Three days later, on June 3, the governor of Antwerp decided to come out in support of Charles III and open his city's gates to Marlborough, thus saving a prolonged siege. It is written that 'My Lord Duke was received at Antwerp with one piece of ceremony which was odd enough, the magistracy of the town marching before him with lighted flambeaux though in the middle of the day, which is looked on as the greatest mark of honour they can show'.

Three of clubs — A few weeks later, on June 21, the French were forced to abandon Ghent at Marlborough's approach. Villeroy had hoped to stay there behind the rivers Lys and Scheldt to cover Bruges, Ostend and Antwerp, but Marlborough's move towards Courtrai to cut off his lines of communication, forced him to abandon the city.

Nine of diamonds — From 19 June to 6 July, 1706, the Dutch field marshall Overkerk's 20,000 besieged the Comte de la Motte's 5,000 in Ostend. The fortress was surrounded by water, marshes and inundations. Nevertheless it surrendered after suffering a naval bombardment and artillery fire from the sand-dunes, with a loss of only 1,600 Allies. A century earlier it had taken three years and a loss of 80,000 to make it surrender. Its capture opened up a direct line of communication between England and the Allied front-line.

Nine of hearts — Marlborough was personally in charge of the siege of Menin from 22 July to 22 August, 1706 (the card wrongly says, 25 August). He surrounded the small town with its superb Vauban fortifications with 30,000 men, while inside 5,500 held out. The French were unable to relieve it as Marlborough constructed lines of circumvallation. The final assault began with the firing of two mines at 7 am, followed by two hours' stiff fighting. The Allies lost 2,620, with the Royal Irish suffering in particular. The garrison was allowed to evacuate to Douai.

Two of clubs — Between 27 August and 9 September, 1706, (not September 5, as on the card), Denermond alone held out in the middle of the nearly conquered Belgian territory, barring the navigation of the rivers Dender and Upper Scheldt to the Allies. Its immense natural strength was due to the water around it. The Allies' 6,000 finally overcame the garrison of 2,000. Marlborough refused to hand the town over to the Dutch afterwards.

Nine of clubs — Meanwhile the Piedmontese army in Turin held on grimly under severe bombardments and assaults throughout July and August, 1706. If the French captured the city, Victor Amadeus of Savoy would lose his throne and the war in Italy would be over. In this allied dark hour, Eugene began his march from Garda, up the Po valley to save Turin. Meeting up with Victor's army in the nick of time, the relief force of 35,000 took on the 60,000 French besiegers. Spotting a gap in the French line between the rivers Dora and Stura, Eugene sent his Prussian bluecoats into the attack, forcing

II ♦
Aeth Taken by ye Lord
Overkerk. Octo. 4. 1706.

III ♦
The Sea fight in ye Mediterranean wherein
Sr Cloudsley Shovel so Bravely
Signaliz'd Himself

IX ♠
What good can you Expect for all your pains
When We are drove in Wooden Shooes & chains
Oh Maintenon Oh Lewis where's your Brains

QUEEN ♠
At first dis honest when I Turkeys fed
Little I thought t'enjoy a Monarh's bed
but now ye dotard's Glutted in a baudy Reign
I may to Turkey keeping go again.

IV ♠
Give Him Blood to Drink

I ♠
The fat Cat denotes ye Partisans Fattend with ye
Substance of ye Nation ye lean Cat ye People of France
Exhausted by heavy Impositions, & ye Blind
Cat ye Ks Councel, who are at their wits end.

I ♥
In ye bright Chariot of the quickning SUN
Does over noisome Clouds and Vapours run
So mighty ANNE on Victory does ride
And tramples down ye Popes & Tyrants Bride

I ♦
Happy ye City ye Victorious made
Like to Augusta both for wealth & trade
The Thames shall glide to France & bring to thee
As Marlbro' does ye fruits of Victory

KNAVE ♦
Every One what he Loves

	the French to abandon the siege and flee across the Alps. The balance of power had been restored in Europe.
Two of diamonds	Hendrik Overkerk (1640-1708) continued the campaign in the north by taking Ath on 4 October, 1706. The town stood on the River Demer, guarding an important bridge. The Allies lost 800 of their 21,000 while the garrison lost only 60 before surrendering.
Eight of diamonds	The year was concluded so far as this set of cards is concerned with the presentation of the keys of Brussels in a 'Gold Basin' to Marlborough on October 27.
Three of diamonds	On 21 August, 1707, Sir Cloudesley Shovell, (1650-1707) attacked the French fleet in its Toulon dockyard basin and did considerable damage. His aim was to land one hundred guns for the siege which the Duke of Savoy was in charge of. This card concludes the list of military events referred to in this pack as the pack was on sale a few months later.
	A number of cards, mainly in the spades suit, are satirical ones directed against Louis XIV and the France of his day.
Ten of spades	The massacre of the Cevennois is the subject of the ten of spades. The Cevennois were 4,000 Huguenots living in the mountainous Garonne. They were also known as Camisards from the white shirts which they wore. They began a revolt against Louis in 1702. Sir Cloudesley Shovell was sent to the Mediteranean with two ships laden with arms, money and agents to make contact with them. As the revolt continued Louis sent the Duc de Villars to quell them in 1704 but as he offered them toleration terms, it was left to the Duc de Berwick to burn them alive and break them on the wheel in 1705. An English attempt to help them in 1706, led by Earl Rivers and 8,000 troops, was a rash project which had to be abandoned.
Seven of spades	Louis' ruthlessness is depicted in a number of cards. The seven of spades depicts him squeezing his officers for ill-gotten gains, while
Six & nine of spades	the six of spades points to the misery he imposed on the people of France. The nine of spades shows the people of France bemoaning their fate under him. Notice the reference here to Madame de Maintenon, who is depicted on the queen of spades too.
Queen of spades	Madame de Maintenon, unofficial wife of Louis XIV, was the only woman who influenced him in the running of the government. She was one of a team of advisers he sought guidance from. She became convinced that the frosts that occurred during the wartime winters were an indication of God's approval of the war. On the card she refers to her humble background; she had once been governess to the royal children and received an estate at Maintenon in reward.
Eight of spades	The eight of spades draws further attention to the plight of French people with their 'paper-pa⁻ to keep their servile pockets thin', as the king says 'I'll have it all'.
Four of spades	Louis is depicted in bed on the four of spades, with the suggestion that the medicine he deserves is blood.

Under these circumstances it is not surprising to find that the ace of spades show Louis having a nightmare.

Ace of spades

The five of spades depicts the wished-for fate of Louis and the pope, both 'drunk with' blood at the hands of the devil before a gloating audience. The devil refers to an anal fistula which Louis developed in 1686 and which confined him to bed. The king's surgeon, Felix, taught himself how to operate for this complaint by reading the Greek physician Galen's report on the operation. He had the necessary instruments made and tried the operation out on as many people as he could find in Paris hospitals before he operated on the king. At 8 am on 18 November, 1686, he began the hour-long operation and received 150,000 livres for the successful result.

Five of spades

Anne's triumph over her enemies, Louis and the pope, is proclaimed by the ace of hearts. The fruits of victory are to be seen poured on London by an angel on the ace of diamonds. Wren's St. Paul's can be seen on the left and Southwark church in the right foreground. The famous London Bridge spans the Thames with the four-storey prefabricated Nonsuch House which had been made in Holland and pegged together on the spot.

Ace of hearts

Ace of diamonds

The pack is completed with the knave of diamonds in which England (E) in the cause of liberty is shown running through ambitious France (F), while the Dutch (D) benefit from the war.

Knave of diamonds

Chapter Twelve

Dr. Sacheverell 1709-1711

This pack is the work of Gabriel Pink, card maker. The engravings are on copper plate and it seems likely that the pack was never put on sale. Today the hearts and diamond suits are to be found occasionally on two sheets, while the spades and clubs suits are in a rare book called, *Playing Cards of Various Ages and Countries*, vol. 1, by C. Schreiber and A.W. Franks.

Most of the cards concern the celebrated case of Dr. Sacheverell (1674-1724), but some cards deal with court intrigues and political events covering the period 1709-1711.

Henry Sacheverell matriculated at Magdalen College, Oxford, in 1689, became a fellow in 1701, and was awarded his D.D. in 1708 when he became his college's senior dean of arts. From 1705 to 1709 he was chaplain at St. Saviour's, Southwark. He was a tall, brawny, well dressed man, but an indifferent scholar. He was bold, insolent, passionate and very vain.

To fully understand the importance of Dr. Sacheverell an appreciation of the position of the Church of England must first be grasped. The national church and the state had formed an alliance, challenged at times, for upholding law, order and morals. Church courts dealt with matrimonial, probate, adultery, and bastardy matters, for example. This alliance had been undermined by the 1689 Revolution settlement. In that year two bills were introduced to settle the problem of the large number of non-conformists in the country. The Comprehension Bill offered generous terms to dissenters to attract them back into the Church of England. For example, they would not have to kneel when receiving communion and clergy would not have to wear surplices. The Toleration Bill offered the licensing of meeting houses for the expected few dissenters who would refuse the other bill's terms.

In the outcome only the second bill became law, so that it came to embrace all half million dissenters. 2,536 meeting houses were licensed in direct competition with the parish churches, and the control of church courts over the lives of the population as a whole was lost. During the subsequent century meeting houses developed more rapidly than churches in the new towns as new churches needed individual acts of parliament.

Under these circumstances the Church of England had either to fight a political battle to regain its position as an all-dominating national church, or enter into religious competition with its rivals and prove its value. Archbishop Tenison had the vision to see that the latter course could lead to a real spiritual revival. His answer lay in the establishment of societies, such as S.P.C.K. (1698), S.P.G. (1701) and the Society for the Reform of Manners to replace the church courts' control of morals.

Other Church of England members fought to re-establish the Church-State authoritatian regime. The Earl of Rochester and Atterbury, future bishop of Rochester, were behind the launching of the new High Church party in 1697. The accession of Queen Anne in 1702 raised their hopes, but she soon disappointed them as she disliked clerical arguments. This led to the High Church party becoming an opposition group, arguing that the Church, and therefore the crown and state, were in danger now that dissenters were allowed official positions in the government.

Between 1708 and 1709 thousands of Calvinist refugees were allowed into the country from Germany, and the Whigs wanted to grant them full naturalization. This meant permitting the receiving of communion at any protestant church to be acceptable under the Test Acts as a qualification to become an MP, and hold official posts. There were rumours of a radical reform of religious tests at the universities too.

In this delicate situation Sacheverell's sermons of 15 August and 5 November, 1709, and his subsequent prosecution by the Whig government before a political court (an impeachment) were political dynamite.

On 15 August, 1709, Sacheverell preached the assize sermon at Derby on 1 *Timothy* 5 v 22. He bluntly called for obedience to authority and warned of the danger of being involved in others' sins. For him all dissenters were sinners and he was not prepared to compromise with them. George Sacheverell, sheriff of Derbyshire, encouraged him to have it printed, and this was done under the title, *The Communication of Sin.*

His second sermon was in similar violent language. The new Tory Lord Mayor, Sir Samuel Garrard, invited him to preach in St. Paul's Cathedral on that essentially Whig celebration day, November 5th. It was a date famous for religio-political events, such as the discovery of the Gunpowder Plot in 1605, the landing of William III in 1688 and the preaching of Bishops Lloyd's sermon

Ace of hearts

Four & two of hearts

Seven of clubs

From hence the Church's Restoration rose, And made Discovery of her Secret Foes.	*Into the Church the Sheriff introduces, The D—r who laments its Foes Abuses.*	*The Derby Sheriff doth of him request, That his Assize Discourse may be imprest.*
A Speech that Shews such Injurys & Wrongs, Calls for Redress, with more then Hawkers Tongues	*Here an Archbishop's son ye Church impeaches, Whose Sire if living would abhor such Speeches.*	*The D—r at the House of P—rs attends, To answer Articles which Com—s sends.*
His Body with Imprisonment is Charg'd, But Souls like his in Prison are enlarg'd.	*He that commands a Sermon to the Press, Ought to stand by the Preacher in Distress.*	*The D—r and his Friends in Consultation, How to reply to Commons Accusation.*

on the Divine Providence Theory in 1689. Sacheverell's text was 2 *Corinthians* II v 26, and its subject was 'on perils of false brethren in church and state'. He drew a parallel between the sad state of the church in Corinth in St. Paul's days to that of the Church of England in 1709. He concentrated on 'false bethren' and proceeded to identify them and show how they threatened the national church. The church had been 'Rent and Divided by Factions and Schismatical Imposters, Her Pure Doctrine Corrupted and Defil'd ... not only by our profess'd Enemies, but which is worse, by Our Pretended Friends and FALSE BRETHREN'. He attacked Church members who favoured a comprehension policy in league with certain dissenter sects. 'This Modern Latitude' was the danger, he said. 'The grand Security of our Government, and the very Pillar upon which it stands is founded upon the Steady Belief of the Subjects' Obligations to an Absolute, and Unconditional Obedience to the Supreme Power'. He went on to criticise the Whig government as avaricious.

His sermon amounted to a re-assertion of the doctrine of non-resistance and passive obedience to a divine right king, the doctrine which had been fundamentally challenged and virtually overthrown by the Glorious Revolution. He seemed to be threatening the Revolution Settlement and the Act of Settlement, a serious matter for it might affect the succession. When H. Clements printed 40,000 copies of it, the Whig government decided to impeach Sacheverell in order to silence him and argue out the lawfulness of the existing constitution and the rights of the protestant succession before the highest court in the land, the House of Lords. An impeachment trial meant that the House of Commons prosecuted the prisoner before the Lords. If the Whigs were lucky they might succeed in pinning a charge of Jacobitism on the Tories.

The dedication of the printed sermon referred to the words, 'By your Lordship's command ...' implying that the Lord Mayor had commanded Sacheverell to have it printed. Although the seven of diamonds indicates the Mayor was happy with the dedication, when he saw these words he was not pleased, claiming that he had not ordered its printing, only saying that he would be pleased if it was published. Sacheverell did not retract on this point and later the same day ordered the second edition to be printed with 'command' still in it. By the end of the trial 100,000 copies in 11 editions in English, French, German and Dutch were on sale for prices ranging from 1d to 1 shilling.

The first move came on December 13, when John Dolben (1662-1710) the younger son of the Archbishop of Canterbury, denounced both sermons as 'malicious, scandalous, and seditious libels, highly reflecting upon Her Majesty and her government, the late happy revolution, and the protestant succession'. With the

Seven of diamonds

Knave of hearts

Eight of spades

acceptance of his resolution for an impeachment by the Commons, proceedings began. The articles, or charges, were agreed to on January 9 in the Commons by 232 to 131 votes, and then presented to the Lords.

Eight of clubs

Knave of spades

Now Sacheverell needed support, but when he had been questioned by the Commons on December 14 about the words 'By your Lordship's command' he found that the Lord Mayor did not support him. The Mayor, fearing he himself would be sent to the Tower, in a strained voice denied that he had commanded the sermon's printing or even desired it. The Commons accepted his denial. From that day until January 12, Sacheverell was held in custody. Then he was granted bail of £6,000 and two sureties, Dr. Lancaster, Vice-Chancellor of Oxford, and Dr. Bowes of All Souls, of £3,000 each.

Three of hearts

Sacheverell had a group of lawyers together with Bishop Atterbury to help him prepare his defence. Sir Constantine Phipps (1656-1723) led the team. Sir Simon Harcourt (1661-1727) was able to defend him until elected to the Commons, and the grateful Sacheverell gave him a silver salver (See also the ace of spades). Duncan Dee (1657-1720) was to speak for four days in his defence too. Dr. Humphry Henchman (1669-1739) was an acute, able and judicious speaker, and Mr. Dodd completed the team. The prosecution was led by the attorney-general, Sir James Montague.

Three & six of clubs

Although some hoped that a scaffold would be needed, the only scaffolding needed was for 400 spectators' seats, which were organized by Sir Christopher Wren in Westminster Hall. The Hall was still decorated with the standards captured at Blenheim.

Three of diamonds

The trial opened at 11 am on 27 February, 1710. Sarah, Duchess of Marlborough, felt that etiquette required that the queen's ladies should stand beside the queen, but after standing for three hours, she asked, and obtained, permission to be seated! At that point her rival, the Duchess of Somerset, arrived and insisted on remaining standing, so suggesting that Sarah was disrespectful. (See also the six of hearts, three of spades). Sarah said Sacheverell was 'an ignorant impudent Incendiary .... a lewd, drunken, pampered man'. However, when he spoke, most ladies present cried.

Nine of hearts

Four of spades

The prosecution took until March 2 to complete its case and as we shall see below, on the night of March 1 the London mob demonstrated its support for the accused. For clarity's sake the prosecution and defence points are taken together here. The prosecution maintained that whoever suggested that the Church was in danger under Anne's administration was an enemy of the Queen, Church and Kingdom, and that Sacheverell's sermons were aimed to 'undermine and subvert Her Majesty's Government, and the Protestant Succession as by Law established.

It was argued that Sacheverell's continued support of the doctrine of non-resistance was virtually sedition, as it logically

Sculpture by this the Workmens Toil displays, That for the Tryall did the Scaffold raise.	Materials for a Scaffold may be brought, Yet He that is Impeach'd be void of Fault;	Without Concern he from his Coach alights To Stand a Tryal which its Hearers frights.
H-d-ly may Sap, and his Associates pull; But Angells interfere and over rule;	The Clock and Pulpit in the Flames expire, That help'd Noncon to set the World on Fire.	When Crouds of Rebels dare assault ye Crown, Tis just that Loyal Guards should cleave em down.
The Waterman and Bailiff on their Knees, Implore their Mercy that upon them Seize.	Law may affix a Padlock on his Tongue, But Innocence will have a Voice thats strong.	Sentence upon Offenders may be pass't, Yet Monarchs Pardon those whom Juryes cast.

amounted to a support of the Jacobites. This charge depended on the identification of the Supreme Power which Sacheverell said was to be passively obeyed. The prosecution argued that it meant the ruler, while Sacheverell said he meant God, and his defence said he meant the legislature.

The prosecution's second point was that he had said that the Toleration Act was unreasonable. To this he replied that he had said that the Act did not give toleration, but merely exempted dissenters from 'penalties of certain laws' as the Act's title said. The prosecution claimed that the legal supremacy in church matters was an essential part of the English political system. To this Dr. Henchman replied that Sacheverell had served the country well by denouncing atheists, deists, &c., who were threatening the spirit of the Toleration Act.

The third article charged him with asserting the Church was 'in a Condition of great Peril and adversity under Her Majesty's Administration'. He replied that it was in danger from vice, infidelity, and atheistical and irreligious principles proclaimed in the press. The prosecution said the Church was in no danger under a pious, generous queen. Phipps replied that Sacheverell had not blamed Anne, but simply said these evils existed, as many others had recently said too.

The fourth article claimed that he suggested that the government was destroying the constitution aided by the maladministration of 'Men of Character and Station in Church and State'. To this he replied that they had misinterpreted his issue of 'False Brethren', and had taken two separate sections of his sermon and fitted them together to misrepresent him.

King &
nine of clubs

During the trial the London mob, some 3,000 strong, demonstrated its support of the accused. On the night of March 1 they attacked the large wealthy Presbyterian chapel of the Revd. Daniel Burgess in New Court between 7 pm and 10.30 pm. Burgess was known for his spirited, amusing sermons. He had once said the Jews were called Israel-ites because God did not want them called Jacob-ites! The mob took the pulpit, pews, cushions and famous japanned clock ('The faithful clock which oft before, Had pointed to the pudding hour') to Lincoln's Inn Fields where they burnt the lot. Half a dozen meeting houses were treated in a similar way.

Queen of
clubs

Threats were made against the mansions of the Whig leaders and the Whig Bank of England. At 9 pm the Earl of Sunderland requested help and Anne sent the Horse Guards, Grenadiers and the Coldstreams to quel the riots. These regiments were the only ones available and their use left the Queen personally defenceless, a fact which worried Capt. Horsey who was in charge of them. However the Horse Guards were successful when they went into action at 11 pm. One rioter's hand was cut off, but none were killed. All was quiet by 3 am. When the Guards returned to their palace duties, the City Militia took over. £100 was offered for the arrest of any of the rioters. The troops had been guided to where the rioters were at work by a certain Capt. Orrell and he may be the man marching in front of the troops on the ten of spades.

Ten of spades

One of the rioters was Daniel Dammaree, a Queen's Waterman, who had got drunk earlier in the evening at the Bell, Water St. Orrell said he saw Dammaree leading the mob and shouting 'I'll lead you on boys; huzza! high church and Sacheverell! God damn them (Meeting houses) all, we will have them all down'. Another rioter was a bailiff, George Purchase, whom Orrell heard shouting, 'I will be for High Church and Sacheverell; I will lose my life in the cause'. An ex-trooper, Purchase, realised that the only way to deal with the Horse Guards was to come up behind them and unseat them. He almost drove his sword through Capt. Hensbrough in trying to do so. Both men were found guilty of treason in waging war against the Queen, condemned, reprieved and pardoned.

Two of clubs

March 1 had also been marked by the publication of a broadsheet about the imaginery prize fight between Sacheverell and Bishop Hoadly (1676-1761). Hoadly was the leader of the Low Church group and had written *A Defence of the Reasonableness of Conformity to the Church of England* (1707). The knave of clubs shows an angel firing at men fighting in a street.

Knave of clubs

On March 20 the final vote was taken in the Sacheverell case and he was found guilty by 69 to 52 (7 bishops said he was guilty, and 6 not guilty). A narrow margin, which some politicians doubtless took as the betting odds on the succession of George or the Old Pretender when Anne died.

Four possible punishments were considered by the Lords. (a) No preaching for seven years; (b) no new benefice for seven years; (c) three months in the Tower and to find sureties for seven years; (d) his sermons to be burnt. On March 23 they announced that he should be banned from preaching for three years and have his sermons burnt. The Tories celebrated this mild punishment as a moral victory, and the Jacobite revival dates from this trial, which also spelt the doom of the Whig government. The trial had cost £60,000 and made Sacheverell a rich man due to the gifts poured on him.

Six & nine of spades

Seven of spades

Ten of clubs

Before turning to the aftermath, a glance at one card concerning the trial is necessary. The five of spades depicts Sir Peter King (1669-1734), recorder of London, who helping to manage the prosecution case with his superb speech on Article II.

Five of spades

'The next that appear'd was the learned Sir Peter,
In antiquity skilful and great,
Who pour'd such charges that wounded much deeper,
But yet he was woundily beat'.

The verdict was celebrated in England and Scotland as the four of diamonds indicates. It depicts the 'Thanksgiving Supper' held at

Four of diamonds

The D—r is preserv'd from being Roasted, For which his Health, a round of Flames is toasted.	Others would Swell with Pride, if thus cares'd, But he bears humble Thoughts within his Breast	His Entry into Oxford here is Shewn: Attended by the Country and the Town.
The College with alacrity receiv'd Her Son return'd, for whom accus'd She grew'd.	At Banbury the Courteous Corporation, Salutes him who returns the Salutation.	St. Asaph's Bishop, for his Flock's Instruction, Allows Him Institution and Induction.
Here Welsh Parishioners attend his Coach, And joy to See their Ministers Approach.	The Mytre in one hand and league in t'other, Shew that the Tubster is a fickle Brother.	Well is the Purse by Majesty bestow'd, On Him that pay'd the Duty which He ow'd.

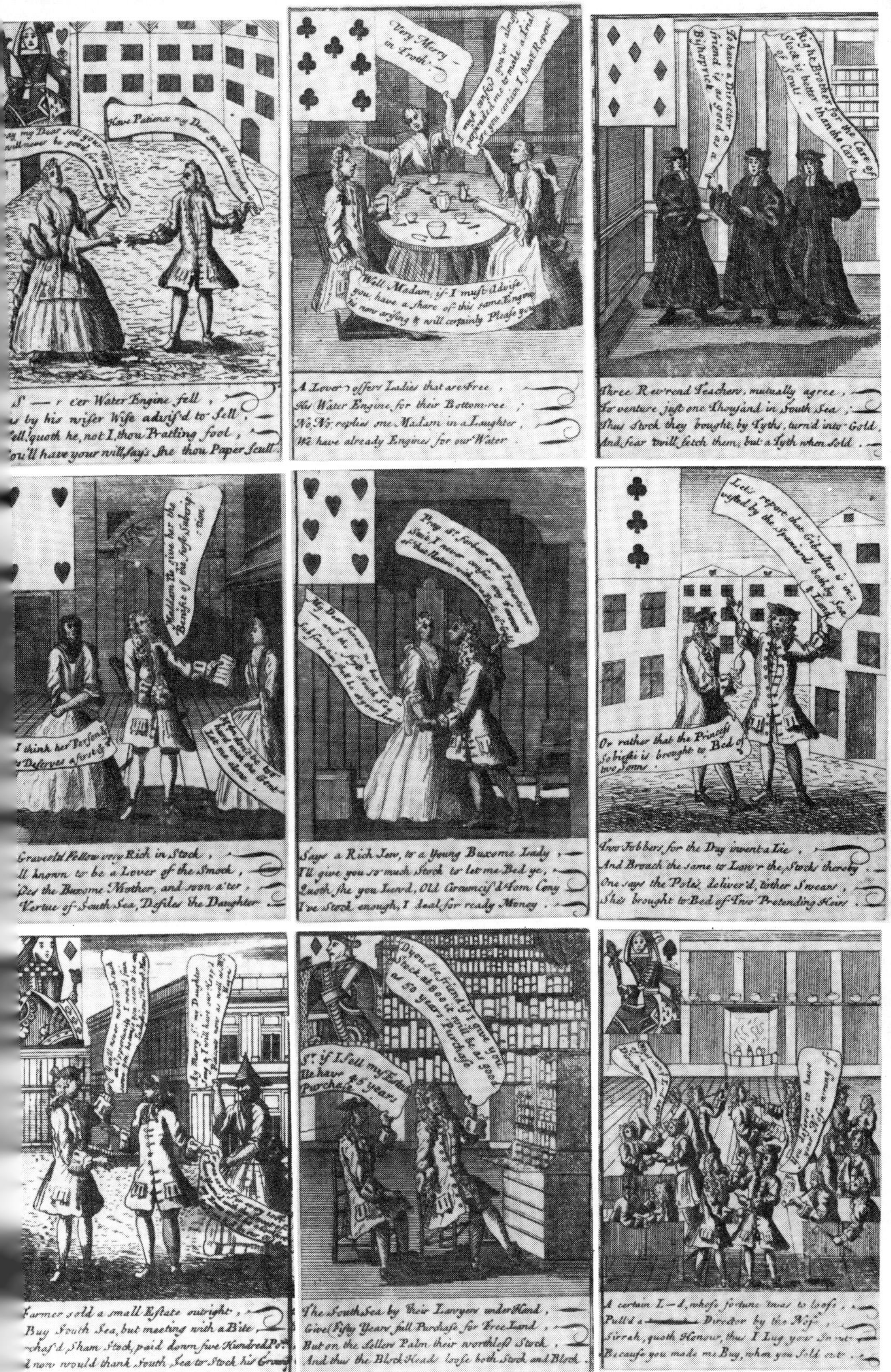
Very Merry in Troth.
Well Madam, if I must Advise, you have a share of this same Engine, now arising & will certainly Please you
A Lover offers Ladies that are Free ,
His Water Engine, for their Bottom-ree ;
No, No, replies one Madam in a Laughter ,
We have already Engines for our Water .
Three Rev'rend Teachers, mutually agree ,
To venture just one Thousand in South Sea ;
Thus Stock they bought, by Tyths, turn'd into Gold ,
And fear 'twill fetch them, but a Tyth when Sold .
Says a Rich Jew, to a Young Buxome Lady ,
I'll give you so much Stock to let me Bed ye ,
Quoth she you Lewd, Old Circumcis'd Tom Cony
I've Stock enough, I deal for ready Money .
Or rather that the Princess Sobieski is brought to Bed of two Sons
Two Jobbers, for the Day invent a Lie ,
And Broach the same to Low'r the Stocks thereby .
One says the Pole's deliver'd, t'other Swears ,
She's brought to Bed of Two Pretending Heirs .
Sr if I sell my Estate We have Purchase 45 years
The South Sea by their Lawyers under Hand ,
Give Fifty Years full Purchase for Free Land ,
But on the Sellers Palm their worthless Stock ,
And thus the Block Head loose both Stock and Block .
A certain L—d, whose fortune was to loose ,
Pull'd a Director by the Nose ,
Sirrah, quoth Honour, thus I Lug your Snout ,
Because you made me Buy, when you Sold out .

rent and the title; for the rest they talk all by the lump, and give forty to fifty years' purchase.

In August the company directors challenged the legality of many of the 'bubble' companies which had sprung up in the wake of their own share boom. The story of what happened to these companies is told in the next chapter. The point is that when the South Sea Company undermined the integrity of its rivals it found its own integrity doubted.

On September 19th, its share quotation was down to £450, and ten days later a mere £135. Ruin came to thousands. Two hundred new coaches, four thousand embroidered gentlemen's coats and three thousand ladies' gold watches were all going secondhand as their proud possessors discovered their new found wealth was elusive. Suicides followed and the government crashed. Aislabie, the Chanceller of Exchequer, was expelled from the Commons for making £750,000. Sir Robert Walpole, returning from his Norfolk estates, acquired the nickname of 'the Screen' for the way in which he shielded MPs who were prepared to support him in the future as prime minister.

The set of cards can be grouped together by subjects, starting with those referring to the buying of shares. Anyone seeking advice was directed to buy South Sea shares according to the five of hearts. Women who followed the advice went so far as to rent a shop a few doors away from South Sea director John Blunt's office in Birchin Lane. They turned it into a club where they drank tea and kept an eye on the share prices. When they had time to spare they gambled for china. Women were able to deal on the Stock Exchange as no-one had thought of banning them from doing so. The ladies of the Prince of Wales' court, the daughters of Earl Ferrers, the Duchess of Rutland, the Countess of Gainsborough, and the Duchess of Marlborough all dealt in shares. But their emancipation did not survive the Bubble.

The two of clubs is an example of a man making £100 by a quick resale. Buyers had to be on the look out for unscrupulous jobbers, men who bought and sold the shares. But those who were slow to buy shares were liable to find the price had gone up sharply. Methods adopted to obtain South Sea shares were varied as the queen of clubs shows. Those who found their normal line of business was failing turned hurriedly to South Sea stock.

Even Welshmen thought it worthwhile to take their money from the Welsh Copper Company (see Chapter 14, nine of spades) and put it in South Sea stock. Investing one's servants' wages was a temptation for some.

Ambitious wives pressed their husbands to invest and make fortunes. An increase in riches naturally led to social advancement and the need for a man to acquire a coat of arms as the three of hearts shows when a nonentity calls at the College of Arms.

Five of hearts

King of hearts

Two of clubs

Eight of clubs

Ten of clubs
Queen of clubs
King of clubs
Ace of diamonds
Two of diamonds
Ace of hearts
Three of hearts
Ten of hearts

A Set of Bubble managers attend
A Lawyer, Fee him well to stand their Friend ;
The Act says he you fear, is coming on ye ,
Will hurt no Fools, but those that have no Money .

A Crafty Jew pretending to retale
Stock at low Price, when he had none to sell ;
The Angry Brokers Merrily Chastiz'd him ,
And in a Horse pond twice or thrice Baptiz'd him .

A Lady Pawns her Jewels by her Maid ,
And in declining Stock, presumes to Trade ,
Till in South Sea at length, she Drowns her Coin ,
And now in Bristol Stones , is glad to shine .

Ladies, whose Husbands are undone by Bubbles ,
Meet at a Tavern to Lament their Troubles ;
At length, they all agree upon Petition ,
To Pray the State to Mend their Bad Condition .

Three Merry Doctors, meet in Consultation ,
To Cure the South Sea Plague, that spoils the Nation ;
But all agreed, the Fools should still endure it
Till Smarting Poverty alone should Cure it .

A Famous Builder of Meridian Coaches ,
To make each South Sea Drab, appear a Dutchess ,
Had Fourty Coaches at one time bespoke ,
But Falling Stock did Thirty Five revoke .

Some Officers of Land grown Rich and Great ,
By Pay and Plunder in the Wars of late ;
Decoy'd by some, behind the South Sea Curtain
Are nothing for New Wars to mend their Fortune

A Jobber for Stock diffrence in a Bubble ,
Is by another Bite haul'd into Trouble ;
The Serjeant grumbles, till he gets Extortion ,
Or else a Jayl must be the Prisoners Portion .

A certain Non Con Teacher growing Poor ,
Forsook his Pulpit, and turn'd Bookseller ;
Failing in that, he Jobb'd a while in Stock ,
But now again Instructs a tatter'd Flock .

Knave of clubs

Knave of diamonds

Queen of hearts

Seven of clubs

Seven of diamonds

Four of hearts

Seven of hearts

Three of clubs

Two of spades

Queen of diamonds

King of diamonds

Eight and queen of spades

Two of hearts

Six and eight of hearts

Nine of spades

Nine of hearts

Women whose fortunes had increased sought peers for lovers in future, spurning their old loves. Irish husbands were sought after by some women. Those who were fortunate secured husbands, coaches and country houses. The merits of Highgate, Hampstead and Richmond were hotly debated.

Water Engine Company shares were not held in high esteem by women it seems. This company was the idea of William Paterson, the intellectual parent of the Bank of England and inspirer of the Darien colony. In 1691 he planned to supply London with water from the heights of Hampstead where the ponds he built as reservoirs still exist.

The clergy were tempted to invest in South Sea stock too, valuing it as high as promotion within the church, and certainly beyond that of the care of souls.

Soon the shares were used as a tempting bribe to secure a bride, or, less honourably to seduce a woman.

Cunning businessmen, finding South Sea prices too high, turned to deception to secure lower prices. To suggest Gibraltar was attacked by Spaniards would shake the stock market, and so too would the suggestion that the Old Pretender's wife, Princess Clementine Sobieski, had two heirs to claim the throne for the Jacobites. Her first son, Bonnie Prince Charlie, was born on 31 December, 1720, and she did have another son, Henry, in 1725, long after this pack of cards was printed. Others suggested that to announce the assassination of King George in Germany would suit their purposes. The two of spades shows the devil muttering that they do not need George.

Naturally there were those who suffered from the cunning of others, such as the farmer referred to on the queen of diamonds One could not trust one's lawyer to judge from the king of diamonds.

Signs of trouble to come are hinted at on the eight of spades, where a lady is warned by her broker, and violence against a director is to be found on the queen of spades.

The act to end the 'bubble' companies, which is fully dealt with in Chapter 14, is referred to as a threat to the South Sea Company, which was behind the act's passing. The challenge to the integrity of one company can rebound on another as the South Sea Company found out.

The remainder of the pack deals with the effects of the disaster. Dutch sailors were affected claimed the six of hearts. Soon one Jewish dealer found he could not hope for the profit he had expected, while another Jew was 'baptised' for his dealings by an angry crowd.

Ruin could mean the sale of one's home and the necessity of seeking lodgings on the less important side of the Thames as the distressed family on the nine of hearts found out.

A Wealthy Cobler which is rarely found,
Had ventur'd in South Sea, Five Hundred Pound,
By Aul, and End, thus prosper'd till the fall
Of Cursed, South Sea, made an End of all.

A Sea-Comander having lost his all,
In Stocks and Bubbles unexpected fall,
Damn'd the South Sea, and swore 't had ruin'd more
Than all the other Seas had done before.

A certain Gold-Smith, when the Stocks run high,
Set up his Coach his Pride to gratify;
But South Sea falling, left his Coach at 'Change,
And Shipping took, the distant World to Range.

A Thriving Gamester quits his Box and Dice,
And with his ready Money South Sea Buys;
But loosing all, he Storms and Curses fortune,
And Damns the Rogues that lurks behind the Curtain

A Ruin'd South-Sea Jobber of Renown,
Leaps from a lofty Window, Head long down,
When taken up, he crys Adzounds I'm broke,
Who gives Eight Hundred Pounds for South Sea Stock

A Busy Fool, grown Rich by Empty Bubbles,
Pursues his folly till involv'd in Troubles;
Then, vexing at his Losses, grows Audacious,
Curses the Law, and damns each Scire Facias.

A Broker went to let a Lady know,
hat South Sea Stock was falling very low;
ays she, then what I gain in my good Calling
y rising things, I find I loose by falling

I John who thought my self of late possess'd,
Of Three times Fifty Thousand Pounds, at least,
Can pay no Parish Debts, but Sigh and Moan,
For want of Money to discharge my own.

A Lady, prompted by an Am'rous Youth,
Ventur'd her Dow'r and lost it in the South;
My Dear quoth he, 'tis time I should forsake you,
Since South Sea has your Gold, may South Sea take yo

Knave of hearts	The woman, who had rejected her old lover on the ten of hearts, found herself spurned on the knave of hearts when she tried to return to him when the crash came. Ladies' jewels soon had to be pawned and stones of lesser value worn. Rich clothes had to go too when the Bubble burst. Some desperate women decided their only hope lay in applying for some form of state aid.

Knave of hearts

Three and six of diamonds

Ace of clubs

Four of clubs

Five of clubs

Six of clubs

Nine of clubs

Four of clubs

Five of diamonds

Eight and nine of diamonds

Five and seven of spades

Ten of diamonds

Ace and six of spades

Three and knave of spades

Four of spades

Eight and ten of spades

King of spades

The woman, who had rejected her old lover on the ten of hearts, found herself spurned on the knave of hearts when she tried to return to him when the crash came. Ladies' jewels soon had to be pawned and stones of lesser value worn. Rich clothes had to go too when the Bubble burst. Some desperate women decided their only hope lay in applying for some form of state aid.

The jobbers found they were no better off than the amateur sharedealers when the share price slumped.

Medical advice for coping with the 'South Sea Plague' varied from saying that it was incurable to saying it could be cured with poverty or by a period in Bedlam, the prison for the insane.

Ruination faced the coachmaking trade. Possession of a coach was akin to the possession of a Rolls-Royce today, and many who had ordered coaches when their shares rose in value now cancelled their orders. Paying one's creditors with stock was the suggestion made to one shopkeeper.

Wartime profiteers thought only another war could save them from the ruin they now faced. Jobbers found it necessary to make themselves scarce when pursued by the sheriff's officers, the sergeants.

Those who had switched their careers to jobbing in shares now found they were back at their old work again. The nonconformist teacher and the sea captain among them.

Rèvenge on those who had brought ruin upon sufferers naturally followed the crash. A broker threatened to cut the throat of a Frenchman, who replied that he will do it himself, according to the seven of spades. The wife referred to on the ten of diamonds says her coach has turned into a wheelbarrow!

Another coachowner, the ace of spade's goldsmith, sought refuge in flight when trouble came his way. Emigration was an obvious way out for many. Suicide by hanging was in the mind of the three of spade's gamester, although such suicide attempts did not always come off it seems to judge from the knave of spades.

It was not always the South Sea shares which were to blame. York Building shares crashed when the company was served with a scire facias writ challenging the legality of its activities. The full story of this company is told in Chapter 14 on the five of spades in that pack.

The natural reaction to news of the Bubble's bursting was that all was lost. Confusion followed, and the victim of the ten of spades lay in bed and bemoaned his ruin.

Loss of one's love followed from the loss of wealth too, it seems, if the king of spades is to be believed.

Two verses form a suitable ending to this tale of ruin. The first is the opening verse of *A South Sea Ballad; or, Merry Remarks upon Exchange Alley Bubbles*, published in September, 1720.

In London stands a famous pile,

>   And near that pile an alley
>   Where merry crowds for riches toil,
>   And Wisdom stoops to Folly.
>   Here sad and joyful, high and low,
>   Court Fortune for her graces;
>   And she smiles or frowns, they show
>   Their gestures and grimaces

The second is from Swift's *The South Sea Project*

>   Directors, thrown into the sea,
>   Recover strength and vigour there;
>   But may be tamed another way
>   Suspended for a while in air.

Chapter Fourteen

All the Bubbles
The Bubble Companies   1720

Ace of diamonds
Knave of spades

The *Post Boy* of 20 October, 1720, contained this advertisement: This Day is Publish'd A New Pack of Playing Cards containing fifty two Copper-Cuts wherein are represented as many several Bubbles, with a satyrical Epigram upon each Card, applicable thereunto; The Lines by the Author of South-Sea Ballard and Tippling Philosophers: The Cards made of Superfine Paper and engrav'd by an able Artist; spotted with the proper Colours so that they may be play'd with as well as Common Cards. Price 3s 6d.

    At Cards and Dice Men fairly may contend,
    And Friend without Deceit engage with Friend;
    But Tricking Bubbles are the Nation's Spoil,
    From L...b...rt's Project, down to Rhadish Oil.

Printed for T. Bowles, Print-seller, in St. Paul's Churchyard; and Eman Bowen, next to the King of Spain's Head at S. Katharine's; where such as take a Quantity, may have considerable Allowance. Sold likewise by Mrs. Guy, at the Archmides and Globe, at the Corner of Exchange Alley, Cornhill; Mr. Deard's Toy shop, at the King's Arms against S. Dunstan's Church, Fleetstreet; Mr. Hannekin's, a Print shop, at the Corner of Hemming's Row, S. Martin's-Lane; and Mr. Mason's Toy shop, the Corner of Spring-Garden, Charing-Cross.

   This fascinating set refers to just some of the numerous companies that have been nicknamed 'The Bubble Companies' because of the way in which they sprang up into an unstable existence at the time of the South Sea Bubble. Stocks for these companies were sold in Exchange Alley and nearby coffee shops for down payments of as little as 6d or 1s (2½p, 5p) in some cases.

Some of the companies were genuine but the majority were not. A Cornhill printer announced that he wished to raise money for 'a Company for carrying on an undertaking of Great Advantage that no one to know what it is', and promised an income of £100 for each share acquired by £2 deposit. He collected £2,000 in one day and then vanished! In all some hundred companies were seeking to raise £300 million in the summer of 1720. The *Daily Post*, a four page paper, was full of the latest offers, encouraging subscriptions for the draining of Irish bogland, the making of silver from lead and insurance against divorce, among other things.

The set opens with a title card which aptly sums up the stock market madness of the year by showing men falling off a tree into the sea. We can group the cards by subjects, starting with insurance companies. *Title card*

The *Daily Post* for 22 April, 1720, contained this announcement: *Six of spades*

> A General Meeting of the Company of Insurers of Houses and Goods from Fire throughout England, (who lately subscrib'd at Sadler's Hall) is appointed to be holden at at their Office on the North Side of the Royal Exchange, this Day, the 22d Instant, at 3 a Clock in the Afternoon, on special Affairs. N.B. None are to be admitted without producing their Receipts for the 5s. per Cent. paid into the Hands of Mr. Stephen Ram.

This company merged with the Royal Exchange Assurance under the directorship of Lord Onslow. He was also engaged in shipping insurance, a business in which the Duchess of Marlborough invested £2,000. The six of diamonds claims that such insurance is pointless as heaven controls the winds which will inevitably sink some ships. *Six of diamonds*

The Rose Fire Insurance also put an advertisement in the same paper on the same day, which read: *Seven of clubs*

> ROSE Fire-Office
> Pursuant to a Resolution of the last General Meeting of the Proprietors of the Rose Insurance of Houses and Goods from Loss by Fire all over England, every Proprietor is to pay 5s. per Cent on his Stock on or before the 2d of May next: And by Direction of the Manager, their Secretary, with a Person belonging to Messieurs Mitford and Mertins, Goldsmiths, will attend to receive the same at the Virginia Coffee house in St. Michael's Alley near Cornhill, on Monday the 25th Instant from 8 a Clock in the Morning until 1 at Noon, and continue so to do so every Day after (except) Sunday) at the same Place and Hours until the said 2d of May.

Such companies maintained their own fire service, which would only put out fires at buildings which were insured with them. The

Insurance on Lives

Come all ye Gen'rous Husbands, with your Wives,
Insure round Sums, on your precarious Lives;
That to your comfort, when you're Dead & Rotten,
Your Widows may be Rich when you're forgotten.

Rose Insurance from Fire

Projecting sure must be a Gainfull Trade,
Since all the Elements are Bubbles made.
They're right that gull us with ye Dread of Fire,
For fear makes Greater Fools, than fond Desire.

Insurance on Horses

You that keep Horses to preserve your Ease,
And Pads to please your Wives, and Mistresses.
Insure their Lives, and if they Die we'll make
Full Satisfaction, or be bound to Break.

Lending Money upon Bottom-Ree

Some lend their Money for the sake of More,
And others borrow to Encrease their Store,
Both these do oft Engage in Bottom Ree,
But often Sometimes the Bottome of the Sea.

Building Ships to let to Freight

Who but a Nest of Block-heads to their cost,
Would build new Ships for Freight when Trade is lost,
To raise fresh Barks, must surely be amusing,
When Hundreds rot in Docks for want of using.

S:r J:n L——ts Improvement of Land

The Famous Knight that is the Sole Projector
Of this New Bubble, is a South Director,
But would be better taken at his Hands,
To raise Poor South-Sea than Improve Poor Land.

Purchaseing of Estates illegally detain'd

You that have Dormant Titles to Estates,
Pil'd on your Closet Shelves to feed the Rats,
Sell them to us we'll gratify your Spite,
And Plague the Rogues that Rob you of your Right.

Royal Fishery of Great Britain

They talk of distant Seas, of Ships, and Nets,
And with the Pils of Royal Gild their Baits;
When all that the Projectors Hope or Wish for,
Is to catch Fools, the only Chubs they Fish for.

Grand Fishery

Well might this Bubble claim the Stile of Grand,
Whilst they that rais'd the same could Fish by Land;
But now the Gam'n lost at the Project Fish,
They've nothing else to cry but Stinking Fish.

Rose badge above the doorway of the building on the seven of clubs indicated that it is insured with that company.

The four of diamonds refers to a company for insuring horses and cattle, which set out to raise a capital sum of £2 million.

The Bottomry company was involved in the insurance of ships and merchandise. Their shares started at £1 and rose to £3.

The company which was set up to build ships to hire out for freight, offered its shares at £1. They soon rose to £15, but in spite of this a petition to continue the company was rejected by the Lord Justices on 14 July, 1720, when the courts clamped down on these 'bubble' companies.

Sir John Lambert's Land Improvement Company began selling its shares at £5, and they rose to £20. The banner displayed on the card refers to the legal steps taken to end the bubble companies, which will be explained at the end of this chapter. We shall meet Lambert again in the whale fishery business too. He was born in 1666 and died in 1723, and was an international stockbroker. He had been educated at Camberwell Dissenting Academy with Daniel Defoe, and he was a director of the South Sea Company from 1711 to 1721.

£1,200,000 was subscribed for Sir James Hallet's company which encouraged people with 'Dormant Titles to Estates' to take their deeds from their rat-invested shelves and sell them to the company.

Land manuring forms the subject of the two of hearts. No artificial manures existed in the eighteenth century so that a scheme offering improved farm land would sound attractive to investors. In contrast the knave of clubs encouraged people with land to spare to turn it into gold for investment in the South Sea Company.

A group of cards are devoted to companies which hoped to develop the fishing industry. Heading the list is the Royal Fishery of Great Britain. The *Daily Post* of 22 April, 1720, carried this advertisement:

> Whereas a Proposition was advertis'd in this Paper on Saturday and Monday last, for taking in Subscriptions at the Marine Coffee-house in Birchin Lane for Ten Millions of Money, for carrying on the Trade of a Royal Fishery, as mention'd in the said Advertisement. This is therefore to acquaint the Publick, that the said Subscription was entirely compleated on Tuesday last, and the Subscribers are to take Notice, That they are to pay £1 5s on each £1,000 Subscription, this present Day, into the Hands of Messieurs Green and Eades, Bankers in Lombard-street, who will depute a proper Person to receive the same, at the Crown Tavern behind the Royal Exchange, and at the same Time 1s is to be paid for every £1,000 Subscription, towards the defraying the Charges the Proposere has been at. Attendance will be given from 9 till 12, and from 2 till 6.

Four of diamonds

Queen of clubs

Seven of hearts

Ace of diamonds

Ten of diamonds

Two of hearts

Knave of clubs

Five of hearts

Two of spades	Its shares sold for £25 at one time, but became worthless when its appeal to continue in business was turned down on 14 July, 1720.

The same paper contained an advertisement for the Grand American Fishery, the shares of which rose from 10s (50p) to £5. The advertisement read:

> Whereas Books were open'd on Monday the 18th Instant, for raising a Joint-Stock of £1,500,000 to be divided into Shares, for the effectually carrying on a Grand American Fishery, at the Ship and Castle Tavern in Cornhill. This is therefore to give Notice to all the Gentlemen concern'd, that the Subscription is compleat, and that the Receipts will be deliver'd out this Day at the Ship and Castle aforesaid, to each Person for their respective Shares so subscrib'd, upon their paying the remaining Sum of 2s 6d per Cent. for each share. Attendance will be given this Day and to Morrow at the same Place, from 10 a Clock in the Morning till 6 in the Afternoon. |
King of hearts Two of diamonds	Sir John Lambert was behind the Greenland Whale Fishery company, which put its shares on the market at 10s (50p). They rose to £3 10s 0d (£3.50), but the company lost its appeal to continue business on 14 July, 1720. The two of diamonds also refers to the Greenland whale fishery business.
Knave of diamonds	An alternative line is offered in the form of coral fishing to be found referred to on the knave of diamonds.
Four of spades	Sir Richard Steele proposed the establishment of a fishing pool to supply fresh fish for London. The proposition sounded so attractive that the shares were quoted at £160 before any money had been paid.
Ace of spades	The need to transport Wigan coal to Tarleton in Lancashire and from thence to Merseyside and Ireland gave rise to the idea of making the River Douglas navigable. In 1720 William Squire, an ex-mayor of Liverpool, spent £900 obtaining an act of parliament for this purpose. The bill claimed that in addition to supplying a waterway for the coal it would also be a 'nurseryes for seamen'. The bill's opponents, the road hauliers, laughed at this suggestion and scorned the bill's claim that the coal barges would be useful to the navy in an emergency. In June, 1,200 shares at £5 each were issued, and in a few days they rose to £70, but by August 18, they had fallen to £3 3s 0d (£3.15p). Shareholders then declared that the scheme was impracticable and was only 'to make a Bubble thereof and to raise money from all such Unwary Persons as they could draw in', and accused Steers of money grabbing. He replied by pointing to the work already undertaken, but what really happened to the £6,000 spent can be charitably left to conjecture. Work did begin on the scheme in 1738.
Nine of clubs	A company was formed in 1720 to supply water to Liverpool from Mosslake. Shares were sold at £10 and rose to £20. A

Whale Fishery

Whale Fishing, which was once a gainfull Trade,
Is now by cunning Heads, a Bubble made;
For round the Change they only spread their Sails,
And to catch Gudgeons, bait their Hooks with Whales.

Greenland Trade

This Project was to Catch to Cut and Boil
Huge Whales, and other Monstrous Fish to Oil,
A Stinking Bubble, tho' of late so Dear.
Yet now the Greatest Sharers Sink for Fear.

Corral Fishery

Corral that Beauteous product only found,
Beneath the Water, and above the Ground,
If Fish'd for as it ought from thence might Spring,
A Neptunes Pallace, for a British King.

Fish Pool

How famous is the Man, that could contrive,
To serve this Gluttnous Town with Fish alive
But now we're bubbl'd by his Fishing Pools,
And as the Men catch Fish the Fish catch Fools.

River Douglas

Since Bubbles came in vogue, new Arts are found,
To cut thro' Rocks, and level rising Ground,
That murm'ring Waters, may be made more Deep,
To drown the Knaves, and lul the Fools asleep.

Liverpool Fresh-water

This Town does to our Western Islands deal,
And Serv's 'em with Malt Liquors, & with Meat,
Both Excellently Good; then how in Nature,
Can People Brew Fine Drink, & want Fresh Water.

York Buildings

You that are blest with Wealth, by your Creator,
And want to drown your Money in Thames Water,
Buy but York Buildings, and the Cistern there,
Will Sink more Pence, than any Fool can Spare.

Water Engine

Come all ye Culls, my Water Engine buy,
To Pump your flooded Mines, and Cole Pits dry;
Some Projects are all Wind, but ours is Water,
And tho' at present low, may rise hereafter.

Temple Mills

By these Old Mills, Strange Wonders have been done
Numbers have Suffer'd, yet they still Work on;
Then tell us which have done the Greater Ill,
The Temple Lawyer, or the Temple Mill.

Five of spades

Four of hearts

Nine of spades

King of diamonds

Nine of hearts

Knave of spades

Seven of diamonds

Knave of hearts

reservoir was built near the site of Gallows Mill in London Road, but in 1742 during heavy rain it burst and flooding occurred.

The large York Buildings company was involved in supplying London with water. It intended to use the land holding powers of its charter, which had enabled it to acquire land forfeited by the Jacobites of 1715, to lay water pipes. The company had been launched by the Duke of Chandos, the biggest money giant of his day. The company set out to raise £1,200,000 and its £10 shares rose to £305. But it was one of the large companies singled out for attack by the South Sea Company in its manoeuvres against 'bubble' companies, and on 18 August, 1720, a writ of scire facias (the words on the flag depicted on the card), challenging the company with misuse of its charter, was served. The announcement of the serving of the writ appeared in the *Gazette* on August 20, and on that day the share price fell from £300 to £200. Two days later there were no buyers at all. Sir Alexander Cam lost £40,000 and Lord Westmorland, £150,000.

In contrast one company was started to pump water from mines and coal pits using hand-operated water pumps. Naturally mining was an obvious opening for 'bubble' companies. The nine of spades shows the arrival of a messenger with scire facias writ for the Welsh Copper Company. The company is referred to on the ace of diamonds of the *South Sea Bubble* set, see Chapter 13. The company was governed by the Duke of Rutland, the Prince of Wales joined the company as a governor too, in spite of Sir Robert Walpole's warning that this would lead to the shares being hawked as 'The Prince of Wales' Bubble'. This did happen, but the shares rose from £4 to £95 too. The Prince resigned on hearing that a writ had been applied for, making a profit of £40,000, which was less than he had hoped to make. On 23 August, 1720, when the writ ordered the directors to appear before the Lord Justices in Council, the company boldly continued to do business. This action was promptly denounced by the South Sea Company, and the company was ended.

The Temple Mills Brass Works was another company which did well during the 'bubble' period. Its shares rose from £10 to £250.

A scire facias writ is to be seen on the floor of the English Copper and Brass Company's furnace building, depicted on the nine of hearts. Its shares had risen from £5 to £105, and it was the only one of the four big companies served with writs on August 18 which was operating legally.

A different line of business is to be found on the knave of spades where oil is being obtained from radish seed. The Rock Salt Project was designed by its promoters to supply the perennial need for salt to preserve meat. The making of salt from earth and water was the ambitious scheme planned for Holy Island. The company wanted to raise £2 million, and their shares started at £5 and rose to £15, a

English Copper & Brass

The Headlong Fool that wants to be a Swopper,
Of Gold and Silver Coin, for English Copper,
May in Change Alley, prove himself an Ass,
And give Rich Mettle for Adultrate Brass.

Raddish Oil

Our Oily project, with the Gaping Town,
Will Surely for a time go Smoothly down,
We Sow and Press, to carry on the Cheat,
To Bite Change Alley is not Fraud but Wit.

Holy Island-Salt

Here by mixt Elements of Earth and Water,
They make a Mud, that turns to Salt here'ter;
To help the Project on among Change Dealers
May all bad Wives like Lot's become Salt Pillars
Since crowds of Fools delight to be Salt Sellers

Rock Salt

You that are willing to Preserve your Meat,
In Winter Savry, and in Summer Sweet,
Encourage this Salt Project, and your Coin
Will turn to some Account, at least to Brine.

Salt-Petre

Come all ye Black Infernal Powder Makers,
And Rocketeers that deal in Squibs and Crackers,
Buy Petre Stock, Let me be your Adviser,
T'will make you (tho' not Richer) much ye Wiser.

Sugar

Fair Tattling Gossips, you that Love to see,
Fine Sugar blended, with Expensive Tea,
Since you Delight in things, both Dear & Sweet,
Buy Sugar Shares, and you'll be Sweetly Bit.

Lute-String

These Crafty Managers have play'd for Years,
The World as many Tricks as Dancing Bears;
By Bubbling too, they've broke their Ancient Rules,
They first made Lutestrings, but they now make Fools.

Puckle's Machine

A rare invention to Destroy the Crowd,
Of Fools at Home instead of Foes Abroad:
Fear not my Friends, this terrible Machine,
They're only Wounded that have Shares therein.

Hemp & Flax

Here Hemp is Sow'd for Stubborn Rogues to Die in,
And Softer Flax, for tender Skins to Lye in,
But should the usefull Project be defeated
The Knaves may prosper but the Fools are cheated

small rise by 'bubble' standards.

Salt-petre was another line of business offering opportunities for profit making.

The demand for sugar to go in tea prompted a company to spring up offering to 'bleach coarse sugar without the use of fire or loss of substance'.

Four of clubs

Five of clubs

Ace of clubs

The most important of the manufacturing companies was the Royal Lutestring, or Lustring, Company. The ace of clubs uses the word 'lutestring' twice, but on sale in the shop is Lustring, a fancy French fabric. It is probably the wit of the poet who was changed lustring to lutestring as the verse is written in mockery of the company. Its shares started at £5 and rose to £120, but being one of the four companies challenged by the South Sea Company, it was served with a scire facias writ. The writ was delivered on August 18 as can be seen in the picture on the card. The company's 10,000 shares, valued at £1,200,000, were then not worth a farthing.

Eight of spades

The invention which would have had an enormous effect on eighteenth century warfare had it been accepted by the military authorities, was James Puckle's 'Defence' machine gun. Puckle, a London solicitor (1667-1724), had invented a patent plastic wood and a patent sword. On 15 May, 1718, he took out Patent No. 418 for his gun, on which he commented:

Defending KING GEORGE your COUNTRY and LAWES
Is Defending YOURSELVES and PROTESTANT CAUSE.

The gun is precisely as pictured on the eight of spades. It could be fitted with a six, nine or eleven chamber revolving magazine with either round bullets for Christians or square ones for Turks. A spare magazine is to be seen on the ground and nearby is the mould for making single bullets. The collapsible tripod is remarkably modern in design. Two were used by the Duke of Montagu in the West Indies in 1727 and may be the two in the Tower of London today. One is a 35 ins. iron-barrelled matchlock and the other a 32 ins. brass-barrelled flintlock. A third, a 28 ins. brass-barrelled matchlock is in Tojhusmuseum, Copenhagen. On 22 March, 1722, the *Daily Courant* contained this advertisement:

Several sizes in Brass and Iron of Mr. Puckle's Machine or
Gun, called a Defence, being now perfected, such Persons
as are desirous, may have a sight of the same at
Seasonable Hours till Friday next the 30th Instant, at the
Workshop thereof, in White-Cross-Alley, Middle Moorfields;
and on Friday following. (Holidays excepted) Attendance will
be given at Mr. Puckle's Office in Pope's Head Alley,
Cornhill against the Royal Exchange, from Three to Five in
the Afternoon to treat with such Gentlemen or Merchants
as have a Mind to be furnished with any of them.

On 31 March, 1722, the gun was demonstrated before the authorities, and, according to the *London Journal,* fired sixty-three shots in seven minutes during a rainstorm, which was considerably faster than a musket of the day could fire. The promotion company's shares rose from £4 to £8, but the gun was rejected by the army and never put into large scale production.

'Malt drying by Air' gave the poet a chance to enjoy himself:
>Of all the Windy Projects now in vogue
>To fleece the Fool, and feed the cunning Rogue,
>The Malting Bubble seems to be most fair,
>Because our Maltsters own they work by Air.

Eight of hearts

Samuel Antrim started a company to raise hemp and flax in England. Its shares started at 2s 6d (12½p) and rose to £1 10s 0d (£1.50), but the company's petition to continue to business was rejected on 14 July, 1720.

Ace of hearts

Thomas Boyd and others started a company for the making and packing of sail cloth in Ireland. The verse refers to Holland cloth which was used by well-off families to cover the furniture in their London homes when they left at the end of the fashionable season to return to their country houses. The company was refused its petition to continue in business on July 14. There is a reference to a person in Exchange Alley selling square bits of playing card with wax impressions of seals representing the Globe Tavern on them for sixty guineas (£63), which he claimed entitled the holder to 'subscribe to a new sail-cloth manufactury projected by a man known to be a man of fortune'.

King of clubs

Joseph Galends started a company to prepare Virginian tobacco for snuff, but lost his petition to continue in business on July 14.

Queen of hearts

A stocking making company referred to on the seven of spades did not have the confidence of the poet to judge from the verse he wrote:
>You that delight to keep your Sweaty Feet
>By often changing Stockings Clean and Sweet,
>Deal not in Stockin' Shares, because I doubt
>Those that buy most, e'er long will go without.

Seven of spades

Nor did the pasteboard and packing paper makers of the two of clubs fare any better:
>As Empty Sayings flow from Windy Fools
>So Pasteboard Bubbles rise from Paper Skulls,
>Madness must surely be the Towns disease,
>When Knaves get Money by such Whims as these.

Two of clubs

A number of cards in the pack deal with trading companies of one kind or another. The six of clubs proclaims a company to fatten hogs, while the ten of hearts refers to E. Jones' firm to export timber from Germany. This firm lost its petition to continue in business on July 14.

Six of clubs

Ten of hearts

The Harburg Company ('Harborough' as the three of clubs puts it) was started by Thomas Burges and others to import linen from Harburg in the state of Bremen. The town stands on the River Elbe

Three of clubs

Irish Sail Cloath

If Good St Patrick's Friends should raise a Stock,
And make in Irish Looms true Holland's Duck,
Then shall this Noble Project by my Shoul
No longer be a Bubble, but a Bull

Cureing Tobacco for Snuff

Here Slaves for Snuff, are Sifting Indian Weed,
Whilst their O'erseer, does the Riddle feed.
The Dust arising, gives their Eyes much trouble,
So shew their Blindness that Espouse the Bubble.

Past-board Manufactory

As Empty Sayings flow from Windy Fools,
So Pastboard Bubbles rise from Paper Skulls:
Madness must surely be the Fomm'd Disease,
When Knaves get Money by such Whims as those.

Fatning of Hoggs

Come all ye Bacon making Greasy Rogues,
That want Good Nurses, for your Meagre Hoggs,
Send them to us, and at a Small Expence
We'll fat em up, with Offal, Blood, and Grains.

Exporting Timber from Germany

You that are Rich, and hasty to be Poor,
Buy Lumber Export from the German Shoar,
For Gallouses, built up of Forreign Wood,
If rightly us'd, may do Change Alley good.

Trade to Harborough

You that delight to take up foreign Linnen,
At Harbrough made, a little Town in Bremen,
Encourage Trade abroad, for times to come
And like Kind Fools, neglect your own at home

Coal Trade from Newcastle

Some deal in Water, Some in Wind like Fools,
Others in Wood, but we alone in Coals:
From Such like Projects, the declining Nation,
May justly fear a fatal inflamation.

Settling Colonies in Accadia North America

He that is Rich, and wants to Fool away,
A Sporting Sum, in North America,
Let him Subscribe himself a Headlong Sharer,
And Asses Ears, shall Honour him or Bearer.

Pensilvania Company

Come all ye Saints that would, for little Pay
Great Tracts of Land, and care not where they lye,
Deal with your Quaking Friends, they're Men of Light,
The Spirit hates Deceit and Scorns to Bite.

beside Hamburg. George I had acquired Bremen in order to give his princedom of Hanover access to the sea via the Elbe. The company sets out to raise £1½ million and its shares rose from £15 to £120. Its petition to continue in business was rejected on July 14.

£3 million was sought by a company which wished to develop the Newcastle coal industry and ship the coal to London.

Colonization in the Bahamas was the subject of the five of diamonds. The shares started at £3 and rose to £40. One 'eminent person' invested £6,000 in this enterprise. The company petitioned to be allowed to continue in February, 1723, but lost its case. The eight of diamonds offered the prospect of colonization in Acadia. Notice the cannibalism going on. In the early days of Virginia one colonist was executed for murdering his wife and eating her as food supplies were so desperate.

The Pennsylvanian Company offered land for sale and proposed importing hemp and flax from the colony. Its shares rose from £2 10s 0d (£2.50) to £28. Notice the reference to Quakers, who had started the colony, in the verse below the picture.

The set is completed with a collection of cards referring to miscellaneous companies.

A company which set out to do something quite practical was the one started to provide a street cleaning service, and the paving of London's streets. It sought to raise a capital sum of £2 million. Notice the woman throwing her rubbish out of the window in traditional style. An inoffensive way of emptying houses of office (lavatories) was the money-making proposal of another company. Problems faced by travellers in the north of Britain was the particular concern of a company which proposed the construction of public conveniences for their benefit.

A hospital to cure victims of venereal disease (clap) was another project of the day. The care of bastards was proposed long before the famous Foundling Hospital was opened.

One of the chief grievances of sailors was being paid with tickets which they could only cash at their ship's home port. Because they might not put in to their home port for months or years on end, they were forced to sell their tickets for whatever they could get for them. The purchasers, such as the Wapping alehouse whores referred to on the eight of clubs, would then arrange for the tickets to be sent to the home ports concerned and collect their full cash value.

Lawrence Braddon (d.1724), the politician and author of *The Miseries of the Poor are a National Sin, Shame and Danger,* 1717, may have started the idea of a company specializing in the care of the poor. No doubt the building on the card is a house of correction. Notice the water pit. Water was fed into it from a conduit and those put in the pit had to keep pumping to prevent themselves from drowning. If one drowned it proved one was

Three of hearts

Five of diamonds

Eight of diamonds

Nine of diamonds

Three of spades

King of spades

Six of hearts

Three of diamonds

Queen of spades

Eight of clubs

Ten of spades

Cleaning the Streets
A Cleanly project, well approv'd, no doubt,
By Stroling Dames, and all that walk on Foot;
This Bubble well deserves the Name of best,
Because the Cleanest Bite of all the rest.

An inoffensive way of emptying Houses of Office
Our fragrant Bubble, would the World believe it,
Is to make Humane Dung, Smell Sweet as Civet:
None Sure before us, ever durst presume,
To turn a ····, into a Rich Perfume.

Errecting Houses of Office in N
Britain for Strangers & Travellers
A usefull Project merrily advanc'd,
Tho' cheifly by Tom-turdmen countenanc'd,
Design'd to Sweeten the North British Nation,
And put Close Stools, and Bed Pans, out of fashion.

Office for cureing the GrandPox or Clap
Come all ye Sparks, whose Noses are in Danger,
And Stroling Jades, that Live at Rack and Manger,
We'll Cure the Sad Effects of all your Poxes,
By Purging Doses, or by Dwiving Fluxes.

Bastard Children
Love on ye jolly Rakes, and buxome Dames,
A Child is Safer than venereal Flames;
Indulge your Senses, with the Sweet offence,
We'll keep your Bastards at a Small expence.

Buying Seamens Tickets
As the Case Stands the Wapping Ale Wives buy,
The Seamen's Tickets for a small Supply;
But tis no matter whether Spendthrift Slaves,
Are Chous'd by Wapping W····s or Bubbling Knaves

Providing for and employing all the Poor in Gr Britain
The Poor when manag'd, and employ'd in Trade,
Are to the publick Welfare, usefull made;
But if kept Idle, from their Vices Spring
W···s for the Stews, and Soldiers for the King.

Bleeching of Hair
Here Dirty, Brown, Dark, Red, and Yellow Hair,
Are Bleach'd, to Colours that are Fine and Fair,
Then Blended so, that half the W····s in Town,
Contribute to adorn one Addl'd Crown.

Furnishing of Funerals to all parts of Great Britain
Come all ye Sickly Mortals Die apace,
And Solemn Pomps your Funerals Shall Grace.
Old Rusty Hackneys Shall attend each Hearse,
And Scare-Crows in Black Gowns compleat the Farce.

useless to the community, but if one succeeded in keeping the water level sufficiently down it proved one was a slothful liar! This technique was used in the Rasp-house (workhouse), Amsterdam, in the late 16th C.

The production of good quality wigs from the bleached hair of whores was another idea. The startling thing is that a man is shown holding two heads which suggests the company intended to operate by decapitating deceased whores rather than purchasing hair from live ones.

Ten of clubs

The queen of diamonds is perhaps a fitting card to complete the set for it offers to supply a funeral service throughout the whole of Great Britain!

Queen of diamonds

The end of the 'bubble' spree was in sight when on 11 June, 1720, John Aislabie and Sir John Blunt of the South Sea Company obtained the royal assent for the 'Bubble Bill' (6 Geo I cap 18), correctly entitled, 'An Act for the better securing of certain powers and privileges intended to be granted by his Majesty by two Charters for Assurance of Ships and Merchandise at Sea, and for lending money upon bottomry, and for restraining several extravagant and unwarrantable practices therein mentioned'. The latter part of the title referred to a clause attached to the act in which the 'bubble' companies were classed as 'Public Nuisances' and 'mischevious projects', and made them liable for prosecution on the ground that they either had no charters, or were acting under the cover of obsolete charters, or were misapplying such charters as they had. From June 24 all such companies were liable to trial in the Courts of Record at Westminster, Edinburgh or Dublin. Anyone then suffering as a result of their continued activities could recover treble damages and full costs of his action. Anyone acting as a broker for such companies was to be forbidden to act as a broker again and be fined £500. Mayors, sheriffs and magistrates were required to help in enforcing this law. The *London Journal* of July 2 recorded that Exchange Alley regarded the proclamation of the new law as the Day of Judgement.

On July 14 a further step was taken against the 'bubble' companies when the Lord Justices in Council rejected appeals to continue in business from thirteen companies, most of which have cards in the set representing them.

Four large companies were vulnerable as their charters were years old and could be proved void from years of non-use or from current mis-use. They were the Royal Lustring, York Buildings, English Copper Company and the Welsh Copper Company. The South Sea Company applied to the Lord Justices for scire facias writs, which were issued on Thursday, August 18. The resulting crashes in the shares of these companies has been recorded above. The Court subsequently decided that only the English Copper Company had been acting legally. By now the 'bubble' companies had crashed and they brought with them the South Sea Company as all faith in the share world had gone.

Bibliography

BOOKS ON PLAYING CARDS

Beal, G. *Discovering Playing Cards and Tarots* (1972)
Benham, W. Gurney, *Playing Cards: Their History and Secrets* (1930; reprinted, 1950)
Compleat Gamester (1674; reprinted 1972)
(1972 reprint by Cornmarket Reprints comes with reproduction of the Popish Plot and Reign of James II, Revolution, packs of cards as possessed by Samuel Pepys)
Franks, A.W. *Proceedings of the Society of Antiquaries* (1892); article on the Meal Tub Plot and South Sea Bubble packs.
Gentlemen's Magazine, vol 32, New Series; article on Popish Plot pack (1849)
Goldsmid, E. *Explanatory Notes of a pack of Cavalier Playing Cards forming a complete political satire of the Commonwealth* (1886)
Hargrave, C.P. *A History of Playing Cards* (1930; reprinted 1966)
Hoffman, D. *The World of Playing Cards* (1973)
Morley, H.T. *Old and Curious Playing Cards* (1931)
Pettigrew, T.J. *Journal of the British Archaeological Association* vol 9, article on the Rump pack. (July, 1853)
Schreiber, C. *Catalogue of the Collection of Playing Cards bequeathed to the Trustees of the British Museum by the late Lady Charlotte Schreiber* (1901)
Schreiber, C. and Franks, A.W. *Playing Cards of Various Ages and Countries,* 3 vols. (1892-5)
Tilley, R. *A History of Playing Cards* (1973)
Willshire, W.H. *Descriptive Catalogue of Playing Cards and other Cards in the British Museum* (1876)

CONTEMPORARY MATERIAL
NEWSPAPERS
Daily Courant, 1705, 1707
Domestic Intelligencer, 1679
London Gazette, 1683, 1685
Mercurius Domesticus, 1679
Observator, 1707
Post Boy, 1720
True Domestick Intelligense, 1679
Weekly Packet, 1720

PAMPHLETS IN THE BRITISH MUSEUM
1. Dr. Parry
   True and Plaine declaration of the horrible treason practised by W. Parry (1585)
2. Meal Tub Plot
   The Midwife unmask'd (1680)
   To Dr. - An answer to his Queries Concerning the Colledge of Midwives, Elizabeth Cellier, (1688)
   Malice Defeated, Elizabeth Cellier, (1680)
   Answer to Certain Scandalous lying Pamphlets entitled Malice Defeated, T. Dangerfield (1680)
   Mrs. Cellier's Lamentation standing in the Pillory (1680)
   Mr. Prance's Answer to Mrs. Cellier's Libel: the Adventure of the Bloody Bladder, M. Prance
   Particular Narrative, T. Dangerfield (1679)
3. Rye House Plot
   Secret History of the Rye House Plot and Monmouth's Rebellion, Forde Grey, Lord Werke (1754)
4. Monmouth Rebellion
   True Account of Proceedings against J. Ayloff and Richard Nelthorp Esquires, at the King's Bench Bar, (1685)
   An Account of the Manner of the Taking of the Late Duke of Monmouth (1685)
5. Queen Anne
   History of Queen Anne digested into Annals, Abel Boyer (1703-12)
6. Duke of Marlborough
   Inscription appointed to be fixed on a Marble Pillar erected at Hochstadt, Mr. Stepney (1705)
7. Dr. Sacheverell
   Dr. Sacheverell's Progress from London to his Rectory of Salatin in Shropshire (1710)
   An Ordinary Journey, No Progress or, a Man doing his own Business, No Mover of Sedition, J. Trapp (1710)
   The Ban-y Apes, or the Monkeys chattering to the Magpie (no date)

REFERENCE BOOKS

Basset, B. *The English Jesuits* (1967)
Carswell, J.P. *The South Sea Bubble* (1960)
Chandler, D. *Marlborough's Wars* (1968)
   Marlborough (1973)
Cobbett, *State Trials*
Cowles, V. *The Great Swindle* (1960)
Dictionary of National Biography
D'Oyley, E. *James, Duke of Monmouth* (1938)
Earle, P., *Monmouth's Rebels* (1977)
English Historical Review, Vol. 40: article by Sir Edmund Warcup 'Journals of the Meal Tub Plot'
Ferguson, J. *Ferguson the Plotter* (1887)
Foley, H. *Records of the English Province of the Society of Jesuits* 7 vols. (1877-83)
Hicks, L. *Dublin Studies,* No. 37, article on 'Dr. W. Parry' (1948)
Holmes, G. *Trial of Dr. Sacheverell* (1973)
Hulton, P.H. *British Museum Quarterly,* vol, 20 (1955) article on Barlow's drawings
Kenyon, J. *The Popish Plot* (1972)
Kunzle, D. *The Early Comic Strip,* 1450-1825 (1973)
Mattingly, G.H. *The Defeat of the Spanish Armada* (1959)
Melville, L. *South Sea Bubble* (1921)
Petherick, M. *Restoration Rogues* (1951)
Roberts, G. *Life of James, Duke of Monmouth* (1844)
Ronalds, F.S. *Illinois Peoria Studies in the Social Sciences* vol. 21, no. 1 & 2, article on 'The Attempted Whig Revolution, 1678-81'.
Scudie, A.T. *The Sacheverell Affair* (1939)
Taunton, E.L. *History of Jesuits in England, 1580-1773* (1901)
Trevelyan, G.M. *England Under Queen Anne,* 3 vols. (1936)
Willcock, J. *A Scots Earl of Covenanting Times: Archibald 9th Earl of Argyll* (1907)
Wroughton, J. *Plots, Traitors and Spies, 1653-1685*(1970)

CARD COLLECTIONS

Collections of the packs described in this book can be seen at the following places. It is usually necessary to make a prior appointment to see them. B.Mus = British Museum.
Spanish Armada: B.Mus., Willshire E185; National Maritime Museum, Greenwich.
The Rump: B. Mus., Schreiber 61; Willshire E195; Guildhall Library, 239
All the Popish Plots: B. Mus., Schreiber 56
The Popish Plot; B.Mus.,Willshire E186, E58 (colour), E 187,

E188; Guildhall Library, 236; Pepys Library, Cambridge
Meal Tub Plot: B. Mus., Willshire E187; Guildhall Library, 238
Rye House Plot: B. Mus., Willshire E189
Monmouth Rebellion: B. Mus., Schreiber E62
Reign of James II, 1685-1688: B. Mus, Schreiber E63, Willshire E190
Reign of James II, Revolution: B.Mus., Willshire E191;
Pepys Library Cambridge
Reign of Queen Anne: B. Mus., Schreiber E64; Guildhall Library, 240
Marlborough's Victories: B. Mus., Willshire E192 & 192; Blenheim Palace
Dr. Sacheverell: B. Mus., Willshire E194, and Schreiber and Franks' *Playing Cards of Various Ages and Countries* vol. 1; Guildhall Library, 241
South Sea Bubble: Guildhall Library 242, 243 and 245
All the Bubble Companies: B. Mus., E66; Guildhall Library 244;
Worcester College, Oxford.

The Popish Plot and the Reign of James II, Rebellion, packs have been reproduced in playable form, together with the *Compleat Gamester* (1674 edition) by Cornmarket Reprints, 1972. The Rump, Marlborough's Victories and the South Sea Bubble packs have been reproduced in playable form by H. Margary, Lympne Castle, Kent.

Index

Italic numerals refer to illustration pages

Abimelech, 144
Acadia, colonization of, 187, *184*
Aesop's Fables, 3, 5
Aislabie, J., Chancellor of the Exchequer, 168, 187
Alancorn, Don, 40
Albermarle, Duke of 95-7
Alford, Mayor, 93
All the Bubble Companies, see Bubble Companies
All the Popish Plots, 5, 36-49, 191
Allen, W., Cardinal, 40, *39*
Ambrose, Father, *see* Oates, Titus
Anabaptists, 26, 79, 102
Anderson, Lionel, *see* Munson, Father
Andrews, Robert, 86
Anjou, Duke of 127, 140, *139*
Anne, Queen, 125-140, 144, 149, 151, 154, 156, 160-2, 190, *126, 129, 131, 135, 139, 145, 147, 158, 161*
Answer to a Certain Scandalous late Pamphlet, 75
Antrim, Samuel, 183
Antwerp, 41, 146
Apostles, Twelve, 7, *9*
Applebee's *Journal,* 166
Apprentices of London, 27, 29, *28*
Apprentices' Parliament, 29, 124
Argyle, Marquis of, 23, 89-93, *90*
Ark Royal, 11, 13
Armada, Spanish, 7-18, 36, 40-3, 191, *9, 12, 14, 17, 42*
Armagh, Archbishop of, 77-8
Arms of the English Peers, 2
Armstrong, Sir Thomas, *alias,* Henry Lawrence, 81, 85, *80*
Arnold, Capt., 74, *72*

Arundell, Lord, 56, 71
Ashby, Richard, *alias* Thimbleby, 54
Assiento, 166
Aston, Lord, 56, 64
Ath, siege of, 148, *145*
Atterbury, Bishop, 151, 154
Ayloffe, Col. J., 91, 190, *90*

Bahamas, colonization of, 185
Baldron, *see* Bolron, Robert,
Balsano, Don, 40
Banbury, 26, 159, *158*
Banb-y Apes, 159, 190
Bank of England, 156, 166, 170
Barcelona, relief of, 144
Barlow, Francis, 5, 7, 36, 64
Barnbow Hall, 73
Barter, John, 102
Bastards, care of, 185, *186*
Bath, 128, 130, *129*
Bavaria, Duke of, 130, 142, *129, 135, 139*
Bedingfield, Revd., 56
Bedlow, William, 53-4, 57, 59, 62, 63, 67, 73, 75, *52, 58, 72, 76*
Beggars' Opera, 3
Belasyse, Lord, 54
Benbow, Admiral, 132, 142, *131, 141*
Berry, Capt., 60
Berry, Henry, 57, *55, 58*
Berwick, Duc de, 148
Black Swan and Bible. 89
Blake, Anne, 70, *69*
Blake, Miss, 94-5
Blasedale, Henry, 67
Bleaching of hair, 187, *186*
Blenheim, battle of, 132, 136, 137, 142-3, 154, 190, *135, 141*

Blood, Col., 71
Bloody Assize, 103
Blunt, John, 168, 187
Bolron, (Baldron), Robert, 73, *72*
Bonn, siege of, 133, 142, *141*
Bottomry Company, 177, 187, *176*
Bowen, Emanuel, 164, 174
Bowles, Carrington, 3, 164
Boyd, Thomas, 183
Bradbury, Capt. James, II
Braddon, Lawrence, 185
Bradshaw, John, 20, 32, 33, *21, 31*
Bragge, B., 138
Brandenburgh, Capt., *see* Busse, Anthony
Brandon, Mr., 105, *106*
Bristol, 40, 75, 130, 134
Bridgewater, 100, *96, 99*
Bridport, 93, *92*
Brooks, Alderman, 60
Broomhead, John, 138
Brown, D., 89
Brussels, 148
Bubble Bill, 187
Bubble Companies, 164, 174-186, 192, *176, 179, 181, 184, 186*
Buckingham, Lord Steward, 160, *161*
Bucklersbury chapel, 122, *121*
Bulls, Bay of, 128
Bulstrode, *see* Whitlock, Sir Bulstrode,
Burges, Thomas, 183
Burgess, Revd. Daniel, 156
Busse, Anthony, 100-102
Bussex Rhine, 100

Cabal, 163
Cadiz, 128
Caill, River, 91
Calais, 13
Califord, John, 88, *87*
Camisards, *see* Cevennois
Campbell, Archibald, *see* Argyle, Marquis of
Cansham, *see* Keynsham
Capel, Sir Henry, 62
Carisbrooke Castle, 22
Cariston, 89
Carlingford, 78
Cass, John, 162
Castlemaine, Earl of, 71, 73-4, 118
Catesby, Robert, 43, 46, *42, 45*
Cecil, Robert, 43-4
Cellier, Mrs. Elizabeth, 66-7, 70-1, 75-7, 120, 190, *65, 76*
Cellier, Peter, 66
Cevennois, 148
Chaise, La, 53, 54, 60
Chandos, Duke of, 180
Chapman, sir John, 115

Charles I, 19-20, 22, 23, 26-7, 29, 32, *28, 31*
Charles II, 23, 35, 36, 48, 50-1, 53, 54, 56, 60-2, 71, 78-81, 88-9, 105, *47, 52, 58, 82, 106*
Charles II of Spain, 140
Charles III of Spain, *see* Charles, Archduke,
Charles, Archduke, 127, 133, 134, 140, 144-6, *131, 139*
Charlie, Bonnie Prince, 170, *167*
Chelsea Hospital, 100
Churchill, Sarah, *see* Marlborough, Duchess of
Clap, *see* venereal disease
Clement XI, 140, 149
Clements, Henry, 153
Coal trade, 178, 185, *184*
Codrington, Col., 128
Coleman, Edward, 48-9, 53-6, 59-60, *47, 52, 55, 58, 61*
Cologne, Bishop of, 142, *139*
Colonization, 185, *184*
Commemorative Medals, 50, 57, 132, 159
Communication of Sin, 151
Como, Cardinal, 37-8
Compleat Gamester, 3, 189, 192
Comprehension Bill, 150
Coningsby, Sir Richard, 4
Conny-catching, 2
Consults, 54, 56, 60, 62, *52*
Conyers, George or John, 53, 56, *65*
Coral fishing, 178, 179
Corbet, Miles, 29, *31*
Cordova, Don Luis de, 16
Corker, James, 63
Corral, Francis, 75
Correction, houses of, 185-7, *186*
Corunna, 41
Council of Six, 79-81, 85, *80*
Country Party, 85, 128, 151, 153-4, 160-2, 166
Coventers, 23, 60, *24, 31*
Coventry, Henry, 68-70
Coverely, Sir Roger de, 3
Cowper, Lord, 160
Coxe (Cock), William, 15, *14*
Cromwell, Elizabeth (Joan), 30
Cromwell, Sir Henry, 29
Cromwell, Oliver, 19-23, 25-34, *21, 28, 31*
Cromwell, Richard, 22, 25, 33
Cropredy Bridge, 25
Cumberland, Duke of, 3
Cutts, Lord, 142, *141*

D'Adda, Comte, 118
Daily Courant, 125, 138

Daily Post, 175, 177
Dalrymple, J., 3
Dammaree, Daniel, 157, *155*
Dangerfield, Capt. Thomas, *alias* Willoughby, 66-78, 81, 190, *65, 69, 72, 76*
Dartmouth, Lord, 113, *114*
Davies, Walton, 88
Declaration of Indulgence, 108
Declaration of William III, 122
Deerham (Deering), Henry, 85
Defence machine gun, 182-3, *181*
Defiance, 11, 43, *12*
Defoe, Daniel, 136, 166, 177, *135*
Delight, 15
Denermond, siege of, 146
Derby, Sacheverell's sermon at, 151, *152*
Derbyshire, Sheriff of, *see* Sacheverell, George
Desborough, John, 25, *24*
Deventer, 40-1
Disdain, 11
Disney (Desny), William, 94, *92*
Dr. Sacheverell's progress, 159, 190
Dodd, Mr., 154
Dog Towzer, 75
Dogger, 94
Dolben, John, 153, *152*
Domestic Intelligencer, 36
Dorislaus, Dr. Isaac, 23
Douglas, River, 278, *179*
Drake, Sir Francis, 7-8, 11-16, 36, 41-3, *12, 14, 42*
Dublin, 20, 22, 27, 77, 187
Dugdale, Stephen, 56, 64-6, *55, 65*

Ecclesiastical Commissioners, 105, 107
Edgehill, battle of, 26, 29
Edinburgh, 23, 91, 187
Edinburgh, Dean of, 91
Edward IV, 1
Elizabeth I, 1, 16-18, 36, 37-41, 132, *12, 17, 42*
Ellis, Thomas, 124
Ely Cathedral, 134
English Copper and Brass Company, 180, 187, *181*
Episcopalians, Scottish, 133
Essex, Earl of, 26, 79, 86, 105, 116, 87, *106, 117,*
Eugene, Prince, 133, *131,*
Evelyn, John, 23, 110, 112, 132, 133-4
Everard, Edmund, 60
Evers (Eure), Francis, 56, 64
Exchange Alley, 174, 183, 187
Exeter, 112, *111*

Fairfax, General, 19, 22, 29, *21*
Farmer, Anthony, 107

Farrant, Amy, 100
Fawkes, Guido, 41, 43-8, *42, 45*
Faversham, 115
Feake, Christopher, 26
Felix, surgeon, 149
Fenwick John, *alias* Caldwell, 56, 60, 62
Ferguson, Revd. Robert, 79-81, 83-5, 93, 98, 102, *80, 96, 101*
Feversham, Lord, 100, *99*
Fiennes, Nathaniel, 26, *24*
Fifth Monarchists, 26, 85, 102
Fire of London, 63, 93, 116-118, *61*
Fire Monument, 63, 116-118, *117*
Fireships, 13, 15, 43, *14, 42*
Fishing, *see* Royal Fishery, Grand American Fishing Co., Greenland Whale Fishery, Steele, Sir Richard
Flax making, 183, 185, *181*
Fly-boats, 13, 15
Flying Horse, 88
Fogarty, Dr. William, 56
Fontaine, Sir Andrew, 64
Fort St. Michael, 142, *141*
Four Knaves, 2
Franks, A.W., 150, 189
Frobisher, Martin, 11, *12*
Frome, 98, *96*
Fullarton, Major, 91
Fuller, William, 134-6, *135*
Fullwood, Samuel, 125
Funeral company, 187, *186*
A Further Discovery of the Plot, dedicated to Dr. Titus Oates, 74-5
Gadbury, John, 71
Galends, Joseph, 183
Gallows Mill, 180
Gang, The, 26
Garrard, Sir Samuel, 151-3
Gascoigne, Sir Thomas, 73, *72*
Gavan, S.J., 62
Gazette, 180
Gentlemen's Magazine, 3, 189
George I, 166, 170, 182
George II as Prince of Wales, 180
George, Prince, husband of Queen Anne, 127-130, *126, 129*
Gerard, Sir Gilbert, 22
Gerard Conspiracy, 22
Ghent, 146, *145*
Gibraltar, siege of, 137, 170, *135, 167*
Gifford, Bonaventura, 107
Giles, John, 74, *72*
Girauld, Father, 57, *47, 55*
Glencoe, massacre of, 3
Globe Tavern, 166
Goat Inn, 67
Godden, Mr., 107, 115
Godfrey, Sir Edmund Berry, 37, 49, 50, 51, 57-9, 62, 67, 75, 93, *47, 55, 58*

Goodwin (Godwin), Thomas, 19, 20, 25, *24*
Goodenough, Francis, 77
Goodenough, Richard, 79, 81, 83-6, 102, *82, 84*
Grace, Richard, 2
Grafton, Duke of, 97, 124, *96*
Grand American Fishery, 178, *176*
Gravelines, battle of, 7, 13-15, *14*
Great Mouth, 78, *76*
Green Ribbon Club, 71, 81
Green, Robert, 57, *55, 58*
Green Lettice Tavern, 66
Greene, Robert, 2
Greenland Whale Fishery, 177-8, *179*
Grey, Lord of Werke, 79, 81, 85, 93, 100, *80, 84, 92, 99*
Grove, William, 54, 60-2, 47, *61*
Growth of Popery, 88
Guildhall, 144
Gunpowder Plot, 36, 43-8, 151, *42, 45, 47*
Guy, Thomas, 166
Guy's Hospital, 166

Haberdashers' Hall, 29, *28*
Hair, bleaching of, 187, *186*
Hales, Sir Edward, 107, 113-115
Hallet, Sir James, 177
Hampden, John, 29, 79
Hampsted, 170
Harburg, (Harborough) Company, 183-5, *184*
Harcourt, *see* Whitbread, Thomas
Harcourt, Sir Simon, 154, 160
Harley, Robert, 160-2, 166, *158*
Harris, Benjamin, 36
Harrison, Thomas, 26, *24*
Haselrigg, Sir Arthur, 27, 33, 34
Hawkins, John, 11-15, *12*
Helderenburgh, 93
Hemp making, 183, 185, *181*
Henchman, Dr. Humphry, 154-6
Henry VII, 1, 120
Henry VIII, 1
Hensbrough, Capt., 157
Herbert, Lord Chief Justice, 107, *106*
Herbert, Thomas, 74
Herbert, Vice-Admiral Arthur, 110
Hesse-Cassel, Prince of, 130, 137
Hesse Darmstadt, Prince of, 137
Hewson (Huson, Hudson) John, 2, 5, 20, 27, 33, *21, 28*
Hewson, L., 5
Hicks, John, 102
High Church group, 128, 136, 150-163
Hill, Lawrence, 57, *55, 58*
Hoadly, Bishop, 157, 159, 163
Hoare, Sir Richard, 162

Hobson (Hopsonn), Vice-Admiral, 132, *129*
Hochstadt, *see* Blenheim
Hog fattening, 183, *184*
Hoistet (Hochstadt), *see* Blenheim
Holbeach House, 46
Holloway, Judge, 110
Hollyday, Richard, 100
Holmes, Maj. Abraham, 79, 97, 102, *101*
Holt Lodge, 100
Holy Island, 180, *181*
Hone, William, 85-8, *84, 87*
Horse Guards, 156-7
Horsey, Capt., 156
Hough (Huff), Dr. John, 107, 118, *117*
Howard, Lord of Effingham, 11-16, 41, *12*
Howard, Lord of Escrick, 79, 85-6, *84*
Hubert, Robert, 116-118
Huguenots, 148
Hunsdon, Lord, 10, *12*
Huy, siege of, 130

Inchinnan, 91
Independents, 23, 29
Insurance companies, 175-7, *176*
Ireland, William, 56, 60-2, *61*
Ireton, Henry, 20, 30, 33, *21, 31*
Irish ruffians, 48, 56, *55*

Jackson, F., 2
Jacobites, 128, 153, 156-7, 170, 180
James I, 36, 43, 44, 46-8, *47*
James II, formerly Duke of York, 5, 32, 48, 51, 53-4, 56, 59, 63-6, 68, 77-9, 81, 86, 89, 99-124, 134, 192, *111, 114*
James, Prince of Wales, the Old Pretender, 110, 112-3, 118-120, 124, 134, 162, 170, *109, 114, 119, 121, 123*
Jeffreys, Judge, 85, 103, 105, 115, 118, 124, *84, 114, 123*
Jenison, Robert, 56, 66, *65*
Jenkins, Sir Lionel, 83, 85
Jenner, Sir Thomas, 115, *114*
Jerusalem, kingdom of, 140, *139*
Jesuits, 18, 37, 49, 53-7, 60-4, 74-5, 78, 110, 115, *17, 61, 69, 119*
Johnson, Sir Archibald, 23
Johnson, Dr. Samuel, 3
Jones, Arthur, 88
Jones, E., 183
Joseph I, emperor of Germany, 140
Judith, 144

Keeling, John, 83
Keeling, Josiah, 79, 83, 86, *92*

Kelly, Revd., 57, *55, 58*
Kelsey, Col., 25-6, *24*
Ketch, Jack, 102, *101*
Keyes, Robert, 48
Keynsham (Cansham), 97, *96*
Killaloe, 22
King, Sir Peter, 157
King's Head Tavern, 62
Kirby, Capt., 132-3, 142, *131, 141*
Kirk, I., 3
Knivett, Sir Thomas, 44

Lambert, Lady Francis, 30, *31*
Lambert, Maj. Gen. John, 26, 27, 33, 34 *28*
Lambert, Sir John, 177, 178, *176*
Land improvement, 177, *176*
Landau, siege of, 130, *129*
Langhorn, Richard, 53
Lauderdale, Earl of, 60
Lavatory company, 185, *186*
Lawrence, H., *see* Armstrong, Sir Henry
Leake, Admiral, 144
Leicester, Earl of, 11, 41, *12*
Leicester Fields, 73, *72*
Lenthall, Willia, 20-22, 29, *28*
L'Estrange, Sir Roger, 74-5
Levellers. 19
Lewis, William, 77
Liege, siege of, 130
Lillybullero, 120-2
Limburg, siege of, 130, 143, *141*
Lime St. chapel, 110-112, 122, *109, 121*
Lincoln's Inn Fields, 74, 88, 122, 156, *121*
Linen import, 183-5
Lisbon, 134
Lisle, Alice, 102-103, *101*
Liverpool, 178-180, *179*
Lloyd, Bishop, 151
London Gazette, 88-9, 98
London Journal, 182, 187
Long Parliament, 20-3, 27, 105, 108
Lords, House of, 125, *152, 161*
Loretto, Our Lady of, 120
Louis XIV, 112, 127, 130
Lumley, Lord, 100
Lustring, *see* Royal Lutestring or Lustring Company
Lutestring (Lustring), Royal Company, 182, 187, *181*
Luzon, Don Alonso de, 16
Lyme Regis, 93-4, 102, *92*

Macdonalds, 3
Machine gun, 182-3, *181*
Magdalen College, Oxford, 20, 107, 118, 150, 159, *106, 117, 158*
Maids of Taunton, 94-5, *96*

Maintenon, Madame de, 148, *147*
Malice Defeated, 75
Malt drying, 183
Mandrana, Don Diego de, 10
Mansell (Mansfield) Col. Roderick, 68-71, *69*
Manuring the land, 177
Marlborough, Duchess of, 130, 154, 162, 168, 175, *161*
Marlborough, Duke of, 4, 127, 130, 133, 136, 137-149, 162, 190, 192, *135, 139, 141, 145, 147, 161*
Marshall, Stephen, 26-7, *24*
Marten, Henry, 22-3, 30, *21, 31*
Mary, Queen, wife of James II, 113, 118, 124, *109, 114, 119, 123*
Mary, Queen of Scots, 38
Masham, Mrs. Abigail, 130, 162, *161*
Maximilian Emanuel, *see* Bavaria, Duke of
Meal Tub Plot, 5, 64-78, 190, 192, *65, 69, 72, 76*
Medina, John Lopez de, 8
Medina Sidonia, Don Alonso 10, 11, 13, *9*
Mendoza, Don Antonio, 10, *9*
Menin, siege of, 146, *145*
Mercurius Domesticus, 36
Meroz Cursed, 26, *24*
Merseyside, 178
Meteran, Emanuel van, 7-8
Midwife, 110, 120, 190, *119*
Mildmay, Sir Henry, 25, 32, *24*
Minerva, 144
Mining companies, 180, 185, *184*
Modena, Duchess of, 110, 120, *109*
Moncado, Don Hugo de, 10, *9*
Monck, General, 23, 32, 34
Monmouth, Duke of, 56, 68, 71, 79, 85, 89-98, 190, *80, 92, 96, 99, 101*
Monmouth Rebellion, 5, 85, 89-98, 137, 190, 192, *90, 92, 96, 99, 101*
Montague, Sir James, 154
Morgan, Thomas, 38
Mosslake, 178
Motte, Comte de la, 146
Mounteagle, Lord, 36, 44, 46, *45*
Mowbray, Lawrence, 73, *72*
Moyle's Court, 102
Muddiman, J.G., 59
Munden, Rear-Admiral Sir John, 133, *131*
Munson, Father, *alias* Lionel Anderson, 73
Musgrave, Mrs. Susanna, 94-5

Namur, siege of 136, *135*
Nassau, Count of, 113

National Debt, 166
Nelthorpe, Richard, 79, 85, 102-103, 190, *82, 101*
Neville, Edward, 38
Newcastle coal, 185, *184*
Newgate prison, 66-7, 70, 73, 75, 85, 88, 118, *106*
Newland, Sir George, 162
Newmarket Races, 81-3, *82*
Nonsuch House, 149
Norfolk, Duke of, 54
Norris, 'Black' John, 10, *9*
North, Lord Chief Justice, 75, *72*
Norton St. Philip, 97, 103, *96*
Nuestra Senora del Rosario, 11, 43, *12, 42*
Nye, Philip, 19-20, 25, 32, *24*

O' Neal, Owen Roe, 32
Oates, Titus, 48, 51-7, 59-60, 62-3, 73, 74-5, 118, *47, 52, 55, 61, 72, 117*
Observator, 137, 138, *135*
Office, houses of, *see* public conveniences
Oglethorpe, Maj., 97, 100, *96*
Old Nol's Fidler, 75
Onslow, Lord, 175
Onslow, Sir Richard, 20
Oquenda, Miguel de, 8
Orange, Prince of, *see* William III
Ordinary Journey, 159-160, 190
Ormonde, Duke of, 128, 132, *129*
Orrell, Capt. Edward, 157
Osborne, Richard, 23
Ostend, siege of, 146, *145*
Oudenarde, 144, *145*
Overkerk, Field Marshall Hendrik, 146-8, *145, 147*
Owen, John, 19-20
Oxford, 19-20, 25, 107-108, 113, 128, 159, *106, 126, 158*
Oxley, Elizabeth, 62

Paget, Charles, 38
Parker, Dr. Samuel, 107
Parkin (Parking), Henry, 100
Parma, Prince of, 13, 15, 40-1, *14*
Parry, Benjamin, 22
Parry, Edward, 22
Parry, Dr. William, 36, 37-40, 190, *39*
Parry's Plot, 36, 37-40, 190, *39*
Pasteboard making, 183, *184*
Paterson, William, 170
Pembroke, Earl of, 25, 59, 98, *96*
Penn, George, 95
Pennsylvania Company, 185, *184*
Penruddock, Col., 102
Pepys, Samuel, 2-3, 26
Percy, Thomas, 43-6, *45*

Peterborough, Earl of, 68, 71, 77, 78
Peters, Hugh, 19, 30, *31*
Petre, Revd. Charles, 110, 122, *109*
Petre Father, 110, 113, 118, 124, *114, 123*
Peyton, Sir Robert, 71
Philip II, 40-1
Philip V, *see* Anjou, Duke of
Philip's Norton, *see* Norton St. Philip
Phipps, Sir Constantine, 154, 156
Pickering, Thomas, 48-9, 54, 60, 62, 78, *47, 61*
Pink, 94
Pink, Gabriel, 150
Pitts, Thomas, 103, *101*
Playing Cards,
  origin, 1
  Worshipful Company of Makers of, 2, 4, 125
  games, 3
  Grace's Card, 3
  Curse of Scotland, 3
  duties on, 3-5
  making of, 5
  books on 189
  collecting, 191-2
Playing Cards of Various Ages and Countries, 150, 189
Plow Alehouse, 57, *55*
Plunkett, Oliver, 77-8, *76*
Pope, the, 7, 33, 38, 40, 64, 118, 120, 140, 149, *9, 39, 52, 65, 119*
Popish Midwife, *see* Cellier, Mrs., and Midwife
Popish Plot, 2-3, 5, 36-7, 48-66, 67-8, 74-6, 191-2, *47, 52, 55, 58, 61*
Port St. Mary (Porta Santa Maria), 128, *129*
Portman, Sir William, 100
Porto Carrero, Cardinal, 140, *139*
Portsmouth, 113, 127, *114, 126*
Post Boy, 138, 174
Post Man, 129
Powell, Judge, 110
Powis, Lady, 66, 68, 71, 77, 78, 113
Powis, Lord, 54, 62, 71, 113
Prance, Miles, 57-9, 63, 73, 75, 190, *58*
Prebyterian Plot, *see* Meal Tub Plot
Price, Mrs. Anne, 64-6, *65*
Pride, Col. Thomas, 23, 27, 29, 33, *28*
Pride's Purge, 23, 27, 29
Primrose Hill, 57, *58*
Prince of Wales' Bubble, 180
Princess Royal of Prussia, 140
Public convenienves, 185, *186*
Puckle, James, 182-3, *181*
Purcell, Henry, 120, 144
Purchase, George, 157, *155*

Quakers, 64, 185, *65, 184*
Queen's College, Oxford, 159, *158*
Queen's Head Inn, 57, *58*

Radish Oil, 180, *181*
Ralegh, Sir Walter, 2
Ramillies, battle of, 144, *145*
Reading, 113, 124, *114, 123*
Reading, Nathaniel, 62, *61*
Recalde, Juan Martinez de, 10, 11, *9, 12*
Riddell, John, 91
Rivers, Earl, 148
Rochester, Earl of, 151, 160, *161*
Rock salt project, 180, *181*
Rolph, Edmond, 22-3, *21*
Rooke, Admiral Sir George, 128, 132, 137, *129, 131, 135*
Rookwood, Ambrose, 48
Rose Fire Insurance, 175-7, *176*
Rota, 128
Rouse, John, 85, 88, *84, 87*
Rowlands, Samuel, 2
Royal Exchange Assurance, 175
Royal Fishery of Great Britain, 177-8, *176*
Royal Lutestring, or Lustring, Company, 182, 187, *181*
Rumbold, Richard, 79, 81-3, 91, *82, 90*
Rumley, William, 63
Rummer Tavern, 85
Rump, The, 5, 19-35, 191, *21, 24, 28, 31*
Rumsey, Col. John, 79, 85-6, *80*
Rupert, Prince, 26
Ruremonde, siege of, 130
Rushout, *see* Rushton, Father
Rushton, Father, 73, *72*
Russell, Lord William, 79, 86-8, *84, 87*
Rye House Plot, 5, 79-88, 91, 98, 105, 190, 192, *80, 82, 84, 87*

Sacheverell, Sheriff George, 151, *152*
Sacheverell, Dr. Henry, 150-163, 190, 192, *152, 155, 158, 161*
Safety, Committee of, 23, 27, 29
Sailcloth, 183, *184*
Sailors' tickets, 185, *186*
St. Albans, 26
St. Asaph, bishop of, 160, *158*
St. James' Park, 48, 54, 60, 81, *47, 52, 119*
St. John's, Clerkenwell, 122, *121*
St. Margaret's, Westminster, 26, 33
St. Martin, 7, 11, 16
St. Omer seminary, 54, 60, 62, 74
St. Paul's Cathedral, 18, 43, 132, 144, 149, 151, 159, *17, 42, 131, 147*
St. Saviour's Southwark, 150
St. Winifred's Well, 120, *119*
Salt companies, 180, *181*

Salt-petre, 182, *181*
Sampson, Jacob, 51
Sampson, Thomas, 77
San Lorenzo, 15
Sancroft, Archbishop, 105, 108, 118
Santa Cruz, Marquis of, 10, 40-1
Savoy, Duke of, 140, 142, 146, 148, *139, 145*
Savoy Palace, 56
Scholers' Practicall Cards, 2
Schreiber, Charlotte, 150, 189
Scire facies writs, 172, 180-2, 187, *171, 179*
Scot, Thomas, 27
Scroggs, Lord Chief Justice, 60. 62-3, 66, 70, 73
Sedgemoor, battle of, 98-100, 103, *99*
Sellatyn, 159, 160
Seven Bishops, The, 108-110, 118, *109, 117*
Seymour, Lord Henry, 13, 15
Shaftesbury, Earl of, 59, 68, 71, 74, 78-9, *69, 72, 80*
Shag's Heath, 100
Sheffield, Lord, 15
Sheppey, Isle of, 115, *114*
Shortest Way with Dissenters, 136, *135*
Shovell, Sir Cloudesley, 148, *147*
Sidonia, Medina, *see* Medina
Somonias, 23, *21*
Skippon, Philip, 25, *24*
Smith, Aaron, 81, *80*
Smith ('Narrative Smith'), John, 78
Snuff making, 183
Sobieski, Princess Clementina, 170, *167*
Solemn League and Covenant, 22, 23, 30, 32
Somerset, Duchess of, 154, 162, *161*
Somerset, Duke of, 162
Somerset House, 54, 57-9, *52, 58*
Sophia of Hanover, 127, 140, *126, 139*
South Sea Ballad, 172-3
South Sea Bubble, 164-174, 192, *165, 167, 169, 171*
South Sea Company, 164-170, 177, 180, 182, 187-8
South Sea Project, 173
Southampton, 26, 137
Spanish Armada, *see* Armada
Spanish Succession, War of, 127-149, *126, 129, 131, 135, 139, 141, 145, 147*
Speke, George, 62
Squire, William, 178
Stapleton, Sir Miles, 73
Stanley, Sir William, 40-1, *39*
Steele, Sir Richard, 178
Stepney, George, 142, 190, *141*
Stocking making, 183
Storm, the Great, 133-4, *131*

Street cleaning and paving, 185, *186*
Stroud (Strode), 67
Suadadoes, 94
Sugar, 182, *181*
Sunderland, Lady, 162
Swift, Dean Jonathan, 160, 173, *158*
Sydney, Col. Algernon, 79, 85

Tale of a Tub, 160, *158*
Tallard, Marshall, 130, 136, 142, *135*
Tarleton, 178
Tasborough, John, 64-6
Taunton, 94-5, 98, 103, *99*
Taylor, Randal, 19, 36-7
Tempest, Lady, 73
Temple Mills Brass Works, 180, *179*
Tenison, Archbishop, 151
Tesse, Field Marshal, 144
Thimbleby, *see* Ashby, Richard
Thompson, William, 85, *84*
Thwing, Father, 73
Tilbury, 11, 16, 41, *12, 17, 42*
Timber exporting, 183, *184*
Tixall, 56
Tobacco, 183, *184*
Toledo, Archbishop of, *see* Porto Carrero, Cardinal
Toleration Act, 150-1, 156
Tonge, Dr. Israel, 74, *72*
Tonge, Simpson, 74, *72*
Torbay, 112, 122
Tories New, 160-2, 166
Toulon, siege of, 148
Traebach, siege of, 137
Trevanion, Capt., 94, *92*
True Domestick Intelligence, 50
Triers, siege of, 137
Tubster, *see* Swift, Jonathan
Turin, siege of, 146-8, *145*
Tutchin, John, 103, 137, *135*
Tyler, Capt., 97
Tyrconnel, Earl of, 112, 120, 134, *121*

Ulm, 130, *129*
Union, Act of, 127-8
Uxbridge, 159

Valdez, Flores de, 8
Valdez, Pedro de, 8, 11, 43, *12, 42*
Vane, Sir Henry, 22, 30, 33
Vauban, S. le Prestre, 146
Venereal disease, 185, *186*
Venloo, 142
Vigo, siege of, 132, 142, *129, 131*
Villars, Duc de, 148
Villeroi, Marshall, 133, 146, *131*
Vincent, Capt., 97

Vincent, Revd. John, 95
Virginian tobacco, 183, *184*

Wade, Capt., 132-3, 142, *131, 141*
Wakeman, Sir George, 53, 54, 60, 62-3, 64, 66, *61, 65*
Walcot, Lt. Col. Thomas, 79, 83, 85-8, *80, 87*
Waller, Sir William, 25, 63, 70, *61*
Walpole, Sir Robert, 168, 180
Walton, Robert, 51
Warcup, Judge, 70
Ward, Sir Patience, 116-118
Warwick, 159
Water Engine Company, 170, 180, *167, 179*
Water pit, 185-7, *186*
Water supply, 178-80
Waters, Lucy, 89
Weekly Comedy, 138
Weekly Packet, 164
Wells Cathedral, 98
Welsh Copper Company, 168, 180, 187, *165*
West, Robert, 79, 81, 83, 85-6, *82, 84*
West Indies, 128, *126*
Westminster Hall, 32, 60, 127
Whale fishing, *see* Greenland Whale Fishery Company
Wharton, Marquis of, 120
Whigs, *see* Country Party
Whitbread, Thomas, *alias* Harcourt, 54, 60-2, 64, *65*
White Horse Tavern, 54, 62, *52*
Whitlock, Sir Bulstrode, 22, *21*
Whores, 185, 187, *186*
Wig making, 187, *186*
Wigan, 178
Wild House, 54, 63, *52*
Wilkes, Mrs. Judith, 120, *119*
Wilkins, Jonathan, 51
William III, 3, 98, 110-115, 122-7, 136, 151, *109, 111, 114, 119, 123*
Williams, William, 102, *99*
Willoughby, *see* Dangerfield, Capt. Thomas
Wilmot, Lord, 25
Win at First and Lost at Last, 32-5
Winchester, 108, *106*
Windsor, 48, 56, 118, 124, 134, *55, 117, 131*
Winter, Joseph, 92
Winter, Thomas, 43, 46, 48, *42*
Withers, Sir William, 162
Worshipful Company of Makers of Playing Cards, 2, 4, 125,
Worsley, Col., 25, *24*

Wren, Sir Christopher, 149, 154
Wright, John, 43, *42*

York, Duchess of, 53
York, Duke of, *see* James II
York, Rowland, 40
York Buildings Company, 172, 180, 187, *171, 179*

Zutphen, 41